COLLISION
AT DAWN

and other thrilling stories of the sea

© 2008, Robert C. Parsons

 Canada Council Conseil des Arts
for the Arts du Canada   Canadä   Newfoundland Labrador

We gratefully acknowledge the financial support of the Canada Council for the Arts, the Government of Canada through the Book Publishing Industry Development Program (BPIDP), and the Government of Newfoundland and Labrador through the Department of Tourism, Culture and Recreation for our publishing program.

Cover design and layout by Joanne Snook-Hann
Printed on acid-free paper

Published by
CREATIVE PUBLISHERS
an imprint of CREATIVE BOOK PUBLISHING
a Transcontinental Inc. associated company
P.O. Box 8660, Stn. A
St. John's, Newfoundland and Labrador A1B 3T7

Printed in Canada by:
TRANSCONTINENTAL INC.

Library and Archives Canada Cataloguing in Publication

Parsons, Robert Charles, 1944-
    Collision at dawn : and other thrilling stories of the sea / Robert C. Parsons.

ISBN 978-1-897174-32-6

    1. Shipwrecks--Newfoundland and Labrador--History. 2. Seafaring life--Newfoundland and Labrador--History. 3. Ships--Newfoundland and Labrador--History. 4. Navigation--Newfoundland and Labrador--History. 5. Newfoundland and Labrador--History. I. Title.

FC2170.S5P362 2008   910.4'5209715   C2008-906130-6

COLLISION AT DAWN

and other thrilling stories of the sea

Robert C. Parsons

CREATIVE PUBLISHERS

St. John's, Newfoundland and Labrador
2008

TABLE CONTENTS

For though we are strangers in your silent world
To live on the land we must learn from the sea.
"Calypso" - John Denver

FOREWORD

The first and most unique sea story of all occurred when someone, some primitive man or woman, first pushed a log or several logs lashed together to form a crude boat, and paddled or drifted across a stretch of water. Since that dateless event, the waters of the world have witnessed an unending drama of mariners and ships. One scene of that lengthy drama played itself out near Newfoundland and Labrador shores between the seventeenth and nineteenth centuries.

Many of the best sea stories have never been, nor ever will be, put on paper. The tale has been lost at sea with the people who went though the event. Others exist as folk tales and legends of seaside towns. Others survive as fragments, pieces and parts of a story that may never be fleshed out entirely. They exist as snippets of information in logbooks, journals, on gravestone inscriptions, incomplete stories in whatever media existed in its time. Exciting stories, no doubt, but to track down specifics is almost hopeless.

From the number of true and lengthy stories that have survived in Newfoundland and Labrador, I have selected sixty, and thus entitled this work as *Collision at Dawn and Other Thrilling Stories of the Sea*. The sea tales fascinated me and I felt that you, the reader, would enjoy them as well. I need not say here what parts of our great province the stories originate in, or the era they represent; that will be obvious when you read them.

However, I will say they are true; yet the word "true" is used with a caution. All are subject to the quirks of human memory and the fallibility of newspaper reporting. Wherever possible, oral retellings, gravestone dates, diary reports, ship loss statistics and scrapbook clippings were spliced with archival newspapers and magazines in an attempt to verify or augment the story. There may be a slight discrepancy with a date, in the spelling of a name, or a location.

There are photos and images that support some of the stories; other photos stand alone, that is, in isolation and without a long story to accompany them. I felt rather than not present the image to you, it would be best to add it and augment the photo with a caption. Also, you will see that many of the stories are endnoted. These notes, while not essential to the story, are unique or interesting facts or anecdotes about the community, the ship captain, the crew, the owner, the family, or the shipbuilder. Sometimes, too, the notes refer to sources, detailing where the story originated or where the background information can be found.

Many people supplied me with photos and information. I am deeply grateful for the opportunity of reproducing it in *Collision at Dawn and Other Thrilling Stories of the Sea*. I have made every effort to identify rightful owners and obtain proper permission to reproduce them. If errors occur in this regard or with the information please notify the author, and efforts will be made in any subsequent editions to correct the errors or omissions.

"Preserving Newfoundland and Labrador's Maritime History, One Tale at a Time"

CHAPTER 1
LITTLE RIVER'S CASE OF SALVAGE

LITTLE RIVER (ST. ANDREW'S): Bound from Montreal to Glasgow in June 1903, the S.S. *Norwegian* struck a ledge off Larkin's Point near Little River, where the Codroy River empties into the sea. Shipwreck and salvage - and therein hangs a tale which ended with disappointment, trouble and lawsuits.

The S.S. *Norwegian* left Montreal on June 11 with a general cargo consisting mostly of hams, flour, bacon, cheese, fruit, canned meats and 650 head of cattle. A ship with this kind of cargo would be a salvor's delight on any coast – on Newfoundland's shores, it would be a picnic.

Captain Whitney and his crew had foggy weather all the way down the St. Lawrence River; some days later, the captain took his bearings and, after consulting with his chief and second officer, agreed the bearings were correct. They were approximately thirty miles outside Cape Ray. In other words, about to turn the corner at sea, well out from the southwestern tip of Newfoundland.

Alas, there was something wrong with calculations, compass bearings, charts or another factor – the ship struck Larkin's Point in the early morning of June 13. It was nine miles northwest, on the wrong side of Cape Ray, and had been running at a speed of twelve knots.

To lighten the ship, 150 tons of cargo were immediately thrown overboard, including flour, canned goods and seven head of cattle. Nearly all of this was salvaged by the people of Little River. Meanwhile the coastal steamer *Glencoe* was passing by Port aux Basques on that Saturday morning and hearing of the wreck, proceeded to *Norwegian*'s side to give whatever aid it could.

When *Glencoe* could not pull *Norwegian* off the shoals, the captain of the stranded ship threw another 200-300 cattle off the ship. These were brought ashore by the Little River people. This lightened the ship somewhat, but it still took on a lot of water in the forehold. *Glencoe* was asked to remain alongside while Captain Whitney, fearing the ship would sink if pulled off from the shoal, got in touch with the owners in Montreal.

Meanwhile on June 14, the Wreck Commissioner for the area, J.W. Keating arrived at Little River with two policemen, constables Sheppard and Wilcox. They listed the names of those in the settlement who had assisted in salvaging the abandoned goods and cattle from *Norwegian*. It was important that their interests, as well as those of the insurance agents, were taken care of.

The fireworks started when the S.S. *Norwegian* was finally towed off the shoals of Larkin's Point. It was patched up and ready to be towed or taken away. The residents of Little River were to have received one third of the salvaged cargo. They claimed a certain amount while the ship owners figured it far differently; perhaps thinking a lot of the work was done pro bono – free.

Little River people were disgusted that the bags of flour which they had saved had not been apportioned to them by the Wreck Commissioner as per the salvage agreement. As a result, they threatened to destroy the salvaged cargo, saying "'T'is just as well we throw this overboard, if we can't have it!"

Of the 650 cattle aboard *Norwegian*, 217 were landed at Codroy and placed on the farm owned by W. Dicks. The people, now fed up with the treatment accorded them, engaged one of the best known lawyers in the country at the time, William R. Howley, who was later to become one of the first commissioners under Newfoundland's Commission of Government.

Howley arrived on the scene about the same time as a Mr. Dobson, who represented the insurance agents. Howley had a difficult time getting Dobson to come to an agreement on the subject of salvage of the cattle. It was agreed, though, that fifty per cent salvage be paid for flour and hams. The cattle, now grazing contentedly on Dicks' farm, represented a value of $15,000.00 and Dobson's goal was to have them shipped out of the valley as soon as possible. Howley, of course, refused to allow this to happen until some security for the Little River people was forthcoming.

After heated battles between Dobson and Howley, and later between Howley and another St. John's lawyer, a Mr. Morrison, King Counsel, acting on behalf of the ship owners, the case finally came to the Supreme Court at St. John's. Meanwhile the cattle were shipped out of Codroy through Port aux Basques and back to Montreal.

In the end it was disappointment for the good people of Little River. Despite the best and earnest efforts of Howley (assisted by lawyer Michael P. Gibbs), the case was dismissed in the Supreme Court and the residents of Little River received nothing legally for their efforts in saving goods and cattle from the wreck of the S.S. *Norwegian*.

However, not all goods found on the shore and brought ashore were declared legally. Many a fine meal of ham, bacon, canned meats and cheese graced the tables of Little River in the summer and fall of 1903.[1]

Notes

1. Early in the 1900s, the name Little River changed to St. Andrew's. It is a farming community situated at the mouth of the Little Codroy River about twenty-five kilometres north of Channel-Port aux Basques. St. Andrew's was named for the patron saint of Scotland, as some early settlers were highland Scots who emigrated to the fertile river valley from Cape Breton Island in the nineteenth century. The first Nova Scotian Scots are said to have arrived in the area in 1844, including branches of the McNeill and McIsaac families, still two of the most common family names in St. Andrew's in 1994. Later families moved in from Acadian Nova Scotia and were Aucoin (O' Quinn) and LeBlanc (White), as well as the Doyle and Tompkins. The present population stands around 230.

CHAPTER 2
LOSS OF THE *BURNHAM H* AND
OTHER WEST COAST SEA TALES

BLACK DUCK BROOK AND BONNE BAY: On January 9, 1907, *Burnham H* left Lark Harbour in the Bay of Islands with a cargo of frozen herring destined for Halifax. Captain George Sheppard and his business, George Sheppard and Sons, had purchased the eighty-seven-ton schooner the previous spring. Outside Lark Harbour, a southeast wind with snow accompanied by frost came on. Sheppard kept his course until he was about twenty miles west by north of Cape St. George, Port au Port Peninsula. Then things took a turn for the worst.

The wind veered, bringing a succession of gales, mountainous seas and intensely frosty weather. Two hours later *Burnham H* was struck by a heavy sea which carried away its bowsprit, headgear, cut water and foresail, causing the schooner to make little progress in the wind and sea. On Thursday, the 10th, the storm increased in violence to near hurricane force. The vessel was badly pounded by monstrous waves. Although Sheppard didn't think his schooner could take much more damage, it happened – the skylight and binnacle (or housing for the compass) were washed away.

By 3:00 p.m. the crew sighted land, but the wind was so fierce, it was impossible to get the canvas up on the ship. *Burnham H* could not be worked or worn away from the encroaching rocks and shoals. Sea water poured over the decks and in the heavy frost, soon froze and the schooner iced up. It was impossible to handle ropes, sails and running gear.

Nothing could be done to save the *Burnham H* and it gradually drifted near shore at Cape St. George and struck the dreaded shoals, "The Chains," about a half a mile off land from Black Duck Brook.

It was then about 7:00 p.m. and for three weary hours the *Burnam H* lay aground and was swept by seas. Captain Sheppard and his crew were up in the rigging, expecting every minute to be their last. But the very seas which had grounded the ship proved to be her salvation. One immense wave, much larger than the rest, carried *Burnham H* 200 yards nearer to land.

Three crew members were then able to man the dory and, with a line, succeeded in reaching shore. Two crew members returned to the wreck and, by

Only the name board for schooner *Conqueror* exists today. The vessel was built over 100 years ago in 1903 by the Wheelers at Bonne Bay. In 1938, the thirty-seven-ton *Conqueror* was wrecked on the west coast. George Osmond of the Osmond Brothers business, Bonne Bay, bought the wreck and repaired it. In November 1942, while bringing supplies from Corner Brook to various West Coast ports up as far as Port Saunders, *Conqueror* was pushed ashore by a storm at Belldowns Point, a settlement located between the mouth of Bonne Bay and Cow Head. The three crew - Everett Osmond (Sr.), Lemuel Osmond and James Parsons, all of Silver Point near Glenburnie, escaped without injury.

The forty-eight-net ton *George L* (right) was built in Shelburne, Nova Scotia, in 1906. In 1917 it came under the registry of Edward (Ned) R. Barry of Summerside, Bay of Islands. There it served as a ferry and mail boat from Curling to the communities on the north side of Humber Arm. At first it was operated by Peter Barriault and later by the owner's brothers, Thomas and James Barry.

In the spring of 1933, the government's Board of Trade decided *George L* was not suited to carry mail and passengers. A protest followed led by letters to authorities by I. J. Hackett in which he said, "*George L*, while not stylish or elegant, is well suited to do its work. Its captain and crew are always ready to do any reasonable act of kindness..."

Its service was retained until the late 1930s; eventually *George L* was replaced and it sank off Summerside. Part of its hull can still be seen underwater today.

making trips to the schooner guided by a rope from shore to the ship, rescued the remainder of the crew.

When they all reached land, they were taken in by the people of Black Duck Cove. Captain George Sheppard wrote a letter to St. John's, describing the loss of *Burnham H*. This tale of an obscure ship and wreck was published in local papers on the day before the death announcement of one of Newfoundland's well-known sons, Captain Arthur Jackman.

The storm swept the West Coast and wrecked or damaged several other schooners. *Ontario*, belonging to McFatridge, Sandy Point, was ashore at Three Rock Cove. *Ontario*, with its cargo of herring for Boston, was a total loss. Within a few days, news from Port au Port said the wreck of the schooner and its cargo would be sold and the crew had already left the scene for their homes.

The report also said the Moulton firm of Burgeo had lost *Romeo* on Codroy Island. Captain M. Rose and his crew had a very narrow escape leaving the wreck. *Richard Wainwright*, with Captain Robert Wadden, ran ashore near The Openings, just outside Sandy Point, Bay St. George. This vessel had a cargo of frozen herring aboard – 1000 barrels below deck and another 150 barrels below deck. More tragic, one of the crew was swept overboard and drowned during the storm.

THE STORY BEHIND A STONE

Towns that send a fleet of ships to the sea have always had shipping losses; the litany of vessels lost with crew or missing without a trace are often reflected in the local gravestones and monuments. So it is with a granite marker in the Glenburnie Shoal Point churchyard erected for a drowned seaman. The inscription reads "Archaleus Osmond...who was washed from the deck of a vessel and drowned October 22, 1907."

During the late summer of 1907, Captain Benjamin Osmond, with four of his sons, on board their little schooner *Young Builder* (twenty-three tons), made their annual fishing voyage up the straits of Belle Isle.

On the 26th of August they returned to Brig Bay where they landed and dried their voyage of cod. On the morning

of October 21, they reloaded their schooner and sailed for Bonne Bay. The wind was east-northeast, a favourable breeze, and the weather looked promising for a quick run home.

At 10:00 p.m. Captain Osmond judged himself to be off the River of Ponds. The wind had hauled to the northeast and increased to a gale with snow. Osmond shortened sail and ran the little vessel under two-reefed foresail until midnight, by which time the sea was in mountains and the wind blew a hurricane.

The crew then took in sail and ran their little craft under bare poles, (with no sail). At 3:20 a.m., with the storm at its height, an unusually high wave broke with such tremendous force on the stern of *Young Builder*, that those on board did not know but their craft was going down stern foremost.

When the ship had freed herself of water, the man at the wheel was gone, the wheel was carried away, the cabin doors smashed, the sliders to the door gone or damaged, and the cabin full of water. The missing man was Archaleus Osmond (identified in some sources as Art), twenty-five years of age, unmarried, and a member of a seafaring and enterprising family of Bonne Bay. At 7:00 a.m. on the 22nd, the storm began to abate, and four hours later *Young Builder*, battered and storm tossed, entered her port with its flag at half mast.

Today the only visible reminder of this sea disaster is a single marker with the story and its attendant grief summarized in a dozen engraved words. Around our island stand many such stones and stories; it is our duty to preserve them.

CHAPTER 3
SYBIL ELOISE'S FINAL HOURS

GULF OF ST. LAWRENCE, CHANGE ISLANDS: Since Newfoundland and Labrador was first settled, people in the remote and isolated seaport towns depended on the sea for transportation and to supply food and goods. The schooner was the main vehicle, sailing to St. John's, Nova Scotia and Prince Edward Island for trade and returning with the necessities of life. By 1960-70s that trade was drawing to a close. The Trans-Canada Highway across the province sent secondary roads into the bays and across the peninsulas. Transport trucks, taxis and private cars brought vital supplies to towns.

One by one the coastal vessels disappeared forever. One of last large vessels built specifically for the coastal trade was the *Sybil Eloise*. This is the tale, in images, of its last hours.[1]

The Elliott business began in Change Islands at the beginning of the nineteenth century with Joseph Edmund Elliott and was passed down to his son, Samuel.
In this Change Islands photo circa 1920s, the house is Ray Scammell's; the building (foreground), owned by Frank Hynes, is the Change Islands Co-operative Store. The schooner is *Helen Vair*, a vessel once owned by Buffett's business of Grand Bank, then by Samuel Elliott. Elliott later sold it to William Collins of Carmanville.[2]
Photo courtesy the Weir family: Reg, Harvey and Joan

Sybil Eloise was built in the spring and summer of 1963 by master shipwright Reg Weir at Western Harbour in Little Bay Islands. The photo shows the harbour-side boatyard, with Weir's office, tool-shed and carpenter shop in the foreground. *Sybil Eloise* is being painted, prior to launching.

Builder Reg Weir employed local carpenters and labourers from Little Bay Islands: Pierce Roberts, Orison Grimes, Stan Rowsell, Clifford Stone, Percey Locke, John and Gerald Simms. Wood for construction of *Sybil Eloise*, apart from the framing, came from Newfoundland Hardwoods in Clarenville. Most timbers were cut by Cyril Pelley from Springdale. This wood, juniper and birch, came from "cut overs" – trees left behind when the fir and spruce were taken by wood harvesters.

At the christening on October 3, 1963, quite a crowd gathered. The Minister of Fisheries, C. Max Lane, gave an address and then Mrs. Sybil Eloise Buffett broke the traditional bottle of champagne on the bow. However, the ship *Sybil Eloise* refused to move and the actual launch came the day after, on October 4.

Sybil Eloise, was originally owned by the G & A Buffett business of Grand Bank and called after Sybil Eloise, wife of manager Wilfred Buffett. At 273 gross tons and 123 feet long, it was one of the largest wooden cargo vessels ever constructed in Newfoundland. In January 1965, the freighter took its first consignment from St. John's to the Grand Bank owners. By the early 1970s the ship was in the hands of lawyers and tied up at Clarenville. It was eventually purchased by Captain Wallace Elliott, of Ontario and formerly of Change Islands.

Captain Elliott had his newly-acquired vessel taken from Clarenville to the shipyard in Marystown where it was put on refit, repaired, and certified seaworthy.

In December 1973, Elliott obtained a charter to take a load of Christmas trees from Halifax to Nassau, Bahamas. However, the stevedores were on strike in Halifax, and *Sybil Eloise* returned to Bay of Islands and anchored off Corner Brook. An assignment came from National Sea Products to deliver barreled herring to Halifax, and on January 27, 1974, it went from Halifax to Burgeo. After three days in Burgeo, it proceeded to Lark Harbour, leaving there on February 14. *Sybil Eloise*'s days were numbered when ice in the Gulf gripped the vessel until March.

On March 27, 1974, the weather was clear and calm; seas, usually boisterous in the Gulf of St. Lawrence, were relatively smooth. The crew was Captain Wallace Elliott, his son Arthur Elliott, Randy Hollett, Halifax, and Reg Galloway, Harbour Grace.

About 1:00 p.m., about fifty miles off the Newfoundland coast, engineer Arthur Elliott came to the bridge to say the hold was filling with water. *Sybil Eloise* was already setting by the bow. The pack ice must have damaged planks and the eleven-year old freighter was filling with water.

Captain Elliott and the crew had no time to gather extra clothes or personal possessions. He got out one SOS and talked to a super tanker located on the continental shelf. That vessel would not have found a white lifeboat amid the white ice.

Then one crewman spotted an airplane and someone found a flare to attract the plane. Elliott put a smoke flare on the water to ensure any searchers could find them.

Gulf ferry *Ambrose Shea* answered the distress call via the flare. The quartermaster on *Ambrose Shea* informed the captain he saw a flare and the ferry swung around to render help.

In the meantime, the crew tried to get out one of the lifeboats on port side. There was enough water on deck that the lifeboat, once freed from its lashings, was on an angle and caused it to jam in the wheelhouse door. The four got the second lifeboat out, rowing away to avoid suction should the vessel go down quickly. Arthur Elliott still had his camera in his winter parka pocket since he had been taking pictures of seals earlier in the day. He took a series of photos of the wallowing *Sybil Eloise*.

Once considerably down in the water, as in the photo above, *Sybil Eloise* seemed to come back up somewhat. However, at this point, trapped air in the holds blew off the hatch covers and the ship dipped lower in the water. Within fifteen minutes after abandoning ship, *Sybil Eloise* went down until only the wheelhouse and the stern showed above water.

Ambrose Shea arrived on the scene shortly after *Sybil Eloise* put up a flare. To ensure the vessel went down (and would not become a semi-submerged hazard to shipping), the captain gently nudged the side of the freighter and then came around to hit the hulk a second time. The shipwrecked crew was picked up and taken to Port aux Basques.[3]

Notes

1. Dating back to the 1920s, Weir's shipbuilding enterprise at Little Bay Islands had built sixty boats, large and small. One of the largest was the schooner *James Strong* (132 net tons and 106 feet long) built in 1925 by Reg Weir's father, James. *Sybil Eloise* was built using top quality local and imported materials and met or exceeded every requirement of the Division of Vessel Construction and the CSI. Others in attendance at the launching were Richard Harvey, Division of Vessel Construction, Gerry Drover, Fisheries Loan Board and Max Burry, Government Vessel Inspector.

2. A footnote to the Collins' connection: In 1933 William Collins purchased the Lunenburg schooner *H. H. MacIntosh*. On May 28 during a trip to Charlottetown, PEI for potatoes, his vessel struck a reef in dense fog near St. Peter's Island. Captain Collins and his crew of Frank Collins, Stanley Collins, Edward Ellsworth of Carmanville and area, David Goshee of Halifax and another Newfoundland seaman were rescued by landsmen from Charlottetown.

3. On September 21, 2007, the author talked with Captain Wallace Elliott in his home in Embree. Further stories of the early Elliott ships can be found in *Salt Water Tales Volume II*. All photos, except one, are courtesy of the Elliott family.

CHAPTER 4
FIRE CLAIMS THE *ALFRED AND EMILY*

CURLING, PORT SAUNDERS, BELLBURNS: It was dark, no moon, that night of Wednesday, October 3, 1951. The Bowater tug *Foundation Lillian*, with an empty wood barge in tow, steamed northward toward the Strait of Belle Isle. Bound for Hare Bay on the northeastern side of the Great Northern Peninsula, it was getting up toward Point Riche.

The man on watch saw a glow on the horizon in a place where no light should be. He called the captain and both saw a flash of light in the black night sky like something resulting from an explosion. As it steamed in that general direction those aboard the tug saw a burning three-masted schooner gradually come into view.

Drawing closer, it could be seen that the vessel was blazing mostly in the stern and that section had burned to the waterline. The forward section appeared to be quite solid. There was no one aboard; nor was there a lifeboat nearby. With the aid of the searchlight on the bow, it could be seen the stern was the *Alfred and Emily*.

A message to Corner Brook said, "*Alfred and Emily* found blazing astern near Point Riche. No sign of crew." When first sighted by *Foundation Lillian*, the blazing ship was about seventeen miles from Point Riche and

Alfred and Emily's crew when it burned on October 3, 1951. All were from Curling, Bay of Islands.
Captain Joseph Wells
Owner Ambrose W. Payne
Mate A. Hackett
Engineer M. Connolly
Cook P. Lynch
Seaman Ed Pike
Seaman Fred Companion

was drifting at about one knot per hour. Several crewmen aboard the tug knew it was owned by Ambrose W. Payne of Curling and that the current skipper was Captain Joseph Wells.

The *Lillian* stood by until daylight Thursday. A search of the general vicinity began. By then word came that the crew, including owner Payne who had been aboard, had been rescued or had made land.

Alfred and Emily was built in Meteghan, Nova Scotia, in 1938. Its career began as a Canadian Naval Training Vessel, *Venture*. With a hull similar in shape and design to the famous *Bluenose*, the vessel looked sleek; however, it was fitted with three masts instead of two like the speedy *Bluenose*. After the war, W.A. Shaw, a Halifax-based ship owner and businessman, purchased the ship. It was renamed *Alfred and Emily* after his son and daughter-in-law.

After a varied career along Canada's east coast, in 1950 the tern was sold to Ambrose Payne of Curling.[1] The ship was put into the coasting trade and it made some trips to the seal fishery.

Like the *Foundation Lillian*, the *Alfred and Emily* had been bound north, delivering coal from Sydney to Hawkes Bay, when it exploded. The crew hastily threw over a dory and rowed to land about twenty miles south of Port Saunders and near Bellburns.[2]

er Brook, Nfld., Canada, Friday, October 5, 1951   TWENTY-TWO PAGES—PRIC

Alfred & Emily On Fire, Crew Said To Be Rescued

News was received in Corner Brook Thursday morning that the three-masted Alfred & Emily, owned by A. W. Payne, Curling, had caught fire late Wednesday night and been abandoned by Capt. Jos.

Alfred and Emily (above) destroyed by fire near Bellburns on October 2, 1951.

Photo courtesy C. A. McBride/Shipsearch MARINE, Yarmouth, NS

In mid-October 1947, *Thomas S. Gorton*, above, went aground on Whaleback, near Martin Point, fifteen miles from Bonne Bay. Owned by Arthur Moses Earle and in command of Captain Abbott, the crew (two from Fortune Bay, one from Bonavista and the others from Carbonear) rowed ashore at St. Paul's and spent the night at Sally's Cove. Eventually, the lumber-laden *Thomas S. Gorton* floated off. A week later it was found by fishermen and then re-claimed by owners.

It is likely that some of the same crew were aboard when the schooner struck an iceberg off Twillingate on June 10, 1956. This time the crew – Captain Frank Poole, Belleoram, mate William Kane, first engineer Bert Power, second engineer C. Power, cook J. Power, seamen G. Blagdon and Fred Saunders – rowed into Twillingate.

Photo courtesy Maritime History Archives, MUN Accession # PF-055.2-K072

Notes

1. According to the booklet *Shipping Casualties off Canada's Atlantic Coast 1896-1980*, at the time of its loss, the 100-ton *Alfred and Emily* was registered in Bridgetown, Barbados. It says it exploded and caught fire two miles from Bellburns.

2. The loss of *Alfred and Emily* was not the only shipwreck that week. In the second, the crew had a closer brush with death through a sinking ship, and then from hunger on the open sea.

The engine of *Inez Eloise*, out of Port Morien, Nova Scotia, gave out about eight miles from Flint Island. Three crew members – Captain Frank Corkum and Morris Burke, both of Drumhead, and Joseph Richardson of Canso, were forced to drift helplessly away from land.

During the night the crew sighted a ship about two miles away and signaled frantically with gasoline flares, and by blinking their flashlights. The vessel did not notice them. Disaster struck when angry seas and a forty-mile-an-hour gale smashed the stern of the helpless craft and, at 10:00 p.m. Sunday, it sank in two minutes.

The frantic crew took to the dory and escaped. But that was the beginning of an ordeal. The men left *Inez Eloise* in a hurry and had on only light clothing. There was no food or water; only a compass and some gasoline. For four days, three men took turns rowing and, during brief rain showers, caught water on the compass face – they had no other container. Finally, at noon on Thursday, they staggered ashore at Kennington Cove. There, they took their first nourishment since Sunday, given by the village postmaster, Sandy MacLean.

CHAPTER 5
THE HAZARDOUS NORTHERN ROUTE

STRAIT OF BELLE ISLE: The S.S. *Mexico* ran full speed into an almost perpendicular cliff on the west end of Belle Isle. The steamer sank almost immediately. It was July 15, 1895, when the British cargo ship attempted to steam through what was termed "the northern route." This took steamers around Belle Isle at the northern tip of Newfoundland. It was a shorter route to Europe by approximately 225 kilometres. However, although shorter, it eventually proved to be even more hazardous than passing treacherous Cape Race and the heavily populated Grand Banks fishing grounds.

The strait is approximately 125 kilometres long and ranges from a maximum width of sixty kilometres to just fifteen kilometres at its narrowest. Navigation in the strait can be extremely difficult, with strong tidal currents interacting with the Labrador Current. Although depths reach several hundred metres in places, sea ice for eight months of the year and variable weather conditions including gales and fog made the run treacherous.

Two dramatic wrecks in 1895, both within weeks of each other, illustrate the gamble captains and shipping companies took to make the run.[1]

Fog, combined with a narrow route filled with rock and hidden ledges, claimed *Mexico*. The steamer, carrying a general cargo including cattle, was never refloated. By August 10, insurance survey people had been to the wreck site. *Mexico*, they said, is partly under water from the fore part of the bridge to the aft of the ship. It rests on the starboard side with several big holes in the bottom.

The most disconcerting news came from fishermen of the area. They saw what happened before the insurance agents arrived. The ship had been set on fire intentionally, they said. "In the thick smoke and lapping tongues of fire, the cattle broke loose. They were running frantically on deck, bellowing."

Several cattle that had received some burns jumped overboard and swam for land. It seemed as if the cows had as clear a conception of self-preservation as any human. A few actually got a foothold on the near vertical cliff and made the top. Others slipped and fell into the remorseless sea to be dashed to pieces against the cliffs.

The cattle held aboard suffered an equally gruesome fate. In the flames the suffering intensified until the trapped cattle perished in the fire.

Within a day or two after the wreck, insurance agents said that local schooners were still at work, fishing flour out of the vessel's hold, although it was expected that the next heavy sea would break up the wreck of the S.S. *Mexico*.

Sir Wilfred Grenfell, the English doctor who, in 1892, had set up a hospital and mission stations along the Labrador coast, commented on the loss of the *Mexico*. His first mission station was located at Battle Harbour, about thirty kilometres north of Belle Isle, where the steamer had struck.

The 227-ton barquentine *Olinda*, owned by Rorke and Sons of Carbonear and built in Nova Scotia in 1899, was wrecked at Francis Harbour Bight, Labrador, in the second week of November 1919. This vessel, never refloated, bears the same name as that in Story 38.
Photo courtesy Maritime History Archives, MUN Accession # 314.01.256a

"Until winter set in," wrote Grenfell, "barrels of flour, uninjured except for a half inch layer of dough coating the outside, were picked up floating to and fro along the coast. For weeks fishermen with improvised corkscrews mounted on long poles were using her hold as a magnified bran pie, hooking up hams, cheeses, kegs of butter and whatever else came up within reach of their tentacles."

A little over two months later, another great liner hung suspended on the Strait of Belle Isle Rocks. On September 24, the S.S. *Mariposa*, a freighter passenger steamer, was bound from Montreal to England. It ran aground five miles west of Forteau Point and was picked clean by the local fishermen before the straits caught over with ice.

On the morning *Mariposa* went aground, Captain William Cave heard the fog horn on Greeley Island. In the dense fog, Cave altered course, but the steamer ran its bow upon a rock, about fifty feet from shore. Apparently strong currents near Grassy Point, between L'Anse au Clair and Forteau, pushed the ship on the reef.

Although the sea was relatively smooth, the rough coastline precluded any attempt at landing until daylight. A breeches buoy – a running, swinging chair – was rigged up and the thirty passengers landed without incident. The next day, September 25, the Allan Line steamer transferred all passengers on board; later the same day, the *Austrian* of the same line took on the crew. No deaths or injuries resulted from the shipwreck.

Aboard *Mariposa*, in addition to 6,000 ton of cargo consisting of flour, grain, cheese and lumber, was a cargo of 2,164 sheep and a few cattle. These were taken ashore by people living in the area on the salvage principle of a share of the full value (not stolen or pirated).

Captain Blandford in the S.S. *Nimrod* arrived on the scene and, although short of winches and hoisting gear, salvaged some cargo. The S.S. *Kite*, under Captain John Bartlett, arrived too late to obtain permission from insurance underwriters to participate in salvage work.

Most activity came from local schooners and fishermen. According to *The Evening Telegram* (October 9, 1895):

There was quite a scene of activity at and near the stranded ship, but all the transactions were straightforward and the work was honestly carried on. There remains on board a lot of flour, grain and so forth, with the value well nigh washed out of it.

Some persons have done well with the furniture and fittings. One gentleman ship owner who signed himself "Taylor" said we have 600 sheep and six head of cattle, saved on the halves and a quantity of lumber and 20 cheese on board.[2]

Notes

1. Scores of Newfoundland Labrador fishing schooners and sealing vessels were lost in the vicinity of Belle Isle and the Strait of Belle Isle. On October 2, 1899, ten days after the loss of S. S. *Scotsman* at Belle Isle, Richard Mills and Company of London, owners of Dominion Line, issued a company directive, "In the future our east and west bound steamers will not use the Straits of Belle Isle route. They will go by way of Cape Race and the southern tip of Newfoundland."

By the 1930s all the larger shipping companies had discontinued using the shorter "northern route" (with the exception of World War II shipping) because of increased hazards and the resultant disasters. Some of the most notable wrecks of great steamers in the general area are listed here.

Steamers Wrecked in or near the Strait of Belle Isle

Ship	Date Lost
Canadian	June 4, 1861
Nipigon	1893
Montreal	August 8, 1899
HMS *Lily*	September 16, 1889
Mexico	July 15, 1895
Mariposa	September 24, 1895
City of Baltimore	July 1897
Ipsden	July 1898
Scotsman	September 22, 1899
Karen Rogenaes	October 1, 1921
HMS *Raleigh*	August 8, 1922
Nordfelt	November 22, 1922
Empire Mallard	September 26, 1941
Empire Energy	November 4, 1941 (chased by enemy sub)
Chatham	August 27, 1942 (torpedoed)
Arlyn	August 28, 1942 (torpedoed)

The tale of *City of Baltimore* gives further evidence of the scope of wrecks and ship loss in the Strait. On August 1, 1897 the Newfoundland steamer *Harlaw* arrived in Sydney, Nova Scotia, with ninety-seven head of cattle on the upper deck, sixty-six below deck as well as thirty-five sheep. Those many live animals would represent a substantial deck load for a steamer much larger than *Harlaw*, but they were all delivered to Sydney without mishap.

The livestock was part of the cargo of the S.S. *City of Baltimore*, aground in the Strait of Belle Isle in the vicinity of Flat Island. Captain Farquhar, managing owner of the steamer, was in the area and had the cattle put aboard *Harlaw*.

A 2,334-ton vessel owned by Furness Withy and Company, *City of Baltimore* was nine years old and 290 feet long. It was on a voyage from Montreal to Manchester, England. Farquhar stood to collect a substantial amount as a salvage claim on the cattle cargo, valued at $8000.

City of Baltimore had been bound from Montreal to Manchester with a full load of grain, lumber deals and livestock. After *City of Baltimore* grounded it landed the entire herd of 205 cattle on a small island. If they had been left there, no doubt most would have perished in a short time, but the *Harlaw* was sent from Port aux Basques to assist the stranded ship and to salvage what it could. In addition, *Harlaw* delivered a quantity of feed and the ten cattlemen who had looked after the animals aboard *City of Baltimore*.

I recently learned that the schooner *All Alone* went missing in the Straits around mid-June 1933. Captain Michael Phillip Gillam, Art Stanley Kettle, St. Lawrence and others were presumably drowned.

2. It is interesting to note that Grenfell, later Sir Wilfred, also commented on this wreck, saying: "Our own nautical outfits profited from the wreck of the *Mariposa*, as gear useful to us but valueless to small boats was brought to our neighboring hospital in lieu of fees."

THREE ARMS, NOTRE DAME BAY, CHAMPNEYS, FERRYLAND: James Norris moved from St. John's to the Notre Dame Bay community of Three Arms when he was a young man. At age twenty he built a schooner which he traded with other communities in the Green Bay area. By 1871 he had established himself in business at Three Arms.[1]

He later supplied crews from nearby communities to the Labrador fishery and the French Shore fishery, establishing branch businesses at Conche and Coachman's Cove, which were later run by his sons, John and Bernard. His eldest son, Stephen, was killed in France while serving as a lieutenant with the Royal Newfoundland Regiment.

The final phases of his shipping business came to an end with the loss of two of his larger and more dependable ships within a seven year period. One was the *Lucania*.

At 4:30 Saturday evening, February 16, 1918, Norris' *Lucania*, laden with cargo, left St. John's. Captain A. Norris of Three Arms was bound southward along the southern shore.

Captain Norris had an experienced crew from Three Arms with him; two were Norris seamen, although it is not clear

Crew of *Lucania*, Wrecked February 1918	
Captain A. Norris	Three Arms
Mate Michael Norris	Three Arms
Cook Willis Wiseman	Three Arms
Bosun P. Wells	Three Arms
Seaman Elias Norris	Three Arms
Seaman William Casey	Conche

what relation they were to the skipper. Deck hand William Casey hailed from Conche.

Up to midnight on Saturday, it was fair winds and good progress. Sunday morning was a different story. By daylight, a stiff breeze blew from the southeast and the sky darkened, showing every indication of a severe storm.

At 8:00 a.m., seas and winds increased to such a force that Norris gave orders to shorten sail. With all light canvas stowed and with the heavy sails shortened down, *Lucania* stood up well against the boisterous seas which threatened at times to pound the schooner to pieces.

Being heavily laden and practically on a lee shore, Norris decided that when the opportunity offered he would run his ship into a harbour – Cape Broyle, Ferryland or Fermeuse. About 11:30, *Lucania* was standing several miles off Ferryland Head. Norris couldn't see it, however, as a blinding snowstorm had come on. For nearly three hours, the schooner had been slowly making its way toward land.

Norris had a notion he was within Freshwater Bight, Ferryland, but by now the snow was so thick he had no idea of his position. It was better to wait out the storm and when the snow let up, perhaps he and his crew would see land.

The anchor dropped, but failed to hold and in less than twenty minutes, *Lucania* was on the rocks. Mate Michael Norris and four others got in. Not wanting to give up his ship too hastily, Captain Norris refused to go. Slowly the five in the small boat struggled to shore and when they made land, reported to those living there that *Lucania* was a wreck.

At the risk of losing his life, Captain Norris stayed with his ship and when the storm abated, a crew from Ferryland took him off. On Sunday evening the crew, except the captain, came into St. John's by the express train. Norris supervised the salving of the cargo which was only slightly damaged. *Lucania* was never refloated.[2]

WRECK OF *ROSSLAND* AT CHAMPNEYS
In late October 1925 a localized severe gale hit Trinity Bay. By November 3 reports trickled in of loss to property throughout northeastern Newfoundland. Captain White, when he arrived in St. John's on the *Ellie West* on November 1, said he had seen the wreck of the thirty-two-ton *Rossland*. It was a total wreck at Seal Cove near Champneys.

White reported that *Rossland* went ashore at Seal Cove on the south side of Trinity Bay. *Rossland*, built at Pilley's Island in 1906 and fifty-four feet long, seventeen foot wide, was registered to James Norris of Three Arms, Notre Dame Bay.

Rossland left St. John's for Three Arms on Thursday, October 29, and made fair progress until the next day, when the wind veered to the southeast with rain. As the day advanced the wind increased in strength, and by nightfall – an unusually dark night – it was a virtual hurricane.

After Captain Bailey and his crew of three had battled the elements for several hours, *Rossland* struck land on Bonaventure Head. The crew, according to the newspaper *Daily News*, "had a trying time for their lives, owing to the heavy sea that ran."

Fortunately, just before the ship grounded, the crew had put up distress signals. These were seen by people along the shore who went to the scene of the wreck. Here the news reports and tales of the people of the area are brief, but it is known they used "ropes and other equipment" to get the shipwrecked sailors off *Rossland*.

Shipping officials at Port Rexton confirmed the loss of the craft and that it was a total wreck. As well, the crew lost all belongings, together with food supplies for the winter for themselves and for their families.

There is one eyewitness account, not of the rescue, but of the salvage of goods aboard *Rossland*. Clayton Moody of Champneys recalled witnessing the wreck of *Rossland* at Fox Island, Champneys when he was a boy. This schooner had many items which people salvaged: leather, butter, flour and coal. The coal was unusual. It burned bright and hot (perhaps hard coal, anthracite) and had been immersed in cold sea water after the wreck. It burned so hot that the stove tops and covers warped from the great heat.

Newspapers of the day verifies: schooner *Rossland*, Bailey master, ran ashore at Champneys on the night of October 29-30, 1925; total wreck, crew safe. This was reported to government officials by A.E. Butler of Port Rexton.[3]

In the era of sail, nearly every town large and small in remote coves, arms and bays around Newfoundland had a shipping business or two. There are many reasons why the enterprises folded, faded and died. In Three Arms, the Norris firm left the village around 1925-6. The rocky shores of Newfoundland were not kind to his ships, and the death of Stephen Norris in World War I left the Three Arms business without a heir apparent. When James Norris died in 1924, the business closed out.

Notes

1. The three arms – the fishing towns of Middle Arm, Three Arms and Western Arm – are a series of long, narrow inlets in western Notre Dame Bay. Three Arms first appears in Newfoundland *Census* of 1845 with a population of twenty-nine.

By 1869 the population was sixty-nine (including the Bartlett, Cooper, Norris, Shearing, Strong, Wells and Young families) and a fledgling Wells' business had been taken over by James Norris. By 1884 there were 102 people living at Three Arms and the community prospered.

In 1935 there were only twenty-three people in Three Arms – the families of inshore cod and lobster fishermen, and by 1945 there were only two families, Moore and Rideout. In time the once viable town of Three Arms was abandoned and most of the homes had been moved to nearby Harry's Harbour.

2. In 1918, forty-three ships were recorded as lost in Newfoundland. Appendix A lists those and the cause of the loss.

One schooner, *Emily M. Anderson*, lost about the same time as *Lucania*, was owned by William H. Hynes of St. John's. Captain Leonard Miller, his brother, bosun Frank Miller, and seaman Edward Cox were from St. John's; cook William Edwards came from Harbour Grace; Thomas Mckinnon, Fogo, and Walter Richards hailed from LaHave, Nova Scotia.

This vessel left Oporto on January 11, 1918, and encountered heavy weather on the eastward trip. On January 25, the canvas was stripped from the schooner and its head gear carried away. For six days the crew pumped desperately to keep the schooner afloat.

On February 1, a lookout on *Emily M. Anderson* saw an auxiliary cruiser. The crew signaled and the cruiser came by. In the gale and with high seas running across the deck of the schooner, no ordinary rescue ship could have taken off the crew, but the cruiser had a large derrick or crane aboard. The crane lowered a lifeboat well out from the side of the large ship, thus preventing it from smashing against the bulwarks.

The Newfoundland schooner was abandoned in the Atlantic at 27 degrees West, 48 North and the un-named cruiser brought the crew to Halifax on February 8.

3. The story of the loss of two of Norris' ships came from three sources: *The Evening Telegram* February 12, 1918; *The Daily News* November 4, 1925; *Globe* November 3, 1925, and personal conversation with Clayton Moody, Champneys.

CHAPTER 7
RUTH HICKMAN'S CREW MEETS THE ENEMY

SPRINGDALE, TWILLINGATE ISLAND: In May 1918 the tern schooner *Ruth Hickman* was overtaken by a German sub. Enemy subs were always on the lookout for ships carrying food and supplies to Europe or salt back to Newfoundland using shells or bombs. Headlines on this sinking say it was torpedoed. *Ruth Hickman* left Newfoundland in January with a load of fish which was discharged at Gibraltar. It then sailed to Cadiz for salt needed to cure the fish back home. Twenty days out, and west of Cadiz, a sub intercepted them.

Seven crew manned *Ruth Hickman*; only four are known: Captain Arthur Snelgrove, Benjamin Bowers and Harris Starkes of Nippers Harbour, Robert Lambert of South Side, and Cecil Anstey, Back Harbour, both towns on Twillingate Island. Not much is known of the experiences of the crew except for the family history of seaman Anstey.

When Anstey arrived back home, he firmly declared that one of the crew of the German sub, possibly the navigator, spoke good English and was probably an Englishman. During the first Great War at sea, the enemy was humane toward the crew of lonely sailing ships it encountered. Often the ship was sunk, but the English crews were given directions to land, given time to gather food and water and generally treated well.

For Cecil Anstey and the rest of the *Hickman*'s crew, the nearest land was the Azores. They were given three minutes to get off *Ruth Hickman*. During that time Captain Snelgrove was able to grab his compass as well as some hard bread (ship's hard tack) and containers of water. It took the crew six days to row the 120 miles to the Portuguese island group.

The only hardships were sore hands, cold and general weariness. According to the family, Cecil Anstey developed kidney stones and passed one in his urine during the long pull to land. He suffered quite an ordeal in personal pain, in addition to the hardships he endured from rowing for nearly a week. At the Azores, the American Embassy cared for them and arranged for passage to New York. Eventually they reached Newfoundland and home.

For Anstey, shipwreck and hardship on the ocean was not a new experience. Family history says he was involved in the loss of his vessels five or six times: *Ruth Hickman* in 1918; the well-documented loss of the S.S. *Ethie* near Cow Head on December 11, 1919; and he was deckhand on *Saucy Arethusa* on November 13, 1929, when it was totally wrecked at Sambro, near Halifax. As well, he was on board two ships that ran into trouble or went aground and were later refloated: the Twillingate schooners *Grace Boehner* and *Bessie Marie*.[1]

In the spring of 1916 George W. Clarke & Sons of Springdale received an order to build a large vessel from A. E. Hickman of St. John's. A tern schooner, *Ruth Hickman*, at 417 gross tons and 148 feet in length, was built and launched at Dock Cove near Springdale by the Clarkes. John Robert Hull, Little Bay Island, was the foreman.

Constructed of local timber and employing thirty to forty men both on site or in the woods, it was launched in September 1917 (as in the photo above).

Both photos courtesy Rob Knight, King's Point, Carl Gillard and the Springdale Heritage Society.

Clarke and sons constructed sixteen schooners (*Ruth Hickman*, above, was the largest). In his personal life, Clarke had tragedy: two sons were killed in 1917 during World War I; another died of consumption at home in 1918.

Ruth Hickman was named for Albert E. Hickman's eldest daughter, who later married Charles R. Bell. *Joan Hickman*, another of Hickman's extensive foreign-going fleet, was named for his daughter Joan.

Schr. Ruth Hickman Torpedoed

CREW SAFE—WAS LARGEST LO
CAL BUILT VESSEL.

The schr. Ruth Hickman, Capt
Snelgrove, has been torpedoed and
sunk by a German submarine. The
crew are safe and have landed a
Angra, Azores. The Ruth Hickma
was one of the prettiest models ever
produced by local builders. The shi
was released from the stocks in No
vember, 1917, at Springdale, N.D.B
by her builder, Mr. Geo. W. Clark
and was fitted out and ready for se
within a month after. She was regis
tered at 417 tons gross and 377 ton
nett, thus at the time of launchin
she was the largest of any ship eve
turned out by any builder in the Do
minion. She was a staunch vesse
easily handled and a quick sailer, he
loss therefore to the trade of th
country is a heavy one. The Rut
Hickman left here in January las
with a cargo of fish which she dis
charged at Gibraltar, from there sh
proceeded to Cadiz to load salt. Afte
twenty days out from the latter por
she was overtaken by a German sub
marine who quickly ended her shor
career. Capt. Snelgrove and cre
reached the land safely, but we ar

"IN FREEDOM'S CAUSE."

Evening Telegram

V. J. HERDER, - - Proprietor
C. T. JAMES, - - - - - Editor

THURSDAY, May 30th, 1918.

Local media headlines report **Schr. *Ruth Hickman* Torpedoed**. In late May 1918, the crew and ship were intercepted by an enemy sub and forced off the ship. They had to row 150 miles to the Azores.

Notes:

1. Despite an extensive search of local papers to see if any reports (and any subsequent tales of privation) were available documenting the return of *Ruth Hickman*'s crew to Newfoundland, none could be located. There was a brief account of the sinking, which in no way describes the arduous experience and long row to safety, in *The Evening Telegram* May 30, 1918 edition. As well there are two or three descriptions of the construction and launch of the tern schooner: *The Daily Star* March 6, 1918; *The Advertiser* of March 9, 1964; and *The Nor'Wester*, Springdale, June 22, 1983. However, I am especially grateful to two people for help in this story – Carl Gillard of the Springdale Heritage Society for photos and John Holwell, who in 2002, sent me invaluable information on his grandfather, Cecil Anstey.

CHAPTER 8
A HARROWING EXPERIENCE ON CHRISTMAS DAY, 1950

PORT ANSON, MUSGRAVE HARBOUR, BADGER'S QUAY: This is a Christmas sea story – an episode of adversity that happened on Christmas Day right about the time when many people open presents, visit with family and friends, hear the story of the Christ Child at church, and enjoy the Christmas Day meal. But peace and festivity was far from the minds of five seamen in December 1950 as they fought bitter winter winds and struggled to keep their ship off the rocks. This is a story of endurance coupled with luck, leading ultimately to survival.

Wilbert "Bert" Wellman was captain of the fifty-ton *Lavinia Bride*. The schooner had been built at Fair Island, Bonavista Bay in 1935 by Job Hunt. By 1950 *Lavinia Bride* was owned and operated by T. J. (Timothy John) Hewlett's business of Port Anson, a community located in western Notre Dame Bay.[1] The seventy-foot long vessel carried a thirty horsepower engine as well as sails, making it an "auxiliary" vessel powered by an engine or by sail.

But neither canvas nor motor was of much use to Captain Wellman on that December 25th day off the treacherous Straight Shore. Weather conditions were described in the papers of the day as "harrowing, a howling storm, with winds from 50 to 60 miles an hour." Indeed the gale had shredded most of the vessel's canvas and the little engine gave out under the strain. On that particular trip, Wellman had with him mate Bert Martin and his son Ed Martin, who was the engineer. The two deckhands were Lauderic Reid of Miles Cove and Albert Morey of Port Anson.

The journey began when *Lavinia Bride* left Port Anson on December 23rd for St. John's to discharge a cargo of salt cod. The first night's anchorage was at Morton's Harbour and the following day the schooner made Seldom-Come-By. It left there early Christmas morning. Captain Wellman hoped to get around Cape Freels and into Bonavista Bay that day.

It was not to be. When Wellman left Seldom the wind, which had been about northwest at thirty miles per hour, breezed up to sixty miles accompanied by snow – the worst of winter conditions. Captain Wellman recalled what happened next:

"Just after the little schooner passed Copper Island, the engine failed and most of the canvas was blown away. Helpless, we were drifting inside of Edward's Reef on perhaps the worst section of the northeast coast along the Straight Shore. Many a ship had piled up on that reef over the years.

"The only thing the crew could do was to try to bring the ship to anchor. It was now dangerously near the reef in a raging sea and a snow blizzard."

This was Christmas Day at sea. Everyone on land was warm and snug at home, with a warm fire going, perhaps cooking or eating Christmas dinner. It was a time to celebrate. Yet on a rugged seacoast such as Newfoundland's, there is always someone, no matter how festive the celebration, looking out to sea; someone worrying and waiting at home. Those waiting anxiously at home were in Port

Lavina Bride (above) in more peaceful times. *Courtesy Jim Wellman and George Yates*

Anson; at Musgrave Harbour someone was watching the mad seas off the northeast coast. Captain Wellman said:

> Both anchors were run out and they held the schooner for three hours, while wave after wave swept completely over it. At 12:00 the strain on the chains became terrific as the winds increased. The big anchor was carried away and the other began to drag. We then dropped a stream anchor attached to a six inch hawser which again held the vessel.
>
> By now the temperature had dropped almost to zero and *Lavinia Bride* began freezing up. Rigging soon doubled in size and tripled their normal size as the schooner wallowed in the waves.

Each man was now fighting to save his life and his ship. Freezing spray coated the decks until they were like glass. There was a real and ever-present danger of being swept overboard as the crew tried to get around to work anchors and to beat ice from the rigging.

At one point the mate was carried off his feet by a sea that washed across the deck. The only thing that kept him from going over the side was that the direction of the wave put him up against the foremast. He was able to hold on and regain his footing.

Edward's Reef can be seen from the windows of many homes in Musgrave Harbour. As dark closed in on that stormy evening, people watched a lonely schooner struggle for life in mad seas near a treacherous reef.

Someone said afterward that "It was only through a miracle that the vessel was not smashed to pieces on the reefs. We did not expect to see her still at anchor the next morning. Certainly none of the crew would live through the night."

But that evening, there was a ray of hope in the series of unfortunate events. As Wellman remembered:

Fortunately before dark the engineer got the engine working and for eighteen hours it ran continuously without a break. That's what saved us.

During the long night following Christmas Day, we were at the mercy of the waves, unable to tell in the darkness whether we were drifting, and we were anxiously awaiting daylight.

By dawn on the 26th, winds had moderated and we were able to chop away the ice from the rigging. It had grown by now to barrel size. I would estimate there was twenty ton of ice that had to be cleared from the decks and rigging.

In addition, water had gone into the forecastle and at one point there was eight inches on the floor. We had to do without warm food for hours.

It was not until one p.m. that the crew had cleared the vessel of ice and they were able to get the windlass working. When the tackle was taken in, it was discovered that only the port anchor was left; both the big anchor and the stream anchor were gone.

Lavinia Bride got under way, using the engine and what was left of the tattered sails. It limped into Badger's Quay on Wednesday evening, December 27. There, Captain Ches Dyke helped them get the schooner back shipshape.

It was a festive season the weary sailors were not likely to forget.

As for the resilient schooner *Lavinia Bride*, it lasted a few more years towing pulpwood from points in Halls Bay to a drum barker in Tommy's Arm. It was then skippered by Bert Wellman's son, Norman. Finally, an old and tired *Lavinia Bride* served as a ferry to and from Little Bay Islands until the mid-1950s when it was put out of service or scrapped.[2]

Notes

1. Port Anson, a fishing and logging community in Halls Bay within western Notre Dame Bay, lies on the southwestern shore of Sunday Cove Island. In fact, its first name was Sunday Cove Tickle, then around 1903, the community was officially renamed Port Anson. The first *Census* shows sixty-three people in 1857.

Early settlers were attracted by the stands of timber as well as by good agricultural land in a location with access to fishing grounds in both Halls Bay and Jerry's Run. In the 1890s and early 1900s several other families arrived at Port Anson, some coming from Beaumont North (Burton and Heath), some from the Twillingate area (Hustins and Rice) and others from Wellmans Cove and Miles Cove (Morey and Wiseman).

By the 1940s five sawmills were being operated by Port Anson residents: J.R. Burton & Sons, Goudie Brothers, George Wiseman, Louis Bown and T.J. Hewlett & Sons. Hewlett's eventually became a major supplier and employer for the entire area.

Since 1974, when a causeway was built across Sunday Cove Tickle, Port Anson has been linked with the mainland. Its present day population is a little less than 200.

2. Captain Wellman's story appeared in the newspaper of the day. Verifying or adding certain details were his two sons, Jim and Norman, and his daughter, Kaye.

CHAPTER 9
LIVING ON DOUGHBOYS

MORTON'S HARBOUR, HERRING NECK: In early December 1902, several schooners got into Seldom-Come-By, near Fogo, out of the weather. *Pioneer, Jessie, St. Clair* and *Nokomis* stayed two days. The morning of Friday, December 5 dawned bright and clear and with fair winds in the offing. Since all four were heading to St. John's, they sailed in company with each other, all expecting to be in St. John's within twenty-four hours.

Jessie had left Gander Bay on Wednesday, December 3, laden with lumber for St. John's and had stopped in Seldom awaiting fair winds. Its crew belonged to Herring Neck, located at the northeastern extremity of New World Island, Notre Dame Bay. Three of them were brothers, Captain Arthur Holwell, mate George Holwell and Claude Holwell and the other sailors were Elijah Warren, Jeremiah Fudge and Elias Grimes.

Captain Kennedy had loaded lumber on the schooner *Pioneer* at Roddickton, White Bay, and set sail for home port in Carbonear. The storm forced him into Seldom too. When the winds abated, *Pioneer* left with the other two, bound eastward. The story of *Pioneer*'s epic voyage is told in Chapter 28 in this book.

The third schooner in that quad of ships about to sail into legend was *St. Clair*, owned in Moreton's Harbour[1] by Dawe Pierce Osmond,[2] under the command of Captain Earle. The story of the terrible experiences of Earle and his four man crew more or less mirrors what happened to the other schooners. In that two week period before Christmas, all three had a terrible time on the vast North Atlantic.

Built in 1900 on Chapel's Island, (between the main land and New World Island) Notre Dame Bay, the seventy-three-ton *St. Clair* was seventy-one feet long, twenty-two wide with a depth of nine feet. The little vessel had a considerable cargo – 1,000 quintals of salt cod, 200 barrels of herring, all below deck and there were forty casks of cod oil on deck.

At 11:00 a.m. on Friday, December 5, 1902, *St. Clair* pulled out of Seldom with the three other vessels, *Jessie, Nokomis* and *Pioneer*. Cape Bonavista was the first important landfall, and by 9:00 p.m. all were off that point.

About that time the wind swung to the south and blew a gale all that night. By daybreak, it veered northeast with hurricane force and blowing snow. Temperatures dropped and Earle and his *St. Clair* were being driven out to sea. High waves pounded the sides of the schooner.

Saturday morning, December 6, became a day to forget for the five sailors. The schooner caught fire. The bouncing of the vessel in the choppy seas caused the stove to overturn. Hot coals, embers, and ashes were flung on the side of the cabin and ignited a pile of oakum.

Their circumstances were not to be envied: being driven out to sea without knowing where they were and not in sight of land; trying to manage a tossing schooner in a mad gale in driving snow; whitecaps occasionally breaking over the deck. Now two or three crew were shouting, "Fire! Fire!"

Fortunately, the crew members were in the cabin when this happened, but had no water at hand to fight the blaze. Blankets, quilts, canvas, and a coat or two were used to smother the flames before the fire got under way too much. The cabin was damaged and filled with thick smoke that drove them out on deck.

That evening, the deck load of casks of oil began to work loose. To save the bulwarks and sides from great damage, the crew decided to let it all go adrift. This wasn't difficult as seas swept over *St. Clair* fore and aft, taking the oil casks with it.

As it was, the crew had to chop out some of the bulwarks to allow the water from the mad seas to run off the decks. By now, temperatures dipped below freezing and ice formed on the cabin, back aft, and the jib boom. Not only was it difficult to walk about on deck, but the ice would make the schooner top heavy and could cause it to roll over.

Water in the holds and the coating of ice pushed the erstwhile schooner down in the water. The crew feared *St. Clair*, now wallowing and labouring heavily, was sinking. Yet they could not turn and head for land; they had to keep the vessel's head into the wind to allow it to labour a little less.

About that time a steamer came by. Earle signalled and it came close. When the ship gave its position, Earle realized he was about fifty miles south of St. John's. There was no hope to get in to port though; they could never sail into the teeth of that gale. In fact, within a day or so, they were driven another hundred miles further south.

Eventually *St. Clair* reached the warmer waters of the Gulf Stream. Ice began to melt and the crew got out the mallets and beat the rest away. In the gales, the foresail had burst. While the schooner was iced up, it had dipped into a trough that broke the jib boom.

Given the ice on the rigging, the crew could not cut the boom away; thus the flinging boom in turn caused the foregaff to break off next. Then to crown it all, the gaff topsail was blown away.

There was little fresh water aboard and the water cask had gone over the side with the oil barrels. The crew had about twenty gallons to do them for whatever period they were at sea (which turned out to be nearly two weeks). Food, meant to last three or four days, ran short.

In fact, it was hunger and thirst and not the wild seas and winds that became their greatest enemy. Often when a sailor became thirsty from working the ship, he could only wet his parched throat. Fortunately there was an adequate store of pork, potatoes, and flour aboard, but no tea.

No warm drink was available for several days. The man assigned as cook decided on a novel way to cook doughboys – steamed balls of moistened flour which in some areas in Newfoundland are called duffs or dumplings. To conserve water, the cook boiled them in saltwater. "If you're hungry enough, you'll eat them," said the cook. He was right; the hungry crew was glad to get them. They had to admit, though, the doughboys had a different flavour.

Through the rationing of food and water, they survived. When they finally reached land, there was one kettle full of water left. Earle and his crew had weathered the storm. They reported seeing a large quantity of lumber floating in the ocean; probably a deck load from some other schooner caught in the same storm.

By Monday, December 8, they had tracked back to within sixty miles of Newfoundland's southern points. They saw a schooner running before the high winds under bare poles, i.e. no sail, just the bare masts. From the general look of the vessel, Earle and his crew thought it might be *Jessie* and the men from Herring Neck. That is, one of the other schooners which had left Seldom with *St. Clair* several days previously. They figured *Jessie* had been driven far off into the Atlantic, as they had been.³

When the heavy gales slackened off somewhat, Earle asked his crew to set whatever bits of the sail remained. Earle beat to the westward for several days, not exactly knowing where they were. The first landfall according to the log and crude charts aboard was Cape Ballard on the southern shore near Cape Race.

It was Wednesday, December 17 – twelve days after leaving Seldom-Come-By. It became more or less routine to sail northward up the southern shore until the jaws of St. John's Narrows opened up. That was their first sight of friendly land, having seen nothing but roiling seas and crashing waves of a mad Atlantic fall upon the little *St. Clair*.

They had all come through with no loss of life and without injury. Despite the wet sleeping quarters and clothes, none of the crew suffered any sickness, not even a cold. Captain Earle jokingly said their constitution must have been toughened from eating so many doughboys boiled in seawater!

Notes

1. Morton's Harbour, a fishing community on the northwestern extremity of New World Island, has the principal settlement on the bottom of the harbour with "Taylor's Side" to the east and "Small's Side" to the west. Both sections were probably named after early settlers. In the 1836 *Census,* the community was recorded as Morden's Harbour. The fishery has always been the community's economic mainstay.

Once established, the community's population increased rapidly, reaching 500 by 1891. The chief merchant families were the Osmonds and the Bretts. Lovell's Directory shows the common family names to be Brett, Hann, Jennings, Osmond, Russell, Small, Taylor, Wall and Woolfrey.

2. By the late 1800s Morton's Harbour had developed into a center for the Labrador fishery, sending nine schooners to the Labrador by 1874. With the need for larger vessels, a shipbuilding industry soon developed. Between 1883 and 1888, sixteen ships were built, eleven of them by master builder Mark Osmond.

An example of the involvement of the Osmonds in the Labrador fishery can be seen in the shipping report for October 1893. The schooner *Verbena*, owned by Mark Osmond of Morton's Harbour, was wrecked on September 18th at Cape Mugford. The S.S.*Windsor Lake* brought home the crew and landed them in various harbours: Master Richard Bonne, Solomon Osborne, Joseph Jewer, John Late

(Layte), Stephen James and Benjamin Lush at Exploits Island; Isaac and Henry Dawe were brought to St. John's.

On November 15, 1895, Louis Osmond's fifty-one-ton schooner *Nancy* was struck by an unknown ship off Torbay. Captain Josiah Noel said that only for the *Nancy* being a new ship (launched earlier that year), it would have sunk at sea and all crew would have been lost.

3. *Jessie*, with its five crew from Herring Neck, had indeed been blown to sea and ran short of the basic necessities of life – food and water. As Elias Grimes said after, "We were down to scraping up the bread dust to eat. And we had a half pint of water a day on the end of it."

Storm-battered and leaky, *Jessie* was abandoned at sea when the steamer *Hornby Castle*, bound for Belgium, came by on December 23rd and rescued the crew. *Jessie* sank in the Atlantic and the crew was landed in Antwerp on New Year's Day, 1903. The thrilling story of how *Jessie's* crew survived can be found in the book *Raging Winds...Roaring Sea* (2000).

Captain Kennedy and his crew aboard *Pioneer* drifted helplessly before the gale for days. After nearly three weeks out to sea, they were plucked off their sinking schooner by the S.S. *Rotterdam*, bound for Holland. *Pioneer's* crew were eventually taken to Halifax and, remarkably, arrived in St. John's in February on the coastal boat *Glencoe* with the crew of *Jessie*.

Nokomis, blown to sea in the same gale, was abandoned 116 miles off the coast of Newfoundland. The S.S. *Peruvian* plucked off Captain Frank Curtis, mate J. Churchill, seamen E. Boyd, R. Brett, C. Pippy and T. Curtis and landed them in St. John's on December 15th. *Nokomis*, laden with lumber, was left a derelict on the high seas. Last registered to Daniel Martin of Codroy, the eighty-six-ton schooner had been built in Mahone Bay, Nova Scotia, in 1884.

Although there is no available image of *Nokomis*, this is the S.S. *Peruvian* which rescued the crew of the Newfoundland schooner.

Courtesy of Capt. Hubert Hall, Shipsearch MARINE

CHAPTER 10
HOW THE *MYRA* WAS SAVED

DURRELL, TWILLINGATE AND CATALINA: John Hillier hailed from Durrell's Arm, since called Durrell, a town near Twillingate. He was an experienced seaman and captain and went through many a storm in his years on the sea. But in December 1899 he had an outstanding episode on the sea which was filled with deviltry and the will to do or die. When it was all over he could smile, for he saved his ship from wreck and ruin and, in addition, fooled potential salvagers.

Back then he was master of the schooner *Myra,* with a crew of four and a pet dog. During Christmas week he was en route from St. John's to Twillingate with a general cargo for Ashbournes, the major fish procurer and supplier of goods and services on Twillingate Island. The food and supplies would be landed on December 23, just in time for Christmas.

When he was off the northeastern Newfoundland's Straight Shore and near the Peckford Islands, he ran into a typical December storm. Hillier and his crew fought the gale but, as was so often the case, the storm prevailed. The force of wind tore the sails from the gaffs and broke or damaged the masts, leaving *Myra* dismasted and at the mercy of the seas.

It lay wallowing in the troughs of the seas with broken spars, gaffs, masts and with the sails and rigging pounding up against the side of the ship. *Myra* was virtually a floating wreck.

At this time the schooner *Specular*, under the command of Philip Wells, sailed north in the same vicinity and also fought the elements. Although owned at the time by Woolfrey's business of Lewisporte, *Specular* had on board a cargo for Hodges business of Twillingate. Wells bore down near the wrecked schooner and hove up as close as possible, signaling that he could take off the crew.

Wells lowered a boat and, with a staunch rope attached, allowed it to drift down alongside. When *Myra*'s crew got into it, the boat was pulled back to *Specular*. But Captain Hillier stubbornly refused to abandon ship. He told his men they could go with Wells if they wished, but he was staying with the crippled *Myra*. Wells had no choice but to leave him to his fate and continue on his way to Twillingate.

But Hillier was not one to give up easily – he wouldn't lose his boat and valuable cargo without a fight. He cut away the spars and other wreckage hanging over the side and allowed it to go adrift. The jib, which had been stowed away when the damage was inflicted, was the only sail left aboard. Hillier planned to use this, if and when the circumstances permitted. The pumps were clogged so he tore up the cabin floor boards and bailed out his ship, bucket by bucket. He found *Myra*, although knocked about and dismasted, was not leaking nor in a sinking condition.

He figured the offshore wind and rising tide would take the lightened ship clear of the rocks and shoals near the Peckford Islands. There was nothing else to do but wait for time and tide to push his schooner further offshore, so he went below, cooked supper and lay down for the night. He knew well the Straight Shore, littered as it is with many charted and uncharted rocks and islets, was inhospitable at the best of times and was downright treacherous in wild weather.

In the morning when he went on deck, he realized he had drifted out to sea. The wind had moderated considerably. He began improvising a jury mast and, using the windlass, ran up a little sail. On Friday he made Bonavista Cape and Saturday morning he was south of Bird Island Cove (today's Elliston) and not too far from the much-frequented and spacious harbour of Catalina. All this time, from Wednesday to Saturday, he was alone and not able to cook his food as he had to bail continuously.

He saw two boats heading seaward and knew the men must be bird hunters. Those hunters, seeing an unfamiliar and curious boat, steered toward the vessel and asked the skipper what he was up to.

Hillier calmly replied he was going to Catalina, but was afraid he couldn't make port before dark. What he didn't say was that his schooner was damaged and couldn't make port unaided. He made a bargain with the men, fixed the price at one dollar each, and they agreed to tow him to Catalina. Had they known the *Myra* was storm damaged and unable to manoeuver properly, the bird hunters could have claimed substantial salvage rights – one third the value of the schooner and its cargo.

The captain and the hunters strung a rope from *Myra* to a line of boats ahead. Late that evening the dismasted vessel dropped anchor off the government wharf in Catalina. One of the first things he did after he stepped ashore was to send a telegram to the owners in Twillingate, stating simply:

"Arrived Catalina, myself and the dog. Vessel and cargo safe."

On December 29, the coastal steamer *Virginia Lake* called at Catalina on its voyage to northern Newfoundland ports and the full cargo of *Myra* was put aboard. It reached Twillingate on the evening of December 31, eight days behind schedule.

Captain John Hillier had saved his ship, the cargo and avoided a large salvage claim on his wrecked schooner.

CHAPTER 11
TWO WRECKS IN THE TICKLE

FOGO: The town of Fogo, with its two accessible harbours, became one of the most important bases for the northern fishery beginning in the mid-eighteenth century. The town became the commercial center for subsequent settlement on Fogo Island. The main harbour, known as Fogo Harbour, is surrounded by rocky headlands and is protected from the open sea by a chain of islands, which make approaches difficult in rough weather. Seal Cove, the other harbour, provides shelter from winds which often make the approaches to the main harbour treacherous.

One entrance to Fogo harbour is between Boatswain's (Bosun's) Tickle (Western Rock) and Barnes Island. That channel has a low water depth of about thirteen feet. Subsequently there have been many shipwrecks in and near Fogo over the years.

One of the earliest recorded near disasters at the harbour entrance was that of the passenger vessel *Tibbie*. At 9:00 on Thursday morning of January 12, 1888, the steam launch *Tibbie*, owned by Robert Scott of Fogo, left Twillingate for Fogo via Beaver Cove.[1]

One of Scott's many ships he had built on Fogo was a little passenger steamer called the *Matilda*; most likely nicknamed *Tibbie*, for short. Netting twenty-five tons, fifty-four feet long and thirteen feet wide, the vessel was classified as "steam/sail." On that January day, it had a crew of two men, including the owner Robert Scott.[2] It carried four passengers, one of whom was a Fogo Island teacher, Miss Ross, who was going to Fogo. Three passengers were landed at 1:00 p.m., and as the fog closed in, the *Tibbie* went no farther than Change Islands that night.

On the next day, the little steamer left Change Islands at 1:00 p.m. and was seen from Fogo at 2:00 p.m. Figuring it was still too foggy to attempt steaming into Fogo harbour, a group of men with John Scott, the son of the owner, went up on a hill to signal the *Tibbie* to go back. However, their signals were misunderstood and the little steamer came on and tried to enter the harbour by the Eastern Tickle. The men were all down at the tickle but the *Tibbie* could not get far enough to communicate with them. It then steamed around to Boatswain's Tickle and the men had to walk around shore.

When the men got round to the Western Tickle, *Tibbie* was being tossed by the waves and those on shore thought every moment that they had seen the last of it. It was 9:00 p.m. when the steamer was rowed to the Boatswain's Tickle, and just as the little ship got into the worst part, some part of its machinery refused to work. *Tibbie* was at the mercy of the waves.

Once those on shore heard screams, one of the men in the area by the name of Robert Irish got his boat out and, with the willing help of the Northside men under the superintendence of John Scott, they got out lines and rescued Robert Scott, Miss Ross and the crewmen.

The timing of the rescue was none too soon for just after they left, *Tibbie* turned bottom up. It is not known if the steam engines blew up when cold water struck

Danish fish carrier *Harriet* aground on Fogo Island in 1920. Courtesy Andrew Shea, Fogo

them, as amid the confusion and noise of the waves a report could not have been heard. A quarter of an hour after the steamer struck, there was not a sign of it to be seen.

The boat with the rescued passengers was hauled ashore and those in it were helped to a house nearby where restoratives were given to those that required them. No one aboard were seriously hurt. The remains of *Tibbie* lies near the wreck of the steamer *Summerside*, lost at Western Tickle in 1883.

The *Harriet*, Twice a Wreck

On December 10, 1920, the Danish schooner *Harriet* ran aground on Light-house Island at the Eastern Tickle entrance to Fogo Island. It was bound for Portugal with a full load of dried cod fish. High seas on the following evening damaged the bottom, and the owners in Marsdal, Denmark determined the costs to repair and refloat the ship were too high, declaring *Harriet* a total loss. Built in 1916 in Denmark, the three-masted, or tern schooner, *Harriet* was 103 gross tons and had an overall length of eighty-nine feet.

During January and February, while Fogo harbour was frozen over, the vessel's rigging was taken down and stored and the cargo removed with grappling hooks – done under the supervision of Fogo's Mark Jones. Salvage of the ship itself seemed possible and in early March, Mr. T. Peckford, the local Wreck Commissioner from Change Islands reported the wreck would be sold at a public auction.[3]

Prospective buyers viewed the ship, concluding that although its bottom was torn out, *Harriet*'s upper section, the sails and gear were in excellent shape. Earle Sons and Company Ltd. successfully bid on the wreck.

When the ice had cleared enough in the spring, the crippled *Harriet*, with its hull temporarily patched, was made buoyant enough to be floated to the west end of Fogo harbour. On May 21, 1921, two shipwrights from Wild Cove, Thomas Roberts and George Payne, and a Mr. Burt of Summerford, came to Fogo to work on the vessel. John Roberts of Twillingate supervised the repairs to the bottom and *Harriet* was re-rigged by Mark Jones.

Finally, in the fall of 1921, *Harriet* was ready to resume work. Captain Ned Jones sailed the tern to St. John's to bring winter goods to Fogo.

Like many other vessels of its time, the tern toiled on in relative obscurity as it continued to ply the overseas trade, taking fish from Newfoundland to Oporto and returning with fishery salt. Not much is heard until December 28, 1923, when news about the tern came from Oporto. Captain Abner Butler and his crew reported that *Harriet* left Newfoundland in the fall of 1923 with a cargo of fish owned by Crosbie and Company.

In a storm the schooner hit the rocks near Sao Bartholomau about thirty miles north of its intended destination. *Harriet* was floated off and beached nearby. But in the terrible raging storm, seas breached over the vessel time and time again.

One wave which boarded the luckless ship smashed the bulwarks and carried nearly everything moveable off the deck. More tragic, one of the crew members, Richard Kenny of Petty Harbour, was swept over the side and was never seen again. A number of the other crew received extensive injuries such that they had to be hospitalized. The survivors were rescued by a breeches buoy.

Unlike its previous wreck in Fogo, on this occasion *Harriet* was never refloated.

Notes

1. This may be today's Port Albert, originally known as Little Beaver Cove after a prominent headland to the southwest. Beaver Cove was renamed in the 1920s, after Prince Albert, husband of Queen Victoria.

The area – Fogo, Twillingate, and Beaver Cove – had a thriving shipbuilding enterprise in the era of wooden ships. It is known that James Elliott of Little Beaver Cove built at least seven schooners there from 1894 to 1907: *Sea Bride*, *Jubilee*, *Bessie Elliott*, *Industry*, *Intrepid*, *Lizzie May*, *Osprey* and *Elrae*. Many of these were built for Earle's business of Fogo and the Elliotts of Change Islands.

2. Robert Scott (1835-1913) was born in Scotland and became an agent for Walter Grieve and Company until around 1865, when he established himself as a ship owner and trader at Fogo. Along with his general fishery supply business, Scott operated a passenger and freight service to and from Fogo Island. He was for many years magistrate, justice of the peace and collector of customs at Fogo. The chart (below) shows other ships registered in his name.

3. Other notable wrecks in the Tickles and around Fogo Island shores are: The schooner *Star*, belonging to the Gardiner family of Grey Islands and Coachman's Cove, was abandoned off Fogo in January 1887 (see clipping page 40); on September 18, 1887, Catalina schooner *Brothers* was lost with all five crew near Island Harbour, Fogo Island; schooner *Lavengro* was lost on Burnt Point during a blinding snow storm on December 11, 1915; the *Fayal*, a motorized vessel from

Vessels Owned and Operated by Robert Scott, Fogo

schooner *Lily*, 43 tons, built in Fogo in 1867
schooner *Harp*, 36 tons, built in 1868, place unrecorded
schooner *Clara Maria*, 113 tons, built in Fogo in 1870
schooner *Fox*, 68 tons, built in Fogo in 1871
schooner *Dove*, 24 tons, built in Joe Batt's Arm in 1871
schooner *Porcupine*, 60 tons, built in Fogo in 1875
schooner *Maggie Briggs*, 33 tons, built in Green Bay in 1880
schooner *Robert Freddis*, 38 tons, built in Exploits in 1883
steam/sail *Tibbie*, built 1884
brigantine *Laddie*, 84 tons, built in Fogo in 1893
schooner *Lassie*, 65 tons, built in Fogo in 1878
steam/sail *Annie*, 71 tons, built in Fogo in 1903

Portugal, became a total wreck on Western Tickle in Fogo harbour on September 4, 1935; the Portuguese motor vessel *Maria Joanna* was wrecked at Western Tickle as it entered Fogo harbour on September 28, 1948, and the *Sunset Glow*, wrecked in Fogo harbour in October 1949. In addition there have been numerous wrecks, many with loss of life, on or near Cann Island on the southern end of Fogo Island.

A gentleman has kindly favoured us with the following extracts from a letter received by him from Barr'd Island yesterday : " On the 22nd of January a schooner was seen outside of Fogo Islands, abandoned. She was boarded the following day by some men from Little Fogo, and later on, by men from here. Her sails and rigging were saved. She proved to be the *Star*, owned by a man named Gardiner, late of Grey Islands, now living at Coachman's Cove. We don't know what Little Fogo men saved. Fenimore & Co., who boarded her, reported to Mr. Fitzgerald.

"On the 28th of January, Miss Meek, school teacher, fell on the ice and dislocated her arm, fracturing the small bones at the elbow."

Evening Mercury of February 26, 1887, describes the loss of *Star* off Fogo.

CHAPTER 12
CLOSE CALL FOR *L.C. NORMAN*

MUSGRAVE HARBOUR AND CAPE BONAVISTA: Today near misses make the news. Headlines like 'Passenger Bus into Accident on TCH. No One Injured' or 'Canada Jet Slides off Runway. All Passengers Safe' are fairly common. But not so for the marine coastal trade a generation or two back. Schooner wrecks, groundings, strandings, and near misses on the sea were so frequent, the events rarely drew a whisper in local papers.

In November 1942, the auxiliary (powered by motor or sail) schooner *L.C. Norman* nearly piled into the bill, or tip, of Cape Bonavista. The occasion was not written up in local papers, but the near brush with death was so traumatic that one of the crew, Stewart Abbott, recalled it from fifty years before as clearly as if it happened yesterday.[1]

The two-masted, cutwater stem *L.C. Norman* had been around a long time; it shows up on Samuel Harris' roster of Grand Bank vessels. Built in1909 in Garnish, it was registered as forty-nine tons. Sometime in the 1920s it was sold to a business on Newfoundland's northwest coast.

In the fall of 1942, *L.C. Norman* was in the coasting trade. The crew consisted of Skipper Jesse West and Elmo Brinson of Carmanville; William and Stewart Abbott, Musgrave Harbour (no relation), and the cook, Charlie Goodyear. Deck hand Dick Saunders from Change Islands was a World War One veteran.

Stewart Abbott, perhaps the last of *L.C. Norman*'s crew alive today, remembered they left Carmanville to get a cargo of lumber at White Bay. The schooner was loaded with wood products at White Bay – scantling or planks in the

Seaman Stewart Abbott and author in November 2006.

hold, lumber piled six feet high on deck with 'wharf sticks', or pilings, on top of the lumber. In addition the small motor boat was lashed on top of the deck load. Coasting schooners were usually well laden in order to make the voyage a paying trip.

Skipper West brought *L.C. Norman* back to Carmanville before proceeding on to St. John's with the lumber. To Stewart Abbott the main sheet or sail looked the worse for wear, and although he expressed his doubts about the seaworthiness of the sail, it was decided not to repair or replace it.

In time the schooner left Carmanville, made its way northeast toward Cape Bonavista, but by this time there was, as Abbott recalled, "a nice breeze of wind from the northeast that came on stronger and stronger." Near the cape, he says, there is the northern bill or extreme edge of land and the southern bill. Sometime that night Abbott was up forward port side, Elmo Brinson was forward too, starboard side – both keeping a lookout for the Cape Bonavista northern bill.

Skipper West was at the wheel. They figured they were past the southern bill; now if they could round the treacherous northern bill, the schooner would be home free with plenty of sea room for the eastward voyage to St. John's. Stewart Abbott recalled the story this way:

> Now the engine we had below on *L.C. Norman* was an old motor, double cylinder, but one of the pistons was 'fooled up' and the engine was likely to give out or stop any time. In those days you went with what you had. It wasn't always easy to get parts and expertise to fix or repair a motor.
>
> Anyway the engineer was down trying to get the engine started again. It was only every now and then the motor would go. If we could get the motor going we could easily keep the ship off the land and clear the Cape.
>
> All of a sudden the skipper called, 'There's the northern bill.' Right away, the northern bill. Right on top of it. Skipper called out, 'Hard down, hard' to Brinson and myself. Then out off the cape, the wind chopped and another storm of wind was right down on top of us, right in our face.
>
> When the schooner came around, it had the mainsail barred across. If you had to reef it or anything in this wind, you almost had to tear your fingernails off to get it tied.
>
> When the schooner turned, up goes the main boom, Bang! It goes forward, strikes the main rigging. The main boom broke off about ten or fifteen feet and then t'was all over the side. A lot of the rigging and sail was all out over the side of her.
>
> Now we couldn't get the schooner around, the old mainsail lashed on the spar was out over the side, half in the water, main boom was broke and the motor wasn't going. *L.C. Norman* began to drift in toward these rocks of the northern bill.
>
> Being a young man then, I was game for anything, so I went out on the spar trying to free it up. I'd say I was five feet out on the spar over the water.

Then the skipper came forward and said, 'Boys, let go the anchor. Let it go about a couple of fathom down to try and keep her steady. That's the only way we might clear Bonavista Cape.' *L.C. Norman* was driving in on the cape by this time.

I came in from the spar and the ship was steadying up somewhat. I went down below forward to where the cook was.

I believe the cook had poor vision; nearly blind. I said to him, 'Now Charlie, it looks like we're going in on Bonavista Head; there's nothing surer than that.'

I explained to him how he could save his life in case we struck under the cliff. 'You follow me. When I go to jump to the cliff, you come right behind me. When the boat surges into the rocks, I'll jump. If you jump when it surges out, you'll be taken back with it. So wait and watch for me.'

I went up and back aft. By this time William Abbott was at the wheel. *L.C. Norman* was no more than fifty or sixty feet from the outermost rocks of northern bill of Cape Bonavista. I thought, 'Well, 'tis all over!'

By this time we did have the foresail and jumbo up, but not the mainsail. That was gone. With that bit of sail, the schooner caught. The wind changed, or slackened or increased or something and the schooner didn't hit the rock. Then, the engineer got the old motor going. The motor gave us a bit more help.

The motor and bit of sail got us out far enough from the cape, the wind caught the foresail and then the jumbo. Then the skipper had us heave away at the anchor. We 'pumped' that up as they call it and got the anchor on the bow. We didn't mind the work now.

As *L.C. Norman* nudged out into open ocean, the wind was still strong and cold. We all worked at the mess of rigging, and got a lot of it, including the piece of the boom, in on deck.

Two or three of us sat on the windlass all that night watching the Cape Bonavista. The topping lift was all fooled up, big sheet (mainsail) useless, water coming in over the side of her and all iced up. But we edged on and edged on and finally we got into King's Cove. We tied on to a wharf there.

One of the first things I noticed was another schooner I knew – the old *Elrae* which is EARLE spelled backwards. It was once Premier Joey Smallwood's schooner that he used to go around in when collecting fish on the northeast coast. I could recall seeing that one in Musgrave Harbour often when it was under skipper Aquilla Hicks of Carmanville.

Now there was no wood (long, heavy, straight sticks) in King's Cove, only what we call 'craddicks.' We went up to this man in King's Cove and asked him if he could find enough wood so we could fish up the main boom – fish it up, put wood around it and repair it.

That's what we did. The next morning we left again for St. John's. When we got out, bless me if the wind didn't breeze up again and we only had a fished-up main boom and a cranky engine for the weather.

When we got up off Conception Bay, we had to run into Western Bay, near Spaniard's Bay and anchor off. The wind was still on the schooner for there was no shelter in that port. It was only what they call a ring harbour.

There was winch or deck engine on deck and with that we got the *L.C. Norman*'s small motor boat off. We went into a beach and then up to the house where Billy Abbott's daughter lived and we stayed the night.

When we left *L.C. Norman* that night in Conception Bay, I didn't expect to see her anymore except on the bottom because she didn't have good anchor chains. But we went aboard the next morning, started it up, proceeded on to St. John's and unloaded our cargo.

L.C. Norman got such a banging up from the storm, the skipper decided to keep it tied up at St. John's for the winter. I came home on the S.S. *Glencoe* and landed back in Carmanville on January 11. The steamer didn't stop in Musgrave Harbour, so I walked all through the country with my clothes bag and suitcase, snow up to my waist.

There is one tragic footnote to this near-miss marine tale as Stewart Abbott recalled. The cook Charles Goodyear (Stewart's first cousin) later drowned on the coasting schooner *Mollie*. On the night of December 19-20, 1944, the vessel wrecked near Grates Cove. Lost with him were Skipper Ross Chaulk, age twenty-six and unmarried; mate James Ellsworth, twenty-five, unmarried; John Goodyear, sixty-one and his two sons Reginald, thirty-two, Charles, twenty-six, both unmarried; and Otto Hicks, a widower with one child. All belonged to Carmanville except Hicks who was a resident of Musgrave Harbour.[2]

Notes

1. On two or three occasions I visited Stewart Abbott formerly of Musgrave Harbour and living in Gander. He was a man who loved a sea yarn and someone to share it with. He could recall nine schooners on which he sailed:

Schooners Seaman Abbott Sailed on:

Vessel	Place	Captain and/or Owner
Mary Greta	Musgrave Hr.	George D. Abbott
Rita Windsor	Carmanville	Don Goodyear
C & A Brown	Carmanville	Theophilus Blackwood
Sam	Carmanville	Harry Guy
Modern Flapper	Carmanville	Jack Goodyear
Alice M. Pike	Carmanville	Arch Blundon
L.C. Norman	Carmanville	Jesse West
Irene May	Lewisporte	Elam Parsons
Clammer	St. Brendan's	Mike Ryan

Another unique ship which quietly departed the scene in Newfoundland Labrador at this time was the little steamer *Walter Kennedy*. It was one of several 100-ton steamers built in Quebec in 1917 for the war effort. They had no name, only a registration number. When the war ended, many were sold to Newfoundland interests and named – the *Wop, H. A. Walker* and *Walter Kennedy*.

The latter (seen above in St. John's and under the ownership of the Bell Island Steamship Company) was named for well-known captain Walter Kennedy of Holyrood. Kennedy began fishing at age fifteen and at twenty-one took charge of sailing vessels. He went to the fishing banks for thirty-two years fishing on the Grand Banks. Several of those years, he owned his own banker (banker vessel) or was captain. In 1915 he was in charge of H.M. Patrol ships in the North Sea, serving until the end of the war.

In March 1907 Captain Walter Kennedy brought down the ten-dory schooner *Hispaniola* from Lunenburg for Patrick Farrell's business of St. Lawrence.

On December 5, 1934, the S.S. *Walter Kennedy* was wrecked at Miquelon Head.

Photo courtesy Maritime History Archive, Memorial University, St. John's.

2. This *Mollie*, an eighty-five-ton vessel and eighty-two-foot long, was built in Shelburne, Nova Scotia in 1905. In 1932 Jasper Chaulk of Carmanville purchased it. The tale of the *Mollie* of Three Arms is found in Chapter 15.

CHAPTER 13
SHIPWRECK AT ST. PAUL ISLAND

PETLEY, ST. PAUL ISLAND, TORBAY AND NEW-WES-VALLEY: St. Paul Island. This rugged crag in the ocean, named by explorer John Cabot in 1497, is located in the Cabot Strait, about forty-four miles from Newfoundland and fifteen miles from the northern tip of Nova Scotia. Its rockface cliff coastline is about three miles long and one mile wide. It takes about two hours by boat to reach St. Paul Island from Bay St. Lawrence, Nova Scotia.

M.V. *Monica Walters* had been built in Petley by James Walters and his two sons, Lawrence and Harry. In this ariel shot taken from a newspaper image, *Monica Walters* is in ice and sinking.

On March 26, 1948, the wreck of a Newfoundland ship off its shores represented the beginning and the end of Dunphy's Limited venture into the seal fishery. That spring Dunphys Ltd., Curling, outfitted the seventy-four-ton wooden ship *Monica R. Walters* for the Cabot Strait seal fishery, putting Captain Fred Hounsell of Pinchard's Island in command.

Any venture at sea has its underlying risks and chance freaks of nature which can bring a swift end to ships and lives. But in winter, with huge rafts and sheets of ice heaving and swaying the tossing Atlantic, it is surely more risky than most prospects.

In essence, *Monica Walters* was not built to withstand the tons of pressure per square inch ice can exert. When this vessel came to doom in the spring of 1948, it was a cold reception for the Dunphys.

It left Port aux Basques in the last week of March and in short time was into the seals. The seventeen men anticipated a quick and profitable voyage. Plenty of seals waited on the great flat sheets of ice. There was no difficulty walking to them and soon the crew had about a thousand pelts "sculped."

Crew of *Monica Walters*: back row, l-r: Engineer Kirk Anderson, Bonne Bay, Bay of Islands; Howard Gill, Pinchard's Island; cook Herbert Norman, Newtown; Victor Vincent, Newtown; William O'Keefe, ? Middle Row, l-r: Hubert Yeo, Torbay; Tom Tuff, Templeman, Bonavista Bay; Captain Fred Hounsell, Pinchard's Island; Gerald Tuff, Templeman; William Tuff, Templeman: Harold Price, Newtown. Front Row, l-r: Cornelius Marshall; Bonne Bay; Charles Codner, Torbay; Robert Codner, Torbay; Philip Thorne, Torbay; Jesse Codner, Torbay; Alex Perry, Newtown. Picture of crew courtesy Winston Perry, Wesleyville.[1]

Sealers were still in the midst of their work with the seals when, without warning, the ice erupted under terrific pressure of the heaving sea. Great pans, several feet thick, buckled and reared up on end. The same pressure began to bear on the wooden hull of *Monica R. Walters*. The ship was not in open water, but in a field of ice about thirty-five miles long and eight miles wide – an ominous sheet that spelled disaster.

Captain Hounsell recalled after that the ice first rafted about 1:00 a.m. Friday, March 26 when *Monica Walters* was about twelve to fourteen miles from St. Paul Island. The vessel was first pushed up, up by rafting ice and it would come down - not in the same shape it went up. He recalled:

> I ordered the men to the ice and all dories and food supplies. Ten minutes later the vessel fell back into the water and we went back aboard.
>
> I contacted Grindstone on the Magdalene Islands and told them we were in a dangerous position and wanted assistance. Twenty minutes later we rafted again and we returned to the dories and our food supplies on the ice. I had told Grindstone the ship was breaking up. It was going down fast.
>
> I was the last to leave *Monica R. Walters*. At that time the bottom was broken out and the mainmast had fallen. It was heaving badly and the escape from a sinking ship was dangerous.

We built a fire on the ice, set up a tent and waited for daylight. At 6:15 a.m. we sighted St. Paul Island some distance off to the southwest. We put all the equipment in the dories and started to haul them toward the island.

We discarded two dories and all of us suffered from the cold. But we arrived at St. Paul at 8:30 a.m.

Fortunately they didn't encounter open water during the trek from the shipwreck to the island. In distance and time it was a short journey, but with the cold and exhaustion, the seventeen sealers were exhausted when they reached safety. Although disheartened at the destruction of a vessel and their potential earnings, the crew was otherwise happy there had been no injury or fatality. As it turned out when they reached the end of the walk, some had to be helped finish by the light keepers on the island.

From St. Paul they were taken by the government icebreaker *Saurel* to North Sydney and thence back across the Strait by the S.S. *Cabot Strait*. Captain Hounsell summarized his encounter with the ice, saying: "It was my first such experience in thirteen years of sailing and I hope it's my last."

Notes

1. Much of the wreck details came from Nova Scotian papers of the day (*Sydney Post Record* March 27, 1948). Winston Perry of Newtown first alerted me to many names of the sealers and provided the photo. Other sealers in the photo were identified by Robert Codner and Hubert Yeo of Torbay.

Of the seventeen crew on *Monica Walters*, it is interesting to note that there were three Tuffs from Templeman, Bonavista Bay and of the five crew from Torbay, three were Codner brothers. The son of Torbay's Philip Thorne married Sheila Copps, the long-time Liberal MP in Ottawa.

CHAPTER 14
ONE SURVIVOR TO TELL THE TALE

GREENSPOND AND CABOT ISLAND: The first reports of a shipwreck on Cabot Island were confusing. There was no doubt that the wreck was the Greenspond schooner *Puritan*. On January 2, 1900, Captain Darius Blandford, born in Greenspond and a Member of the House of Assembly, sent word to St. John's that the schooner *Puritan* was lost with only one survivor out of the nine men believed to be aboard.

When he heard of the disaster, Blandford had taken the S.S. *Alert* from Greenspond to Cabot Island on New Year's Day, but was unable to land on the island due to high seas. From a distance, no doubt aided by a telescope, he saw only one person moving on the island. He could not say for sure where the rest of *Purtian*'s crew were; they may have been sick or disabled.

Blandford had also received a report from the government steamer *Virginia Lake* that eight people had been seen on the island, and there was concern over who was captain of *Puritan* when it had sailed from St. John's to Greenspond in late December 1899. One thing was certain – all aboard *Puritan* were from Greenspond, a town situated on the northwest side of Bonavista Bay.

Puritan, built in New Perlican in 1890, began its career as one of Edwin Duder's extensive fleet. At twenty-three feet wide, eight feet in depth with an overall length of sixty-five feet, it was well-built in the Pittman shipyard in New Perlican. By 1899, the sixty-seven-ton vessel was owned by Captain Alexander "Sandy" Carter of Greenspond. *Puritan* finished the summer fishing season and in the late fall of 1899, with the Carter mariners in command, had gone to St. John's for winter food and supplies.

Then on January 3 Magistrate Seymour at Greenspond wired St. John's, saying the S.S. *Alert* had arrived from Cabot Island:

"Alert *brought (to Greenspond) one survivor, John Hoskins, and the body of Eli Allen. The following crew and passengers have all perished, bodies driven to sea: – Frederick John Carter, married, no family; Kenneth Carter, married, two in family; Edgar Dyke, single; Job Burton, single; Ludwig Harding, single; George Young, single; Robert Lush, married, no family. Eli Allen leaves wife and daughter.*

"Puritan *lost last Tuesday night (December 26, 1899) at 7:00 p.m. in heavy sea. Hoskins leaped from main boom to landwash. Boat containing the others stove in and all perished. Writing further particulars by mail."* [*Evening Herald* January 4, 1900]

It was soon determined that *Puritan*'s owner and captain, Alexander Carter, was not on the vessel. He had been ill and remained ashore, giving command to his brother Fred. Fred Carter had been married one month prior at St. Thomas Church in St. John's. After the wedding his wife, Beatrice (Peckford) Carter, had gone home by another train and would have taken the ferry from Port Blandford to Greenspond. As a result, she was not on *Puritan* when it wrecked on Cabot Island.

By January 8, survivor John Hoskins was able to relate the awful particulars of the loss of the schooner and the deaths of eight shipmates. *Puritan* left St. John's on Christmas Day at 4:00 p.m. for Greenspond. Weather was fine, until at night, when about halfway across Conception Bay, there was thick fog.

Tuesday noon, *Puritan* passed Cape Bonavista – barely seen though the haze – and ran inside the Old Harry, a dangerous shoal hazardous to shipping. Course was altered for home port, northwesterly across Bonavista Bay to Greenspond.

Captain Fred Carter, like all masters of vessels in that era, relied on his experience as captain gathered from years before the mast as a sailor and had learned the lore and skills of navigation from other experienced captains. In those days of few charts and many ocean hazards, knowledge of landmarks, beacon lights, capes and headlands was vital.

But in the fog of 5:30 p.m. December 26, the glimmer of a light could be seen in the distance. The captain and crew believed this to be from the lighthouse on Puffin Island, not far from the entrance to Greenspond harbour. The two islands are ten miles apart and the lights flash at different intervals, but in fog and poor weather conditions a tragic error happened.

The attempt to avoid Puffin Island sent *Puritan* near the rocks of Cabot Island. The nine people aboard came on deck, expecting soon to be safely in port. At 7:15 *Puritan* struck the rocks bow on with terrific force at Southwest Cove, Cabot Island.

Immediately, instant decisions had to be made; first to save lives and then the ship, if possible. A tremendous high sea was running, great white combers ground against the rocks of the island. Strange to say, as Hoskins related, "No one on board heard the breakers before the vessel struck." According to a report in *The Evening Herald* of January 8, 1900, which describes Hoskins' ordeal:

> ...*Captain Carter was forward on the jibboom at the time; his brother Kenneth had the helm. Immediately the boat was hoisted out, three jumping into it, while two others, in trying to do so fell into the water and were quickly drowned. The boat and its occupants were swamped in a few moments.*
>
> *Survivor Hoskins, Captain Carter and George Allen were now on the quarter, and the last seen of poor Allen was while he knelt by the fore rigging praying. Hoskins ran to the lee side to see if he could manage to jump on a rock, but knowing it meant instant death to do so, clambered out under the main boom. This was across the vessel and to which he held with his hands and feet.*

Hoskin's escape was nothing short of miraculous for it was not just a matter of crawling over the boom to the rocks. The vessel was surging back and forth, white foam ran the decks and as often as not, the boom was under water, then above as waves pounded it and the remains of *Puritan* against the shore. The boom itself was a tangle of sail and ropes. Nevertheless, Hoskins saw his only chance to live.

When about halfway out on the boom, with a hold that was anything but secure, he was immersed in water and almost smothered as the hull rolled. He once lost his grip, but held on with one hand.

He eventually reached the end of the boom and, waiting until a comber receded, dropped on his face and stomach into comparatively shallow water – waist deep – and waded to the rocks, about thirty yards distant.

He was met by James Bishop, the light keeper on Cabot Island who brought him to his home and cared for him. Up to then, Hoskins still thought that the schooner had struck Puffin Island.

About ten minutes after the wreck an enormous sea struck the vessel, demolishing it. For a few moments the agonizing cries of the captain could be heard as he was tossed about by the sea on a portion of the wreckage. The other crewmen had probably perished by this time. John Hoskins and Captain Carter were the only two of *Puritan*'s fishing crew from the summer who were on board. The others, except Allen and Burton who were passengers, had joined *Puritan* when it sailed to St. John's for winter supplies.

Hoskins, who had a wife and six children, lost all his personal effects, as well as his winter supplies and food which he had on board. When he arrived in Greenspond, he was utterly destitute and had to wear clothes supplied by a friend.

Only Eli Allen's body, washed in on the rocks of Cabot Island, had been recovered. There was not much left of the once proud ship *Puritan*; much debris was swept out to sea although its spars drifted into Pool's Island, ten miles away. On February 14, 1900, three people living in Greenspond at the time -- Methodist Minister Thomas B. Darby, Darius Blandford and S.A. Dawson – set up a fund for charitable donations with contributions collected and dispersed by John Cowan, M.H.A. for Bonavista district.[1]

Notes

1. This tale of tragedy came from *The Evening Herald* of January 2, 3, 4, 6 and 8, 1900; *The Evening Telegram*, undated article; family genealogy of the Blandford and Carter family from Craig Morrissey and Linda White.

CHAPTER 15
"OUR FATE WOULD BE SEALED"

GREENSPOND, GOOSEBERRY ISLANDS, THREE ARMS: Greenspond Magistrate Isaac James Mifflin sent an urgent message to the Minister of Marine and Fisheries, T. J. Murphy. Dated December 13, 1902, it read:

> Inhabitants here at Greenspond report seeing a light on Offer Gooseberry Island last night and saw a flag this afternoon. The S.S. *Dundee* is now here. Arrange with the Reid Newfoundland Co. that she may go off there immediately.

A subsequent message said that two nights earlier, Wednesday, people on the Inner Gooseberry Island had seen a large fire on the Offer islet, a barren rock rising out of the sea, two miles from the Inner Gooseberry.[1]

Dundee had passed the islets on its coastal run and brought the news to Greenspond. Finance Minister Jackman and Murphy went at once to see the manager of Reid's and they arranged to have the steamer sent to the Offer Gooseberry Island.

Captain Blandford and the *Dundee* arrived back in Greenspond at 10:00 p.m. Saturday night. Minister Murphy received this missive:

> Have just returned from Gooseberry Island. Found the crew of the schooner *Mollie*, John Norris master. The vessel took fire on Wednesday last (December 11) when she was beached there. The crew was all saved but, owing to the big sea, we only succeeded in getting the master tonight. We will try again after daylight. The crew are in camp and have plenty of provisions. The vessel is a total wreck.

By Sunday, the remaining four crew had been taken from the bare Gooseberry and *Dundee* continued its eastward route to Port Blandford. The crew, who all belonged to Three Arms, caught a westbound train. Captain Norris, the owner of *Mollie*, went to St. John's. There he filed a report on the loss of *Mollie*.

Mollie, said Norris, was laden with a full load of winter supplies. "We were on the way from St. John's to Three Arms, Notre Dame Bay. Even the cabin was full of cases, boxes and bags of food and supplies. We hit a storm of wind and snow in Bonavista Bay which the *Mollie* could have weathered, but there was no one in the galley at the time when the stove upset in the gale."

> The squall which first struck the vessel must have overturned the stove. It was freezing hard at the time and there was a big fire on. We threw water down the companionway, but without effect. We cut holes through

The steamer *Dundee* which brought the shipwrecked Captain Norris from Gooseberry Island to Greenspond.
Photo courtesy of Maritime History Archives, MUN Accession # PF-001.1-J39b

the deck and poured water down from four or five different points, but the flames still gained headway.

One of the crew now informed us that there was a keg of twenty-five pounds of gunpowder only a few feet from the bulkhead. If the fire reached it our fate would be sealed.

It was 10:30 a.m. Wednesday and the snow cleared somewhat and land could be seen in the lee. I feared the ship would be blown up at any moment and ran for the land. At 11:00 a.m. it was clear enough to see this was Offer Gooseberry Island.

By now the fire had burnt through the deck and caught the foresail and other head sails. We provisioned the punt with food, supplies, an axe, a flag and other gear, preparing it for launching. *Mollie* was luffed about the point of the island to gain smooth water.

Then a wave boarded our ship, tore the stem out of the punt and washed what was left overboard, aft of the main rigging. The only hope now was to beach the *Mollie* and, accordingly, it was run ashore on rocky bottom.

A succession of heavy waves threw her within eight feet of land. Now, while beaching, the vessel was heading into the wind and smoke and flames were thrown aft to where we were huddled.

We crossed the dangerous spot where the powder lay below deck and clambered out on the bowsprit.

Captain Norris said, "At this point we were terrified the gunpowder would explode at any moment." They had to get off the ship and soon. Norris offered to attempt the dangerous crossing to land first. The crew lowered him down and he swung on the rope as far as possible; then dropped and waded to land.

The rope was set taut and the other crew climbed ashore. About ten minutes after landing, the keg of powder exploded. Norris said after, "It blew the little schooner to smithereens from the pall post to the taffrail, throwing the foremast over the port side."

The crew was now on a barren island without shelter from the wind and snow. From the wreck they gathered two half bags of bread, a box of Christmas fruit, two barrels of flour and a cask of kerosene. This was all secured and kept dry from the wind and wet weather as well as possible. There was a crude hut on the island and about 3:00 in the afternoon they lit a fire.

ANOTHER WRECK !

SCHOONER ON FIRE

IS BEACHED !

The Crew Saved

At 5 p. m. Saturday Mr. T. J. Murphy, Minister of Marine and Fisheries, received the following despatch from Magistrate Mifflen, of Greenspond :—"Inhabitants here report seeing a light or offer Gooseberry Island last night and we can see a flag this afternoon. The s.s. Dundee is now here; arrange with the Reid Newfoundland Co. that she may go off there immediately." Immediately upon the receipt of this message Ministers Jackman, and Murphy called upon Messrs. Reid and Captain Blandford was instructed to visit the place. At 10 o'clock Saturday night another message was received which read "Have just returned from Gooseberry Island; found the crew of the schooner Mollie, John Norris, master

The beaching and burning of *Mollie* is featured in *The Daily News* December 15, 1902.

For two days the shipwrecked crew of *Mollie* lived on soaked bread and fruit. Two pieces of cloth – material for making dresses – drove ashore and from this they made a flag. On Friday the castaways made a huge fire of boughs soaked with kerosene. This fire attracted the people of Greenspond; by Saturday; rescue efforts were underway.

Captain Norris said that when the steamer *Dundee* arrived, its crew put off a boat, but could not approach the rock due to seas. For three quarters of an hour it lay by, until finally he jumped and reached the boat.

John Norris was carried to Greenspond and, when the wind abated, set out with the *Dundee* on its second trip to get the crew. "After a hard time," said Norris, "they were rescued , but they spent a fearful time on the island from Wednesday to Sunday morning."

Built the year previous at Three Arms, *Mollie* netted fifty-six ton with an overall length of sixty-four feet. It was registered to James Norris, Captain John Norris' father. Although the schooner was insured and the cargo partly covered, the loss to the Norris' business was devastating. Captain Norris had to duplicate the cargo, arranging to have it shipped to Three Arms via the railway and the steamer *Clyde*.

For twenty-seven years the Norris' shipping enterprise rarely experienced a loss at sea. That all changed in November 1902. The Norris' carried a load of fish to St. John's just as a downturn in the price of salt cod came. Profits were slim. James Norris was on his way home to Three Arms when he heard of the wreck of his schooner *Allright* on December 5.

E. Norris was in command as *Allright* carried supplies to Notre Dame Bay and, while sheltering for the night at Catalina, ran aground in the harbour. Some cargo was salvaged, but the schooner was a total loss. A few days later *Mollie* met its end.[2]

Notes

1. Gooseberry Islands are situated in Bonavista Bay to the east of Hare Bay, Bonavista Bay, and to the north of Eastport. Captain Norris, an expert seaman and experienced captain, had saved his life and that of his crew beaching the schooner without running aground on a ledge or rock many feet off the island.

According to a description in the *Newfoundland Encyclopedia*, "Offer Gooseberry is so encumbered by shoals that it is not navigable without detailed knowledge of the region." Inner Gooseberry was inhabited up to the mid-1950s.

2. *Allright* was built in South West Arm, Notre Dame Bay, in 1894. This vessel too was a considerable size – fifty-eight net tons and sixty-three feet long. Chapter 6 relates how other Norris' ships met their end.

CHAPTER 16
A DARK AND STORMY EVENING

BARROW HARBOUR, BIG AND LITTLE: Many years ago, the ten gun brig *Black Prince*, of 380 ton and carrying eighty men, came under the command of Guy DeVoux. DeVoux was no ordinary captain; rather he was regarded as the terror of the Atlantic and one of the most desperate pirates of his day. His name was familiar to every merchantman on the seas. But Guy DeVoux was soon to become synonymous with Barrow Harbour, Newfoundland – especially the narrow parcel of land that separates Little Barrow Harbour from Big Barrow Harbour.

It was October 30th; the year 1780. *Black Prince* sailed in a time of lawlessness and piracy on the high seas and when many a snug hidden harbour around Newfoundland became a refuge for desperados and fugitives.

Barrow Harbour was one such hideaway. Today it's an abandoned settlement on the southeastern tip of the Eastport Peninsula, Bonavista Bay, and it once had close economic ties with Salvage. During the Napoleonic Wars, 1796 to 1814, Barrow Harbour was used as a refuge for ships because it could be easily defended against French naval attack. Its main use in later years, however, was a supply and trading depot for fishermen in Greenspond, King's Cove and vicinity.

But back on that October day, *Black Prince*'s lookout suddenly shouted, "A sail ahead!" From out of the blackness of a foggy Atlantic day loomed the hull of a brig, which DeVoux recognized as a Newfoundland merchantman. It proved to be the *Scotch Lass* from Bristol, laden with general cargo, consigned to two branch trading houses in Bonavista Bay.

Like a shot *Scotch Lass* slipped by *Black Prince*. DeVoux gave the order to bear away and soon the pirate ship was in full pursuit of the gallant merchantman. The fog lifted and the wind freshened, giving *Scotch Lass* enough energy to outwit and outsail the dreaded pester of the north seas.

Scotch Lass was about three miles ahead when it rounded Cape Bonavista. In the late evening the pirate ship had gained to within a half mile of its prey. The latter had prepared for eventualities and he knew the coastline well, but Captain William Snow, its commander, knew that unless his ship outsailed *Black Prince*, he was doomed.

The pirate was a mile behind as both sailed southeasterly into Bonavista Bay. Snow set his course for a nest of rocks and shoals which must be navigated to reach Rocky Bay, his haven of rest. Snow felt that should Guy DeVoux follow, the *Black Prince* would find its grave in that treacherous region.

All went well until Willis' Reach, the mouth of the trap, was within ten miles of *Scotch Lass*. The wind veered northeast, with light snow. Within a short time the squall had grown into a hurricane and the merchantman, within sight of safety, was compelled to bear away before the howling northeasterly.

Then, in the midst of the snow squall, *Scotch Lass*' mate John Crotty gave the alarm, "Land on our lee!" to be instantly followed by the captain's command –

"Hard a starboard, stand by the anchors." A minute or so later, "Let go the anchors; give every inch of chain."

Within four minutes the wily Captain Snow had *Scotch Lass* saved from shipwreck and it hung by the anchors in a snug and grand harbour, know to us as Big Barrow Harbour, near today's Salvage.

Meanwhile Guy DeVoux, following close on the heels of Captain Snow found himself in the same snow squall that raged when John Crotty had shouted, "Land on the lee." Those on *Black Prince* lost sight of *Scotch Lass*. The pirate ship ran a few yards further north than the merchantman and without warning *Black Prince* grounded on the sandy bottom of Little Barrow Harbour. By a slight change in course, it had gone a little north instead of south of the point of land that separates the two Barrow harbours.

Scotch Lass was safe, sheltered from the howling hurricane. Guy DeVoux, when his ship struck, believed it to be at least ten miles from any land. He had no idea where the wily merchantman was. Little did he know Captain Snow was "riding it out" snugly behind a headland and within 200 yards of *Black Prince*.

DeVoux fortunately found his stranding place was sand, not rocks which saved his ship of ten guns from being broken into fragments on a granite ledge or under some cliff – those abounded to his right and left.

Seventy-eight of the pirate's crew reached shore safely. While battling waves, two crew members were struck by pieces of wreckage, one of whom was DeVoux's second in command. Their bodies were recovered on the beach hours later.

Within two hours of stranding, the gale abated. *Black Prince*'s hull was intact, but all boats had been swept away or smashed beyond repair. Some pieces of sail were recovered; thus the crew had some shelter to protect them for the rest of the cold night.

At daylight, October 31, the storm was over and all were astir to determine what damage had been done to *Black Prince*. At noon, one of the crew on some height of land spied the merchantman making its way down the bay. In the gentle western breeze *Scotch Lass* was not long arriving at its destination no worst for wear for the chase and the hurricane. Snow believed his feared adversary had made its last chase.

Meanwhile, DeVoux had set about refloating his gallant ship. There was no damage to the bottom, but the topmasts and yards were gone and the several tattered sails were replaced by a second or spare set.

But all his best efforts to float *Black Prince* were useless and, with a heavy heart, he decided to unship his ten cannon. He would also place all empty casks available under the ship to await a spring tide. The guns were spiked (vents plugged to render them useless) and cast over the side. At last the ship floated free; then was fitted and made ready to sail. The cannon could not be recovered.

For a few hours before sailing, the desperate sea rovers forgot their calling, their vulnerable and isolated conditions, and gently carried the remains of the two drowned sailors to their grave sites. Choosing a clearing in the woods nearby, they gently laid each in his own grave, not knowing that eighty years later Newfoundland settlers would be on that very location.

The spot chosen for burial was on the point of land separating Big Barrow Harbour from Little Barrow Harbour, which was later occupied by a settler family named Crocker.

Black Prince was never again known to cause trouble in the North Atlantic. It was said that DeVoux shaped his course for South America where he eventually fell into the hands of a British frigate.

In 1840, sixty years after the stranding of *Black Prince*, Henry Wells settled upon the point of land containing the pirate graves and discovered them while clearing land. Digging nearby he found brass buttons and other trinkets. The graves were left untouched and could be seen for years after; indeed they were called "Frenchmen's graves" by local people.

An adopted daughter of Wells married a Mr. Crocker. Both knew the location of the graves, and for many years possessed the property found at the site. David Smallwood (the grandfather of former Premier Joseph R. Smallwood) once visited the location, searching for pirates' hidden gold. This plunder he expected to be found at Denier Island, two or three miles distant, but he was intrigued by the tales of pirate or "French" artifacts at Barrow Harbour.

Other residents of Barrow Harbour found clay pipes, pieces of iron and large wrought nails which were always identified by inhabitants as "French pipes" and "French nails."

Another early settler of Little Barrow Harbour was William Hefferman (Heffern) who moved there in about 1845 from Bonavista. The piece of land which he cleared for a cabbage garden was the site of the pirate's camp used at the stranding of *Black Prince*. He and his children found pipes, nails and pieces of iron in the garden.

John, the son of William Hefferman, while fitting out his schooner in the spring of 1880, happened to look overboard on a calm clear day. He saw something unusual lying on the bottom directly under the schooner, which was then hauled in near his stage. He and his crew decided the strange sight must be a cannon.

Eventually they succeeded in pulling it on to dry land. The piece was eight feet long and took about a six-inch ball. Spiked and plugged tightly with cork, no water had entered the cannon. The iron was not corroded, but so soft that for two or three days pieces of iron could be cut off with a knife. Then it tempered as hard as flint.

In time, a mooring chain entangled around the cannon and during a storm it rolled into the water. Yet at low tide the gun could be examined. John Hefferman subsequently made a thorough examination of the area and discovered nine more cannons in about fifteen feet of water; seven of which were tumbled across each other in one spot.

Thus today on the bottom lie the jettisoned guns, nearby the remains of two of *Black Prince*'s crew – all that's left of a pirate ship which once stranded at Barrow Harbour on the dark and stormy evening of October 30th, 1780.[1]

Notes
1. This story was adapted from a report written by Sir W.F. Coaker, founder of the Fishermen's Protective Union.

CHAPTER 17
TWO BONAVISTA CATASTROPHES

BONAVISTA, ST. JOHN'S NARROWS: Delivering fish in through the busy St. John's Narrows in the era of all sail schooners was fraught with danger: a narrow opening, one of the busiest seaports on the eastern North American seaboard, unpredictable winds and the difficulty of maneuvering sailing ships in wind and current. In 1889, there was another in a series of shipping disasters off St. John's – this one with devastating consequences for Bonavista.

The Bonavista craft *Psyche*, left Baine Johnson and Company's wharf on October 18, laden with winter supplies. It was manned by five Bonavista seamen – Captain William Carroll, age fifty-eight and a widower with four children; his son Joseph Carroll, age twenty-eight, married with one child; James Powell, age thirty-eight, married with seven children; George Ryan, age forty-two, married with five children and James Pardy, age thirty-one, married with no children.

Around 6:00 p.m. when *Psyche* was outside the Narrows, the crew put their light, a candle, within a glass lantern in the port rigging. A light draft of wind came from the south southwest. Off Blackhead, the southern cape of Pouch Cove, Powell was at the helm. Joseph Carroll was on look-out while the captain supervised the trim of sails. Ryan was below, while James Pardy was getting ready to come on deck.

Carroll saw a large ship which later proved to be the S.S. *Falcon*, Captain Richard Pike, coming from Heart's Content to St. John's. Those on *Psyche*'s deck watched the steamer loom closer through the night and could see its two lights for ten minutes.

When it came too close, one of the Bonavista men called out, "Swing to the port!" The steamer failed to respond, but kept coming head on toward *Psyche*. The wind was so light, the schooner had no power to answer its helm or to avoid the onrushing *Falcon*.

Falcon struck *Psyche* on the port quarter at an estimated speed of eight miles an hour, at an angle so forcibly that it turned the small craft completely over. The ramming happened so quickly the schooner seemed to sink immediately beneath the feet of the crew.

Psyche went down stern foremost, then bobbed back up, bottom up. Ryan managed to grab hold to a part of the schooner's bulwarks. He kept his head above the surface of the water, although at times he went down with the bobbing wreck and came back up. When a boat came from *Falcon*, he was pulled from his precarious position.

Joseph Carroll clung to the wreck in the same way as Ryan until rescued. James Pardy, who had just climbed the companionway when the steamer hit, was a good swimmer. He went down, seemingly for fathoms, after *Psyche* heeled over. He fought his way to the surface, swam alongside the wreck and climbed on the bowsprit until he was taken off.

Bonavista in the 1940s, taken from the Ragged Rocks, Canaille, showing the Mockbeggar breakwater in the background. Near the flake (foreground) is where the marine service facility is located now.

Courtesy Gordon Bradley

Captain Pike claims he reversed the engines immediately after impact and had a boat lowered. Three survivors were taken on board and, after a lengthy search could only find three of the five aboard *Psyche*. Captain William Carroll and Joseph Powell were never seen after by those in *Falcon*'s boat, nor by the survivors.

Not much has been recorded of the loss of the fishing vessel *Haskel*. It is known that the vessel left Griquet near the tip of the Great Northern Peninsula on the third of November 1919. Captain Robert Durdle of Bonavista and his crew had been fishing on the Labrador. Some reports claim the schooner had at least fifteen people aboard, although it is more likely it had at least eight to ten crew aboard.

From Griquet on the French shore, the voyage home would take another two or three days sail. Loved ones and relatives became anxious; there was no word, no report for weeks.

By November 25, many towns en route – St. Anthony, Little Bay Islands, Twillingate, Seldom-Come-By – had been contacted to see if any other ship had seen or knew of the whereabouts of *Haskel*. But there was no word, a silence from the great deeps, and the fate of the sailing schooner *Haskel* remains a mystery of the ocean.

to bring death. The sympathy of the whole country goes out to Dr. Lehr in the sad news.

No News of Missing Craft.

No tidings of the schooner Haskel, Robert Durdle, master, have been received. This schooner left Griquet on the third of November, Polling Day, for Bonavista. Although various places along the shore have been wired-to, and other steps taken, no news of the schooner has been received.

One of the mysterious gaps of the loss of a schooner and full crew: *The Evening Telegram* of November 25, 1919, says **No News of Missing Craft**. Very little was said of its crew, whether lost or if they returned safely to port.

CHAPTER 18
THE PRIDE OF THE FLEET GOES DOWN

PORT UNION: William Ford Coaker, (Later Sir William Coaker) was the founder of the Fishermen's Protective Union. A politician, businessman and reformer who understood the problems of the powerless and poor fishermen, Coaker attempted to rectify their subjugation by the merchants by unionizing them, especially on the northeastern and northwestern coasts of Newfoundland.

Coaker's Fishery Regulations, introduced in 1919, were attempts to control and reform Newfoundland's salt fish trade. As president of the Fishermen's Protective Union, and as Minister of Fisheries from 1919-23, Coaker established minimum export prices. By the winter of 1921, these regulations were disregarded or not complied to (especially by independent fish exporters on the south coast) and were later repealed.

Union headquarters were set up in Port Union[1] along with a productive shipyard. Coaker had fishing, coasting and foreign-going vessels built through the Union Trading Company and the Port Union Shipping Company. In total about fifty ships were either built or purchased by Coaker's business network.[2]

One of the finest vessels constructed in Port Union was *Sir William*. Built in the spring and summer of 1930, this 100-ton sealer was classified as an auxiliary vessel – it had a steam engine, yet carried masts, rigging and sail. *Sir William*, designed for the seal fishery, was ninety-two feet long and twenty-three feet wide. On its only trip to the sealing front in 1931, the sealer carried twenty-eight men, mostly from Port Union and area.

On Friday, March 6, "the pride of the Port Union sealing fleet" (although it was basically untested and was on its first trip to the ice floes) left the Fishermen's Union Trading Company wharf at Port Union. By the next evening it was off

Sir William on the stocks at Port Union with the great Union Trading Company stores, left. The light pole of the Port Union Electric Light and Power Company (which was operational in 1925) can be seen, right.
Photo courtesy Maritime History Archives, MUN Accession # PF-001.1-Z39b

The thirty-seven-ton *A and D Russell*, built in 1935 in Princeton, Bonavista Bay, by Arthur Russell. It was sixty-one foot long, twenty foot wide with a depth of nine foot. It was eventually sold to the Fishermen's Union Trading Company at Port Union. On October 8, 1954, it began to leak while in the Lewisporte Run. Laden with heavy burden of limestone, *A and D Russell* went down quickly.
Photos courtesy Lorin Russell

Peckford's Island. Captain Ned Quinton decided to anchor there until daylight.

On the morning of the 8th, *Sir William* left and by the next day, the crew sighted the blue water around Belle Isle in the Strait of Belle Isle. Quinton and some of the crew went ashore to the island's lighthouse keeper with the idea of getting a sealing report from the wireless operator.

A storm of strong easterly wind forced Quinton to bring *Sir William* to the eastern side of Belle Isle and down the Great Northern to anchor near Green Island, Flower's Cove. At this point the ship became jammed in ice, drifting back and forth in heavy ice until the morning of the 16th.

After scouring around in company with the S. S. *Imogene* and sighting only a few old seals, Captain Quinton decided to reverse his course and, on March 19, entered the ice floes about fifteen miles to the northeast of Horse Island, White Bay. *Sir William* was then about two miles from another sealer, the S.S. *Eagle*.

Again the Port Union ship became jammed in ice. The next night the usual watches were set and all aboard felt there was no danger from heavy ice damage. Yet they could feel and hear the ice pounding hard on the sealer's sides.

All went well until 4:20 a.m. on March 20, when Master Watch William Norman heard the splashing of water in the forecastle. Upon investigating, he found water over the floor. Everything was not as it should be and Captain Quinton called all crew on deck. Manning the pumps became the order of the day.

Pumping was useless, and the crew was ordered to prepare to abandon ship. Within thirty-five minutes *Sir William* filled with water. It did not sink, however, due to the pressure of ice on the hull, keeping the brand new sealer afloat. About noon, the ice slackened, pressure on the ship's side lessened, and *Sir William* immediately sank.

Using two dories, the crew took refuge on the ice. At daylight, the *Eagle*'s crew went to the aid of the marooned men, and by 7:00 a.m., all were safely aboard. Later that day the *Eagle*, not having enough accommodation for an extra twenty-eight men, contacted the sealer *Sagona* and the *Foundation Franklin* to get *Sir William*'s crew transferred.

All agreed that had the *Eagle* not been within two miles of the sinking sealer, the situation could have been very serious for the men stranded on the ice. At 10:00 p.m. Monday, March 23 *Sir William*'s crew were all back in Port Union – sixteen days after leaving for the front – with no ship and no seals. According to the local media:

> This ended the short career of *Sir William*, as fine a vessel as ever sailed from Port Union and the pride of the Port Union sealing fleet. Such incidents as the sinking of *Sir William* are reckoned as "all in a day's work." The lure of the seal fishery is hard to explain, but nevertheless it still exists in spite of the many disasters and loss of life.

Notes

1. Port Union was an unoccupied area in the southwest arm of Catalina harbour prior to a 1915 land purchase by William Ford Coaker. The site became the commercial headquarters for Coaker's Fishermen's Protective Union (FPU) and the Fishermen's Union Trading Company. The harbour was normally ice-free from April to December, large enough to afford anchorage for 100 or more vessels and had a nearby river with potential for generating hydro-electric power. In May 1916 work commenced on building the town, which was named Port Union in December that year.

By 1919 there were about 400 people in Port Union employed in various Union operations. Many of the common surnames were from the fishermen like Diamond, Lodge, Norman, McNamara, Penney, Russell, Sheppard, and Sutton, many of whom had come from Union outports along the northeast coast. For example, from New Bonaventure came (Charles King); Greenspond (Herbert Burry and Edgar Gibbons); Little Bay Islands (James Jones); Port Rexton (Joseph Bailey and Edmund Butler); Wesleyville (Peter Carter); and Windmill Bight (Abraham Goodyear). William White moved from Bonavista to work in the cooperage and blacksmith Michael Noble brought his family from Nippers Harbour.

2. *Sir William* was called after F. P Union President, Sir William Coaker. Indeed several of Coaker's fleet carried names of the enterprise or the people associated with it. *Nina L. C.* (Coaker) was built in Port Union in 1918; *F. P. Union* built the next year and one vessel was named *Roy Algar R.*(Russell, a manager of the Fishermen's Protective Union). The schooner *Port Union* was destroyed by fire in 1923. One of the largest ships built in Port Union was the tern schooner *President Coaker* (1919) and ironically it was the one that brought the greatest tragedy to Coaker's ventures.

While returning from Brazil in early 1924, the schooner became way overdue. On February 1, pieces of a wrecked ship and other debris, later identified as that of *President Coaker*, were discovered at Shoe Cove, near Cape Race. Not one of its six crew survived. Lost were Captain Norman Sheppard, his brother and mate Harold Sheppard, bosun Alfred Sheppard, cook George House, all of Port Union or Catalina, as well as Israel Downey, a resident of Port Rexton, and John Kelly, Black Duck Cove, on the island of Ireland's Eye, Trinity Bay.

In contrast, on July 8, 1919, the FPU tern schooner *Nina L.C.* was abandoned in the mid-Atlantic while delivering fish to Europe. The crew – Captain Rose, mate G. J. Matthews, bosun John T. Norman, seamen P. Hiscock, J. Manuel, S. Courage, T. Lodge and Selby Russell – was plucked off their sinking schooner by a passing vessel and returned to Port Union in August 1919.

CHAPTER 19
OLIVIA, A WRECK OFF WESTERN HEAD, RANDOM ISLAND

RANDOM ISLAND AND SOUTH RIVER: The rocks off the point near Western Head of Random Island proved to be the undoing of the schooner *Olivia*. On the evening of December 29, 1898, it was bound for Random Sound in Trinity Bay for a load of timber. The owners, Thomas and George Hussey of South River, Conception Bay, left home port the day before. The Husseys lived in the Salmon Cove area of South River – the river from which the community takes its name. The river flows through a broad valley into a large harbour pond south of Clarke's Beach, known as Southern Gut. South River includes the areas known as The Gut; Salmon Cove, located northeast of the river; and Springfield, which is inland, along the river valley.

On the outset of their two-day journey, the weather was great; seas fairly calm and there seemed to be nothing to prevent the Husseys from reaching their destination. But often, even when rocks and weather are not threatening, the whims and caprice of nature and equipment breakdown step in. The schooner was stretching in toward land, with a fair breeze from the northwest. The schooner had to tack in to Random Island, but the main sheet, or rope, broke and within a twinkling the position of ship and crew became fraught with danger.

Immediately the crew lowered the mainsail. *Olivia* would not wear clear of the cliff looming a few feet ahead of the schooner; thus the skipper ordered the staysail and foresail lowered and the anchors let go. Ordinarily perhaps, the anchors would grab the bottom, but in this case they dragged and the vessel struck on the point. Part of the keel broke off as the schooner breached one ledge, but stopped across another submerged raft of rock.

Olivia remained there, gradually sinking. Before giving up their ship altogether, the Husseys put out a chain and ropes to pull *Olivia* off the ledge. It was fruitless. Within a short while it was resting on the bottom. The Husseys and their crew had no time to save any provisions and very little clothes. After they left the vessel, they rowed over two miles in a small boat. By then the wind and seas were much heavier.

That night, December 29, they landed at Fox Harbour (today's Southport). Meanwhile *Olivia* settled on the bottom until its cross trees were only four feet above water. The next morning the crew went back to the sunken vessel and with the assistance of some men of the area and a couple of boats, succeeded in trawling some gear with grapnels.

Olivia was partially insured in the Newfoundland Mutual Marine Insurance Company; thus the retrieved gear was sold for the benefit of the underwriters.

The loss of a small schooner didn't receive much ink in Newfoundland newspapers of the day, but one news item did – penny postage. Businessmen and the public complained that on Christmas Day, 1898, penny postage came into effect in Newfoundland. Letters could be sent to Great Britain, parts of Africa and other distant parts of the world for one penny. That was fine. But letter mail from one destination to another in Newfoundland cost a three-penny stamp. One person commented that to send a letter from Brigus to Cupids, less than two miles away, cost three cents, but to send the same letter to British East Africa cost one cent. To reduce postage within Newfoundland and to provide a uniform rate of one penny would cost the mail service between $7000-$8000 a year. Despite the objections, the protest to the government fell on deaf ears.

GLOVERTOWN, CLARENVILLE AND FERMEUSE: On Tuesday, November 16, 1982, a storm nearly put an end to the *Dorothy Marie II*. But the oft-repaired veteran of the sea proved to be a tough opponent. *Dorothy Marie II* was on its last Newfoundland journey from Clarenville to Florida via Boston.

National Convention's Life Line

- **Winter of 1946-47** Built at Glovertown's Burry Shipyards by Edgar Paul
- **1947** Job, Frank and Lawrence Hiscock of Coward's Island name it *National Convention*
- **1947-53** Fished the Labrador under Captain Job Hiscock
- **1954** Purchased by Captain William Bridgeman, St. Brendan's
- **1959** Purchased by Captain Charles Rogers, renamed *Dorothy Marie II*
- **1959-60** Repaired extensively, engine installed, mainmast and foremast shortened
- **1960** Purchased by Captain Lester Andrews for coasting trade
- **1975** Purchased by Ralph Mercer of Clarenville Dockyards, lay a derelict, for a time was partially underwater
- **1978** Purchased by John Andrews, St. John's
- **1979** Purchased by William Jones of California, undergoes further repairs
- **1982** Storm-damaged and nearly sunk en route to Boston, repaired at Fermeuse
- **1983-today** Completed its voyage to the United States, repaired and re-fitted again as a pleasure and touring craft.

In the twenty-foot swells and raging 100-kilometre winds, the ninety-foot mast was splintered into five pieces. Deckhand Boyd Rideout, in an interview with the author in 2005, recalled, "We were lucky the mast didn't hit the windshield of the cabin. The cables and stays were spread all over the deck and we were dragging pieces of the mast on the port and starboard sides."

The beleaguered ship, once the ninety-six-ton fishing schooner *National Convention*, was built in the winter of 1946 at the Burry Dockyard in Glovertown and named for the National Convention assembled in June to decide the type of future government that would best suit the Dominion of Newfoundland. In 1959 the schooner was renamed *Dorothy Marie II*.

Dorothy Marie II's final crew – owner Bill Jones, Watson Goodyear, Bob Balsom, Roger Bursey and Boyd Rideout – guided the vessel from Clarenville on Monday, November 15, unaware that a typical fall storm was brewing. It was clear with light easterly winds and no heavy weather in the forecast, but at 2:00 a.m. Tuesday, a gale warning was issued. Within an hour, with *Dorothy Marie II* off the southern Avalon, a storm struck with fury.

When the great swells hit the mast, the shattered pieces fell across the cabin, splitting both sides above the cabin doors. The greatest danger was the seawater in the ship's hold as waves breached across the stern. With wave after wave coming over the deck, there was about four feet of water in the engine room.

Boyd Rideout, recalling the voyage in later years, said he, Balsom and Bursey began bailing and throwing buckets of water out of the hold through the cabin. When Bursey became fatigued and couldn't continue, owner Jones joined the bucket brigade.

With *Dorothy Marie II* tossing wildly and Goodyear clinging to the wheel and trying to keep the vessel's head into the wind, Jones, Balsom and Rideout were being thrown about below as they tried to bail.

Ship's gear, food, and supplies were afloat. Jones assessed the damage done to the 250 hp Mercedes Benz engine. He shut it down, but worried that the cables and stays from the damaged mast dragging along the side would foul in the propeller.

Dorothy Marie II (ex *National Convention*) **final Newfoundland Crew**:
Captain and owner, Bill Jones, USA
Bob Balsom, Clarenville
Boyd Rideout, Lady Cove
Roger Bursey, Clarenville
Watson Goodyear

When the gale struck, the crew had attempted to shelter in Fermeuse but, in the limited visibility, couldn't find the leading lights into the harbour. As winds

Dorothy Marie II off Elliotts Cove, Clarenville after repairs. The square stern has been changed to a yacht-like stern, the steering wheel cabin has been removed for a stylized cabin. The two masts are replaced by one – a BC fir, hollowed out and laminated.

Photo courtesy Boyd Rideout, Lady Cove

intensified, they headed out to sea. After firing several distress flares about 4:00 a.m. the crew took their chances on the open ocean, rather than face the land and rocks near the southern Avalon Peninsula.

About ten miles southwest of Fermeuse and with no radar or radio because of the damaged mast, *Dorothy Marie II* was spotted by a longliner owned by Ralph Keats. Then, an oil rig supply vessel moved in, as well as the coast guard vessel *Bartlett*.

Later, owner Jones stated that the ship's engines were started and, towing the pieces of the mast and the anchor which the crew had dropped to slow the vessel's drift, they motored into Fermeuse at one knot per hour.

At the Lake Group fish plant wharf, the weary crew rested on Thursday, then repaired some damage. Most had not slept in three days. *Dorothy Marie's* equipment and tools were in disarray, all supplies and food were ruined and everyone's clothes and bedding were soaked.

Eventually *Dorothy Marie II* finished the journey to the United States, leaving behind the memories of an eventful final Newfoundland trip. As it steamed away from the south coast for the last time, a local newspaper commented: "Another bit of Newfoundland heritage and tradition has left our shores."[1]

Notes

1. I first met Boyd Rideout at Clarenville. In December 2006, we exchanged information, Boyd supplying the personal information and also his photo of the vessel. Other details came from *The Evening Telegram*, November 20, 1982 and the Watermarks website "From Glovertown to Boston: *National Convention*'s Long Voyage."

CHAPTER 21
THE LOSS OF *H.F. WILSON*

LONG BEACH, HODGE'S COVE AND GREY ISLANDS: Perhaps we are lucky in a way that over one hundred years after a ship was built there is someone to tell a story of its last moments. William Vey of Long Beach recalls what happened to the schooner *H.F. Wilson* in June 1944.

By the time William Vey sailed on *H.F. Wilson* in June 1944, the schooner was over forty years old, a veteran of the Labrador fishery. A thirty-eight-ton vessel and fifty-eight-foot long, it was built in Happy Adventure in 1901 by the Turner family and was first registered to Thomas Turner.

The *H.F. Wilson* is listed as being at the Grenfell Dock in St. Anthony for repairs in September 1940. At that time, Patrick Hanlon was master and it was owned by the Ryan Brothers of Trinity.

Those aboard the *H.F. Wilson* on its last voyage:
Skipper Hayward Vey, Long Beach
his brother Harold Vey, Long Beach
father and mate Herbert John Vey, Long Beach
William "Bill" Cooper, Hodge's Cove
Bill's sister, cook Mary Cooper, Hodge's Cove
Cyril Smith, Hodge's Cove
Len Stringer, Hodge's Cove
Sam Holloway, St. Jones Within
Adam Rogers, ?
Passengers
Wilson Vey, Long Beach
William Vey, Wilson's son, Long Beach
Ronald Vey, Wilson's son, Long Beach
Tom Smith, Island Cove

It was later owned by Herbert John Vey of Long Beach. William Vey remembered:

> We were going up to the Labrador, recalled Vey, to build up a "room" in Batteau, that is, to fix up a place for fishing – a cook shack, a stage, flakes, and a rough shed to store the fish.
>
> The men and boys of our family got a passage down on the *H.F. Wilson* with skipper Hayward Vey of Long Beach, Trinity Bay. We left around June 15.

William Vey and the author, November 2007.[2]

We were basically passengers – my father Wilson,[1] my brother Ron Vey and Tom Smith of Island Cove. Herbert John Vey, who owned *H.F. Wilson* had eight of his people aboard, including his son Hayward, who was skipper.

William Vey recalled that their load of lumber was on deck, as well as three boats belonging to Herbert John Vey – a thirty foot boat for fishing, another boat of twenty-six feet and a seventeen foot punt. In tow behind the *H.F. Wilson* was Wilson Vey's thirty-two foot motor boat.

When they reached Seldom-Come-By on Fogo Island (which the Trinity Bay fishermen called "Halfway Point" being halfway between Trinity Bay and the Labrador coast), there were several other schooners, all waiting to make the last leg north. Wilson remembered:

> We left Halfway Point early. There was ice in the northward run, bergs, and a southeast wind blowing in on the land with a big swell on, and fog. About six that evening, we were outside Grey Islands, taking a course for St. Anthony.
>
> Someone caught a glimpse of southern Grey Island (Bell Island), but only saw it for a minute when the fog came in again. Now it's two or three miles across the tickle between islands, so we went on, but it was foggy.
>
> From about six in the evening, the skipper reefed his canvas, double reef in mainsail and foresail. The skipper thought he was around the northern island (Groais Island).

Then we saw something white like an ice berg. The schooner was "hove to" – it was hardly moving with not much headway, not much canvas. Someone called out to the fellow steering that there was an iceberg ahead. We saw it and cleared around the berg. Then the land of the northern island loomed up. There was ice lying in by land and we were going toward it.

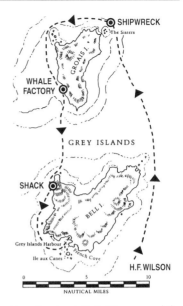

The schooner had a twenty Atlantic horsepower engine, and the engineer went down to start the motor, to put it in reverse to back away from the ice. Instead the motor caught in forward gear and that drove the vessel ahead somewhat.

Our schooner was now in on several big boulders, lying half exposed in the rough water. In front of us was a square cliff with no beach below it. By now the H.F. Wilson was rolling back and forth. We

Map of route of *H. F. Wilson* around the Grey Islands.

expected every minute the spars would come out of her and blocks, tackles and booms would come down on our heads.

Then there was two or three hard knocks on the big boulders under water and there were holes in the schooner by now. Some of the crew and our crowd got below to get clothes and some didn't. I had my warm clothes and cap.

The high seas hove the vessel in broadside on the great boulders dotting the island's shoreline. The crew could hear the grind and crunch of planks and timbers on the rocks. *H.F. Wilson* began to sink and went down partway.

As the schooner was on its side, rolling in the waves, and with the spars threatening to fall any second, there was no way to get the two large boats off deck. The punt was too small to accommodate all. The only recourse was to pull in the boat that been in tow behind *H.F. Wilson*. Vey said of the abandonment of the schooner:

Our motor boat, which had a five horsepower Hubbarad engine, was in tow. That boat saved our lives. Had there been any bad sea on, it would have swept over the schooner while we were trying to get this boat ready and we probably would have perished.

It was attached by sixty fathom of strong rope. We wanted to haul the boat up to get in it to rescue ourselves from this disaster. Five or six of us pulled in about half the rope and it wouldn't come any further. The rope must have been pinched under the iceberg that we were near.

So we called for everybody – the twelve men and girl cook – to pull and we were all strung on deck hauling. Then the rope unhooked from whatever it was caught in and the motorboat came up alongside. The only damage done was a counter knee broke out of her.

Now the crowd below had no chance to get any clothes; only what they had on. Someone picked up the lady cook and put her down in the motor boat. We shoved off from the old schooner. It was still afloat, but we wouldn't stay aboard for fear the spars and blocks would come down and kill us.

When we left, pieces of wreckage, oil drums, the lumber we had on deck to build a shack, all floated away. With no compass – no chance to get that – the thirteen of us kept off from the island, using the two pair of oars. We kept five or six miles from the mainland, staying away from the island, rocks and breakers until daylight. Then perhaps, we would see what to do or where to go.

But at daylight, it was still foggy. The shipwrecked mariners rowed to the south end of the northern island and rowed across the tickle, three or four miles, then to the southern island. By then the sun came out. William Vey recalled that they couldn't use the motor in the trap skiff as it only had five gallons of gas in the motor:

Somewhere along the inside of the southern island we came to a gulch and saw a fisherman's shack on the land. So we landed, broke down the door, went into the shack and lit a fire. This gave us a chance to dry ourselves. We stayed about two or three hours. When we left, we decided to use the motor, as by then we had probably rowed fifteen to eighteen miles.

About 8:00, just as we reached the entrance to the harbour (French Cove) at the end of the southern island, our gas gave out. We knew that there were twenty-five families or so living on the south end. We rowed into the first wharf we saw.

There I saw a sight I have never forgotten, for there was a man on the wharf tarring the iron shoes on his hand slide. He was putting tar on them, I guess, to keep them from rusting during the summer.

"Come up to our house," he said.

"No," we told him. "There's too many of us."

So seven families there each took so many of us. We stayed two weeks until the coastal steamer *Northern Ranger* came in. That took us to Battle Harbour, then Forteau, across the Strait to Flower's Cove and when it went south along the west coast of Newfoundland, we were landed in Humber Mouth. We took the train to Northern Bight station (nearest Long Beach), arriving home July 15, 1944.

H.F. Wilson stayed on the rocks – a partially sunken wreck for a few days. The Veys learned the people from Conche and Crouse visited the site. Using hooks to

A painting of *Edward VII* hangs in the home of William Vey.

pull up goods from the sunken wreck, they salvaged some material from the wreck, including clothes boxes.

According to William Vey, there was a good amount of salvageable goods as there were thirteen people with all the clothing and fishing gear they needed for a summer's work. All their cod traps were lost. Some lumber went down with the wreck, but a great deal drifted away.

The only thing the Veys saved was their father's motor boat, which had been left behind on the Grey Islands. On its next trip northward, *Northern Ranger* picked up the boat and brought it to Newfoundland.

Notes

1. Eleven years previous Wilson Vey had another traumatic experience on the high seas. His schooner *Edward VII* left St. John's on November 25, 1933, heading for Long Beach. With him were mate Daniel Vey, John Gosse, John and Llewellyn Barfitt, all of Long Beach; John Brown and Edmund Allen Lambert, Hatchet Cove; George Smith, Island Cove and Josiah Drover of Hodge's Cove.

In a sudden fall storm, *Edward VII* was blown to sea. In the gale the schooner became leaky, storm damaged and had to be abandoned. On December 6, while out in the Atlantic, the freighter *Maine* came by, rescued the crew and took them to Wilmington, North Carolina. It was December 22 before they reached St. John's again. The longer story can be found in my book *Survive the Savage Sea* (1998).

2. On November 2, 2007, I visited William Vey at Long Beach. As we looked out over the beach where fish flakes once stood, we talked of the wreck of *H.F. Wilson* and of how they "made a go of it" or earned a living with their summer's work lost.

His father, for example, went to work on Ropewalk Lane in St. John's. William Vey found carpenter work in the Clarenville shipyard, helping construct three of "Splinter Fleet" – the *Trepassey*, *Bonne Bay*, and *Glenwood*. He earned ninety cents an hour and stayed in "camps" or tents for the workers. Eventually he returned to the fishery.

CHAPTER 22
ONE SAILOR TO WORK THE SHIP
DUCHESS OF FIFE

BONAVISTA, NEW MELBOURNE, BROWNSDALE: On the morning of Monday, September 16, 1907, two schooners chartered to Philip Templeman of Bonavista had loaded fall provisions in St. John's harbour. Both were bound for Bonavista. *Transvaal*, at twenty-three ton, was built in Seal Cove, Bonavista Bay in 1900 and the *Duchess of Fife* – the latter schooner, at fifty-three ton and sixty-four-feet long, was the larger vessel.

Built in 1902 at Nippers Harbour, *Duchess of Fife* was named for Princess Alexandra, a member of the British Royal Family. Aboard were Captain Thomas Pye, Edgar Pye, both of Brooklyn, Bonavista Bay; mate John Pardy, Bonavista and deck hand Joseph Reader of Musgravetown. Fanny Chalk, a girl of fifteen years, was a passenger, probably going to some community in Bonavista Bay. As it turned out, Fanny became quite a heroine, drawing the praises of the seamen.

By the next day, both ships battled a typical fall storm. *Transvaal* lived through the gale and eventually reached port without incident. When two miles from Green Island, Catalina, *Duchess of Fife* ran into trouble. In the winds, the main sheet shackle burst, causing the mainsail to go out across the rigging.

Captain Pye ordered the schooner be brought around on a wind, and put out to sea farther from the land until the crew could secure the sail. By this time they were past Catalina, a sheltered and much frequented harbour in the era of sail.

On Wednesday the wind veered around. *Duchess of Fife* was put under single reefed sails as the wind had moderated somewhat. Before dark that day, another gale came on. The mainsail had to be taken in. The foresail was double reefed; the captain steered toward land.

Just before 9:00 p.m. the storm burst upon the ship and the crew, who had been labouring at the sails and at keeping the ship trim for several hours, was exhausted. Nevertheless, in the powerful winds, the foresail now had to be taken in. *Duchess of Fife* ran under bare poles, i.e. just the two masts with no sail.

While the crew worked about deck, securing any moveable gear and lashing up the sails, a great sea broke across the deck, sending two or three crew up against the bulwarks. Captain Pye had his leg broken in two places and mate Pardy had a broken leg; two other crew were pinned down with debris. When they were freed, it was discovered that Joseph Reader had broken his leg. Edgar Pye was severely bruised and battered, his leg or hip was twisted or out of place, but he had no broken bones.

The captain and the others were helped into the cabin and made as comfortable as possible. This comfort was little indeed, as the sea which boarded the schooner had nearly demolished the cabin and partly filled it with water. Worse yet, the wheel was carried away and the binnacle which held the compass was smashed. The large light or lantern used at night to help the crew with chores was broken.

At least no lives had been lost. In all this the young girl, Fanny Chalk, had not murmured or complained. What was the point; the crew had all been disabled and one deck hand was left to manage a schooner. Fanny came up on deck, helping the injured get below and did all in her power to manage the ship. She also tended the injured as best she could, considering everything was filled with water. There was no hot tea or food nor a pain killer; not even an aspirin.

Edgar Pye began to pump and, in between, to clear away the debris on the deck. He spent Wednesday night in wet clothes, with no light and all the crew in the cabin. He still had to keep the ship's head to the wind and pump whenever he could. If there was any consolation, it was that the wind had pitched down.

When daylight broke, Edgar, with another crewman who was able to do a little work, managed to fit out a makeshift rudder over the side. One of them pumped as best he could, for water was gaining in the hold. Captain Pye, suffering in the cabin, agreed that they find land to run the *Duchess of Fife*, now a floating wreck, into some cove or harbour.

At 2:00 that afternoon, Edgar sighted land and he put up part of the staysail to give the ship some extra manoeuverability. He sailed the schooner for a cove. As it turned out, that cove was Lance Cove.[1]

A welcome sight it was! The injured had been lying in the cabin now for seventeen hours, wet and no fire to warm them up. Perhaps, they prayed, they would survive a wreck; perhaps if the vessel went to pieces, they could get off.

Lance Cove, near New Melbourne, has a gentle beach and the schooner grounded as gently as possible, considering the circumstances. The people of Lance Cove removed the crew from the wreck, sent for the doctor, took the crew into their homes and did everything possible to comfort them.

To prevent looting, Constable Dwyer, stood guard over the beached *Duchess of Fife*. Two doctors of the area, Macdonald and Pickard, did all that was possible, knowing the injured had to be taken to better medical services.

Soon the chief merchant of the area, M. Button and Sons[2] of New Melbourne, took control of the situation. Button asked for the government tug, the *D.P. Ingraham*, to come to Trinity Bay to convey the injured to the St. John's General Hospital.

He sent this message to Minister of Marine and Fisheries saying:

> September 21. Schooner *Duchess of Fife* went ashore, yesterday, at Lance Cove; total wreck. Loaded with provisions for P. Templeman, Bonavista; goods practically intact. Captain and two of the crew with legs broken... Today, another wreck near Lead Cove; twine, spars, fish, etc., floating about; particulars unknown. a disaster is feared."(signed) E. Button.[3]

On September 28 the tug bearing three injured men arrived in St. John's. Government members for Bonavista district, Donald Morison and Sydney Dara Blandford, met them. The ambulance was waiting to take them to the General.

The people of Lance Cove had one final detail on the wreck. *Duchess of Fife* was unwittingly driven upon Lance Cove Beach, which was the only place within miles where it was possible to beach a schooner for a crew to be saved.

Notes

1. The name Lance Cove existed until about 1910 when the name changed to Brownsdale. A community on the east side of Trinity Bay, twelve km (seven miles) southwest of Old Perlican. Tradition has it that the first settler, John Brown, migrated from Old Perlican around 1820. During the next few years he established a sawmill there and eventually became the first merchant. The community, however, was very slow in developing and by the year 1845 there were only two families there.

Today some of the more common family names are: Austin, Francis, Harris, Hopkins, March, Matthews and Thorne.

2. The chief merchants of New Melbourne were the Buttons. Moses Button was the first teacher there and later became a Justice of the Peace for the area. From the late 1800s W.J. Button had a general store in the community, called M. Button and Sons. By 1921 he owned a liver factory, a lobster cannery, a sawmill and Labrador schooners.

3. The disaster Button refers to turned out to be far worse than the loss of *Duchess of Fife* and the injuries to its crew. Schooner *Effie M.* of Trinity, Trinity Bay, was lost with crew while returning from the Labrador fishery. The same storm which wrecked the *Duchess* overwhelmed the vessel, pushing it onto a reef or cliff. Wreckage of *Effie M.* was located at Lead Cove and Broad Cove, near Old Perlican, on the eastern side of Trinity Bay.

Lost were Captain Fred Morris, James R. Morris, Robert A. Morris, Walter Brown, William A. Miller, John R. Miller, James M. Miller, John Ash, James Janes, George Hiscock, single, son of Robert; James Woolridge, married; James Fleet, Cuckold's Cove; John Pinhorn; Arthur Sexton and his son. Most were from Trinity and area.

CHAPTER 23
HELPLESS IN THE NORTH ATLANTIC

CATALINA, GRAND BANK: The schooner *Thomas A. Cromwell* left St. Pierre for Oporto on December 22, 1917, with a cargo of cod. Captain William Haynes of Catalina was in command and with him were south coast seamen: mate Henry Anstey, cook William Grant, seamen Harry Thomasen, Max Douglas and Charles Blagdon. They were from Grand Bank, except Blagdon, who lived in Fortune.

Built in 1906 at Essex, Massachusetts, *Thomas A. Cromwell* was bought by Simeon Tibbo of Grand Bank in 1914. The schooner was a large one at 119 tons and 110 feet long. In season, the vessel fished the banks with twenty-one crew, but in late fall, it was pressed into service to deliver cod to war-torn Europe. The *Cromwell* was certainly able to handle ordinary weather and seas; however, that December the elements conspired to defeat the schooner.

On December 26, fair sailing weather changed for the worse: a continuous spate of high winds, great combers, seas that seemed to come from every direction. At 3:00 a.m. a high sea washed away the lifeboat and the vessel began to leak, increasing so that the men had to pump 250 strokes (on the pump) every hour. The other small dory aboard *Thomas A. Cromwell* was damaged but, if repaired, could be serviceable in case the crew had to use it.

In his log of the wreck of *Thomas A. Cromwell*, Captain Haynes reported:

> We were then in latitude 40.35 North. The next day, December 27th, it was still blowing from the northeast and we hove to under a reefed foresail. At 2:00 a.m. the rudder gave out and the ship became unmanageable. It was now leaking 300 strokes per hour.
>
> The 28th and 29th were still stormy with a heavy gale blowing from the northeast. It was impossible to repair the rudder. By December 30th and 31st it was still stormy and the ship leaked at 600 strokes to the hour. There was no other ship in sight, but lookouts were posted.
>
> On January 1st, the weather cleared somewhat with light rain. The crew manned the pumps continuously. On the 4th, a steamship was sighted about two miles away. We tried to signal her but she did not answer. The next day was calm and a smooth sea with the crew manning pumps as before.
>
> A heavy gale came up from the southeast on January 6th with a heavy sea running and the same conditions on the 7th and 8th. It was hard work at the pumps and an anxious lookout kept for assistance. The next day a strong gale still blew from the southeast which continued until midnight. The lookouts could see nothing; the ship was still leaking badly.
>
> At daybreak the lookout observed a man-o'-war off the port quarter. We signaled her at 8:00 a.m. and launched a dory. We pulled over to it and stated the condition of the five crew.

An indistinct photo of schooner *Thomas A. Cromwell* (but perhaps the only one available).
Courtesy Kathleen Eveleigh whose grandfather, Joshua Matthews, also captained this vessel.

Haynes ended his report saying he set the *Thomas A. Cromwell* afire so that it would not become a menace to shipping. He and his crew had been adrift twelve days, rudderless, drifting broadside at times to the pounding of the relentless Atlantic.

Due to wartime restrictions, the captain's report does not state the name of the vessel; however, Harry Thomasen, who later became a captain, says it was the American four stacker *Seattle*, bound westward to America.[1]

When the ship first approached the *Cromwell*, it kept going full speed around the sinking schooner. Through a megaphone the captain asked if they wanted to abandon ship. He also said that he must retain his speed in case there was an enemy sub near. He told them to row out in the dory and prepare to jump aboard the *Seattle* when it came close enough.

The patched-up dory could only hold four of *Cromwell*'s men, so Thomasen, Henry Anstey, Max Douglas and William Grant went first. Douglas and Grant climbed on the deck of the cruiser first; Thomasen and Anstey rowed back for the captain and Charles Blagdon, who were still aboard the wallowing schooner. The next time the cruiser circled, the dory was there again waiting. The last four climbed aboard.

One unusual but valuable document of this dramatic shipwreck was the affidavit, or declaration, given by the American captain to Captain William Haynes when the warship docked at Halifax. It was a certificate completed in four points, verifying the conditions when the schooner sank. However, the American ship is identified only as "_____" as wartime restrictions prevented it from being named.

CERTIFICATE VERIFYING THE LOSS OF
"THOMAS A. CROMWELL"

1. This is to certify that at 6:30 a.m., the 10th January 1918, while at sea, the "_____" sighted the schooner "Thomas A. Cromwell," making signals of distress. We went close to her and the first mate came on board and stated that it was necessary to abandon the schooner, as the rudder was gone and the ship was leaking badly. They had been pumping for twelve days. The position of the ship was longitude 42 degrees North and latitude 43 degrees West.

2. The first mate was informed that the "_____" would take the crew on board, but that they would have to expedite, and make but one trip with their boat which was a small dory, having lost their lifeboat previously. The dory returned to the schooner and all the rest of the crew came aboard the "_____," bringing practically nothing with them.

3. The master reported that before leaving the schooner, it had been set on fire and smoke was issuing from the hatches as the "_____" steamed away.

4. The following men were taken on board "_____:" William Haynes, master; Henry Anstey, mate; William Grant, cook; Harry Thomasen, Charles Blagdon, Maxwell Douglas, seamen.[2,3]

Notes

1. Harry Thomasen later described his version of the twelve days adrift on the *Thomas A. Cromwell* in an excellent and informative book *Captain Harry Thomasen Forty Years at Sea* by Andrew Horwood, 1973. One slight difference in the two accounts was that Thomasen identifies one fellow crewman as Ben Brady. Captain Haynes says his seaman was Charles Blagdon.

2. Mate Henry Anstey told shipping officials at Halifax, it was the second incident for the *Thomas A. Cromwell*. The winter previous, while in the Mediterranean delivering fish, they were nearly sunk by a submarine. Anstey said the schooner often went on foreign-going voyages in the fall and was provisioned accordingly for a six month trip.

On a Sunday morning at 9:00, he said, at a point 200 miles east of Gibraltar, they sighted a steamer coming toward them. When it was about a mile away, the crew heard a gun fired and the steamer came to a stop. Later they sighted a submarine on the far side of the steamer.

About an hour later, there was a loud explosion and the ship was blown up, sinking almost immediately. Meanwhile, they had not noticed the approach of another vessel, as their attention was attracted by happenings near the steamer. This second ship was a man-o'-war from Gibraltar, which rapidly approached the sub.

The sub submerged. If this friendly British ship had not appeared, Anstey and the Newfoundland crew were sure they would have been next to be sunk.

3. Captain James Edgecombe, another well-known Catalina mariner, had a similar experience when his tern schooner *Gladys M. Street* went down in mid-ocean on March 20, 1920. James, his son Caleb Edgecombe, and four other seamen were picked up by the United States freighter *Major Wheeler* and taken to Havana, Cuba. There the British consul arranged transportation to Boston; thence to Yarmouth, Nova Scotia, on to Halifax and home by coastal steamer to St. John's.

James Edgecombe had gone to sea for forty years and the loss of the *Gladys M. Street* was his first sea mishap. He had crossed the ocean several times by schooner during the war years. The newspaper clipping details the trip from Yarmouth to Halifax.

paid /by the Dominion Coal Co., for
all /classes of labor, and the provisions in the new schedule as recom-
mended by the conciliation board,
of which Judge Patterson is chair-
man, Prof. Howard Murray repre-
senting the Scotia Co., and J. C.
Watters the Scotia employees.

Crew Of Abandoned Schooner Landed At Yarmouth

YARMOUTH, April 21—Captain James Edgecombe, and crew of five men, of the St. John's schooner Gladys M. Street, arrived here this morning by the Prince Arthur from Boston. This schooner was bound from St. John's to Gibraltar and was abandoned in a sinking condition on March 20, in Latitude 43 north and Longitude 18 West. The crew was picked up by the United States freighter Major Wheeler and landed at Havana, from which port they were sent north by the British consul.

CHAPTER 24
EXPLOSION IN TRINITY

TRINITY: Hundreds of ships wrecked around Newfoundland's coast went down from four chief reasons: stranding on offshore reefs, near land or by ice; sunk, that is abandoned at sea through leaks, heavy storms or destroyed by enemy forces; burnt or in collision. Perhaps the fifth way is more obscure – destroyed by explosion. Maybe that category fits under burning.

Explosions were caused by oil or gas in drums and barrels, coal dust, or gunpowder. Sailors knew well the danger of gunpowder, often carried aboard vessels to free it from crushing ice. They treated the explosive with respect and handled and stored it carefully.

One of Canada's most dramatic ship explosions happened off Newfoundland's northern coast in March 1931, when the sealing ship *Viking* blew up, killing twenty-five. The remaining survivors, approximately 125, walked six to eight miles over Arctic ice to the Horse Islands.[1]

At the time and in later years it became a widely publicized tale of shipwreck. This was due to the fact that among the dead were two American filmmakers who were producing a movie, *White Thunder*, about the seal hunt. The disaster was caused by gunpowder stored below and used to produce dramatic effects with icebergs or to free the ship from encroaching ice.

Another, more obscure account of a ship destroyed by gunpowder happened many years ago in Trinity, Trinity Bay. Initially the ship's agents confused the date of the wreck, saying the ship was wrecked on January 5, 1859. That was when the tidings of the disaster reached St. John's, but, according to Walter R. Smith, the loss of brigantine *Emily Tobin* actually happened on December 28.[2]

Walter Smith says that when he was boy, he lived in Trinity and could verify what happened and when. That particular day, he says, was "Innocents Day" and there was a church service. It was between 8:00 a.m. and 9:00 a.m. and he stood at the window of the Parsonage at Trinity West, waiting for the time to go to church. Presumably his father was clergy in Trinity at the time.

Smith, observing Trinity harbour, was much taken up by events in the busy shipping port. One of Mr. James Slade and Company's brigs, (as writer Walter Smith says) the *Trinity* was leaving for Poole, England, and was taking Alexander W. Bremmer, an agent for Slade, as a passenger . His fellow employees were at Slade's "room," giving him a memorable send-off and firing a small cannon as a parting gesture. Smith said, "The cannon charges from Slade's premises were loud as I heard them."

The brigantine *Emily Tobin* was also in Trinity at the time, having arrived in port on Christmas Eve. *Emily Tobin*, of eighty-six tons, had been built in St. John's in 1844. McBride, a merchant in St. John's (on Water Street at what later became McBride's Hill) owned the sixty-five-foot long vessel.

Built in England as a WWII mine sweeper, the 227-ton M.V. *Fenmore* (shown above at Clarenville) was later converted to an Icelandic trawler. In 1956 Captain John Blackwood bought the ship to carry coal from North Sydney to Newfoundland.

Blackwood left North Sydney on Thursday, October 13, 1960 with coal destined for Trinity. He carried a Newfoundland crew: mate James Sturge from Gambo; chief engineer Roland Clarke; second engineer Fred May, both of Twillingate; cook Herbert Burrage; seamen Don Legge, Joe Clarke and Hedley Keats, all from Dover, Bonavista Bay.

About 9:00 p.m. on Saturday October 15 , while steaming toward the entrance between Trinity's Skerwink and Admiral's Island, *Fenmore* struck a hidden rock or reef and sank with no loss of life.

Photo courtesy Bruce Neal

It had been up in Trinity Bay for a load of lumber and firewood and was bound for some port in Conception Bay where most of the crew lived. It had a passenger aboard, Captain James Pittman of New Perlican. Ordinarily *Emily Tobin* would not have stopped in Trinity, except one of the crew needed medical attention. He had his leg injured when the deck load of lumber shifted during a wind storm.

With Slade's brig out of the harbour, *Emily Tobin* hoisted its anchors from where it was anchored off Stoneman's Dock in Trinity and slowly sailed away. The hull of *Emily Tobin*, says Smith, "had just passed out of my sight around the bend of the "Nudick" when I saw a column of smoke ascend up, apparently from its deck. This was followed by a report, which to me did not appear to be as loud as that from the cannon fired for Mr. Bremmer."

At first the sound of the explosion seemed to be from a swivel cannon, says Smith, perhaps fired from *Emily Tobin* to also honour Bremmer. This was not the case; the brig had been destroyed by an explosion of gunpowder. Smith describes what happened:

In an unused berth in the cabin were two kegs, each containing twenty-five pounds of gunpowder. One was full and unopened; the other was open and a small amount was taken out of it. A candle had been left alight on the table in the cabin.

As the ship heeled over in the light breeze as it sailed out of Trinity, the lighted candle slid off the table and into the opened keg of powder. A large part of the stern of *Emily Tobin* was blown away, together with all the deck aft of the companion way.

The remainder of the deck, as far forward as the main hatch, was thrown up, though not broken off. This section was left tilted on a steep angle. The tiller was broken off short at the rudder head.

Someone had to be at the steering wheel at this point and the unfortunate wheelsman was the captain's brother. He was thrown up in the air several feet and came down across the main gaff. To get the body free from the debris, the gaff had to be lowered.

Captain Pittman, a passenger, had a narrow escape. He was on deck helping the captain and crew secure the anchor. Pittman, walking back aft at that moment, reached as far as the main hatch when the powder barrels exploded. Walter R. Smith says that Pittman was very lucky, coming out of the explosion with only minor injuries.

Curiously, he concludes his report with a concern for the brig *Trinity*. On the evening it sailed from Trinity, a strong gale of wind came up and a tremendous snow storm. The Smith family and others in the town seemed to be more anxious for the safety of Mr. Bremmer than concerned of the wreck of *Emily Tobin* and the death of a crewman.[3, 4]

Notes

1. The list of those killed by the explosion on *Viking* has been presented in various books and publications. I have yet to see the list of survivors. Much too long to present here, it is found in Appendix B.

2. When Walter R. Smith reported on the loss of *Emily Tobin* he was writing as the Reverend Walter R. Smith from Portugal Cove, presumably as a clergy in that community.

3. Walter Smith also summarizes some of the ships built in around Trinity in the 1850s. *Trinity*, one of the ship's described in his narrative, was built by Charles Newhook for McBride and Company, St. John's. It was launched near Stoneman's Dock. *Trinity* was a pretty craft and well built, Smith says, "but was never a favourite with Trinity people. Several vessels had been owned or built with the same name and all had come to unfortunate ends."

Smith was there at the launching on February 10, 1857, of the 180 ton brig *Henry Thomas* at Stoneman's Dock. Smith recalled that *Henry Thomas* – also built by Charles Newhook for the seal fishery in the spring of 1860 – brought in ten thousand pelts while under Captain Terence Halleran.

The first vessel Smith ever saw launched was the *Isobel*, belonging to Slade and Company. The 140 ton, ninety-eight-foot long brigantine slid down the ways at

Trinity in 1855. *Isobel* was first commanded by Captain N. Facey. "He was very successful," Smith says, "and came in loaded with (seal) fat often."

It is not clear who shipwright Charles Newhook is. The *Newfoundland Encyclopedia* says Charles Newhook, a shipbuilder in Trinity, (the second of his name) was killed in St. John's in the spring of 1839 when he fell from the mast of a wrecked vessel on which he had been working.

4. One of the earliest and most tragic shipping accidents in Trinity occurred in April 1845, when a Trinity vessel was lost off Cape St. Francis. On board were eight people: Captain Thomas Verge, his youngest son, and Denis Cashman, who were the crew. Passengers were Mr. Stoneman; John Pilgrim; Henry Burnell, the police constable in Trinity; Burnell's young son; and John Hill. The Constable was in charge of John Hill, a man with mental problems who was going to St. John's.

In a storm on Friday, April 18, the ship was pushed against a pan of ice off Cape St. Francis, foundering almost immediately. Six of those aboard perished; two, Stoneman and Cashman, managed to get up on a pan of ice. There they remained from about twelve midnight on Friday, until 7:00 a.m. Monday.

On Sunday night around dusk, the *Orion* – owned by Captain Murphy and Mr. Moores of Bay de Verde – found the two survivors. Due to encroaching darkness and rough ice conditions, Murphy could not do much. However, he kept a light burning all night so the two survivors could see it and remain heartened. At daylight Monday, he successfully reached the two and carried them to safety.

Captain Verge, who died with his son, was described as an old and respected inhabitant of Trinity.

CHAPTER 25
PRIMROSE WRECKED NEAR
BACCALIEU ISLAND

TRINITY, BAY DE VERDE, BACCALIEU: Captain John Dewling, his brother Joseph Dewling and seaman William Hiscock arrived in St. John's on the coastal boat, the S.S. *Ethie*. They had only left St. John's a week previous in their own schooner, the *Primrose*, bound for Trinity. *Primrose* had a full load of general goods owned by a Mr. Grant and slated for local firms in the Trinity area.

It was 8:00 a.m. Tuesday when *Primrose* slipped past the Narrows. Sailing was great, that is the schooner had "a good time along" until it was well across Conception Bay. Off Baccalieu Island, however, the wind veered off shore, blowing strong about west by north.

Baccalieu Island, (named for the Spanish word *bacallo*, meaning 'codfish') lies off the southeast corner of the extreme tip of the Bay de Verde Peninsula. Its southern extremity, which played a part in this drama of the sea, is just over one and a half miles east of Split Point, the nearest land.[1]

The three seamen took double reefs (the sail was lashed twice around) in the mainsail and foresail, took down the jib and lashed it down. In spite of extra precautions, the extra force of wind split the foresail. Dewling's attempts to sail down into the safe shelter of Bay de Verde failed.

Three times the schooner "mis-stayed" – the sails swung over the opposite way – and it became necessary for skipper Dewling to "wear" the schooner down through Baccalieu Tickle. It had been his intention, given the strength and direction of the near gale, to take *Primrose* out to sea, away from the land.

In the Tickle, Dewling found a comparatively sheltered area called the Jewes. That night about 10:00, the two anchors were dropped over the side; both caught a good holding ground and the three crew settled down for a hard night of wind. There was lots to do as they waited for daylight. The rent in the foresail had to be repaired.

About midnight the wind suddenly came up with increased intensity from the north. Worse, it was accompanied by snow squalls. The three seamen decided it would be best to run up into Conception Bay. Accordingly they hauled up the anchors – the smaller one first. Just as they hove up the second which now had considerable strain on it, the cable burst. At that moment a sudden squall of wind pushed the *Primrose* toward the mainland south of Baccalieu.

Before the men could get up any canvas in order to obtain wind power to pull away from the land, the schooner was carried before the wind and perilously close to the rocks. The one anchor remaining was dropped, but it wouldn't hold. At that very moment when they realized the second anchor was not holding, it was a matter of life and death and a time of quick decisions. The ship had to be abandoned immediately before it piled onto underwater ledges.

The two Dewlings and Hiscock had a difficult task to get the dory over the side and get into it in the wind and high seas. The three jumped and landed in the dory. For the next four hours it became a desperate struggle, in the bitter wind and cold, to keep off the rocks.

All three pulling at the oars could make very little headway and it was necessary to keep the little craft head on to the lop to keep from swamping. In the darkness and blinding snow, it was difficult to see anything and they had to guess at their exact position.

After getting up around Split Point, some two miles to the leeward of the wreck of *Primrose*, the three found a sheltered cove. There they could keep control of the dory until morning. At daylight they got out onto the rocks and walked to Bay de Verde.[2]

The coastal steamer *Ethie* was in Bay de Verde on that day and was about to continue its regular run to St. John's. Three shipwrecked mariners, cold, wet and exhausted, boarded the steamer. *Ethie*'s officers did what they could, suppling the three with dry clothes.

Dewling wired Mr. Grant in Trinity, informing him of the loss. No insurance was carried on the cargo which was substantial. Reports of the day on the wreck reported: "Local dealers, too, lost heavily as the schooner was fulled to the hatches with a general cargo, principally of the Commercial Stores, Mrs. Eriksen and the whale factory. None of the cargo was insured."

In turn Grant sent a message to St. John's to the Member of the House of Assembly for the Bay de Verde district, Jesse Whiteway.[3] Whiteway notified officials in Bay de Verde who appointed someone to look after the wreck. Not much was salvaged by the owners; however residents of the area reaped an unexpected bounty from the sea in the fall of 1909.

Skipper Dewling lost heavily: his source of employment was gone as was much of his summer earnings. William Hiscock lost a considerable amount of money and his extra clothing. His supplies and food, which he was taking to Trinity for the winter, had gone to the bottom with the *Primrose*.

Notes

1. Baccalieu Tickle, a deep water run with few natural hazards, shortened the sailing time and distance between Conception Bay and Trinity Bay. It saw a great amount of sea traffic throughout the centuries. But sailing ships also contend with wind, wave, tide, fog, snow and ice and this, along with human error, accounts for many of the shipwrecks that occured in the area. The tales of shipwreck, survival, tragedy, death and epic struggles are almost countless. Below is a brief mention of some of the more tragic that occurred on or near Baccalieu Island:

Ship Fatalities at or near Baccalieu Island

Date	Ship	Lives Lost
February 1706	frigate *Langdon*	70 deaths, approx.
March 1823	sealer *Active*	25 deaths
January 1882	sealer *Lion*	60 deaths
July 1891	schooner *Pubnico Belle*	7 deaths
October 1902	schooner *Lilian*	3 deaths, Grates Rock
December 1944	schooner *Molly*	6 deaths, Grates Point

2. There was another brief tale of shipwreck which happened on October 20, 1931, in almost the exact same circumstances. The schooner *Dolloman* with Skipper John Smith and his crew of William Smith and Theophilus Smith of Green's Harbour went ashore in adverse weather at Split Point. The cargo of 130 quintals of fish and all the crew's personal effects were lost. However, the three men made it to the shore and reached Bay de Verde without injury.

3. Jesse Whiteway (1863-1940), born in Musgrave Harbour, moved to St. John's around 1881. He established a clothing business and in 1908 entered political life, being elected to represent the district of Bay de Verde. After defeat in 1913, he was appointed to the Legislative Council and, soon after, left that for a life in business and with the church.

CHAPTER 26
BAD LUCK AND SPONTANEOUS COMBUSTION

GRATES COVE, BACCALIEU ISLAND AND ST. JOHN'S: Veteran captains and seamen knew that coal stored in a vessel's hold could burst ablaze without a match or an open flame touching it. Coal was known to sometimes catch fire without apparent cause. Mariners didn't use the words "spontaneous combustion," but that's what it was. Spontaneous combustion happens when a substance undergoes slow oxidation and heat builds up, and temperatures inside a tightly sealed cargo hold full of coal did build up, especially in warm weather. If heat is not released, ignition occurs which soon becomes a blaze.

Wiley captains gave coal plenty of ventilation. Apparently when "slack" or dusty coal was the cargo, the fine dust could ignite from spontaneous combustion. To reduce the likelihood of explosions, captains gave soft coal lots of ventilation. Some skippers kept a hatch cover loose.

On Friday the 13th, September 1918, the wooden steamer *Gordon C* set sail from St. John's to Bonavista. Most captains of that era did not consider Friday the 13th unlucky – that idea is a more modern superstition. But about 1:00 in the morning, Captain Perry noticed fire coming through the deck from the forward hold.

Peter H. Cowan and Company of St. John's owned the *Gordon C*, a vessel built in Sheet Harbour, Nova Scotia in 1917. This was a relatively large ship, grossing 255 tons and measuring 121 feet in overall length. Cowan had the engine of the *Sunbeam*, a British hospital ship which had been sold, remodelled and re-named *Czarina* in Newfoundland, installed in *Gordon C*.

Gordon C was one of the first vessels to reach survivors huddled on the deck of the wrecked *Florizel* on February 24, 1918. Captain Perry and seaman Budden maneuvered the vessel to within 450 feet of the wreck, lying off Cappahayden. They made four trips from *Gordon C* to the *Florizel*, taking off Minnie Denief and Kitty Cantwell – the two women survivors – first. On the fourth trip, raging seas overturned the dory, knocking Perry and Budden semi-conscious. They were thrown into the water, but were rescued by seamen from other vessels standing by.

But it was coal, not the rocks and winds off Newfoundland that hastened the demise of *Gordon C*. Seven months after the *Florizel* event, *Gordon C*'s final voyage of seven days began at the coal chutes of Sydney and continued to the Avalon Peninsula, where the schooner stopped at St. John's for fresh water.

On the evening of September 13 – *Gordon C*'s last and unlucky day – it made its way to Bonavista to deliver 280 tons of coal for Swyers business. That night it lay to under the shelter of Baccalieu Island.

At midnight, when about ten miles north east of the great island, flames broke out and soon spread over the forward part of the ship. In less than five minutes

A Newfoundland passenger and freight steamer fueled by coal from the *Dominion Coal Company No. 3 barge*. This image, circa 1920, was taken in Sydney Bight.

Image courtesy Yvonne Burke, Gander

Gordon C was all ablaze, forcing the crew to leave in two dories, abandoning a third. They lost all possessions except the clothes on their backs. Perry and his crew discussed and analyzed the source and cause of the fire, finally agreeing it had to have started with the coal in the hold.

About 3:45 a.m. they reached Grates Cove, but owing to the heavy seas running on the rugged coast, had much difficulty landing their dories. After some time they were piloted in by the fishermen of Grates Cove. Even these men, with all their experience landing on that rugged shore, had two fishing boats smashed up in the rescue process.

Captain Perry and his crew – mate Davis, chief engineer Ernest Martin, second engineer W. Ring, third engineer Flemming and the other seamen – were treated with considerable kindness and hospitality. On Saturday evening, another ship arrived in St. John's, reporting that *Gordon C* was still afloat and burning.

Some weeks before *Gordon C* burned and sank off Baccalieu, owner Peter Cowan had a deal all but wrapped up to sell *Gordon C* to an American firm. Wisely, he had the vessel and the cargo of coal insured. The loss of *Gordon C* was not the only piece of misfortune for Cowan. A year later, he received a message from Captain Nathan Gillingham that his schooner *Gondola* had gone ashore at Fleur de Lys. *Gondola* left St. John's in early October for Battle Harbour where it took on board 1700 quintals of fish for the Labrador Store Limited.

CHAPTER 27
COLLISION AT DAWN

GULL ISLAND, BURNT POINT AND TWILLINGATE: It wasn't quite daylight when Captain Philip Rideout slipped the moorings of his sixty-ton schooner *Somerset* from the wharf of Harvey and Company, St. John's. He shaped his course northward to round the tip of Cape St. Francis. His schooner had a full load of fall provisions aboard belonging to William Waterman and Company, Twillingate.[1] Built in Loon Bay in 1875, *Somerset* was owned by the Hodge brothers' business – Thomas of Fogo and Richard of Twillingate.

The weather was fine and clear, the moon shining and a slight breeze came from the northwest. Also enjoying the same sailing conditions was the *Mary Ann*, described only as a seventeen-ton fore-and-after. A small vessel, perhaps best classified as a large skiff, it had quite a company of people aboard – twenty-two men and one woman. They ranged in age from teenagers to a seventy-year-old man. All belonged to two towns on the north shore of Conception Bay, Gull Island and Burnt Point.[2]

They had been engaged in the fishery during the summer at Northern Bay. Before returning to Gull Island with the results of their summer's voyage aboard – about 200 quintals of fish – they sailed to St. John's to deliver the fish.

Mary Ann sailed all night and everything went well until a grey dawn was just breaking and the breeze was strengthening. The vessel was approaching Sugar Loaf, a prominent headland a few kilometres north of St. John's. *Mary Ann*, with its living freight, was sailing along easily under jib and mainsail. The foresail had been taken down as a squall was in the offing and the mast was considered too weak to take a force of wind.

Charles Tucker was at the helm and when *Mary Ann* was off Sugar Loaf, he

Survivors of Sinking of *Mary Ann*, September 24, 1886

Burnt Point
John Davis, married
Andrew Milley, single
Charles Milley, married
Charles Tucker, married
Thomas Tucker, married
Jasper Wicks, married

Gull Island
Mark Delaney, married
James Doyle, married
Jonathan Doyle, married
Peter Doyle, married
Thomas Fahey, married
Pat Hogan, married
Gregory Layman, married
Bartlett Oliver, single
John Oliver, married
William Oliver, married
Michael Percy, married
Leander Stockwood, married
Sam Stockwood, married

could see another ship, later determined to be the Twillingate schooner *Somerset*, bearing down on them. Tucker immediately put the helm hard down and kept his craft up in the wind. As *Somerset* came near, Tucker and others called out to those on board the larger craft to port their helm to avoid a collision.

There seemed to be some confusion or hesitation aboard *Somerset* and it kept on the same course as *Mary Ann*, overtaking the latter and striking it with considerable force on the port side. *Somerset* almost cut the skiff in two pieces.

At the time of collision, a number of *Mary Ann*'s people were below in the cabin, as many as could stow there. Realizing the danger from the shouts of those on deck, many scrambled up from below. Four failed to make it and perished in the attempt. They were prevented from getting out as the mainsail fell across the companionway door and blocked it off.

THE EVENING MERCURY.

Lines Written by W. S. on the Occasion of the Collision Between the 'Mary Ann' of Burnt Point and the 'Somerset' of Twillingate.

'Twas a cool September morning,
Just the eve of dawning day ;
And the stars no more adorning
Nature's treasures, fade away.

And the waves with gentle ripple,
Swiftly float along their way,
Vessels laden deep with treasure ;
Toys with which the breezes play.

But nearer than all others
Comes a vessel on her way ;
Like a sea-bird gaily skimming
Through the riplets of the Bay.

The Captain treads with eager step
The deck. The seamen gaze
With joyful faces lit with hope,
Shining through the misty haze.

No thought of death or danger
Came o'er them as they sailed ;
They little thought of shipwreck
Till Sugar-loaf they hailed.

Those who perished were Charles Wicks, aged fifty, married with a family of children; Nicholas Milley, aged thirty, married, no children; Leander Milley, seventeen years old, single; and Jane Fahey, aged forty-five, married with no children. Mrs. Fahey belonged to Gull Island while the three men belonged to Burnt Point.

Within five minutes from the time *Mary Ann* was struck, its stern settled under water. In the meantime the survivors managed to get on board *Somerset*. It fortunately remained alongside the sinking *Mary Ann* as its anchor was entangled in the skiff's rigging. This kept the small craft afloat a little longer and to this providential occurrence, twenty people owed their lives. From the time of impact to when *Mary Ann* sank, twelve minutes had elapsed.

All survivors were brought back to St. John's. Gregory Leamon (or Layman) of Gull Island was seriously injured when the broken end of the mainmast struck him in the stomach. He was hospitalized. The husband of Jane Fahey survived, but was crazed with grief by the loss of his wife. As she struggled in the water, he grabbed her hand, but water rushing aboard *Mary Ann* tore her away and he saw her go down.

Seventy-year-old Charles Milley of Burnt Point survived by a miracle. He was in the cuddy, an enclosed space in the forward part of a small vessel, and tried to get up when he was forced back by onrushing water. He managed to catch hold of the legs of the man before him, who in turn grabbed a man's hand on the deck of *Somerset*. The two of them were thus rescued.

In St. John's, the wrecked crew was taken care of and placed in boarding homes by Alexander McNeily, the government member for the Bay de Verde district. When asked where the blame lay for the sinking of *Mary Ann* and the death of four people, authorities seemed to fault the larger vessel. Neither had any lights burning. But at the time of impact, all *Somerset*'s crew were aft reefing the mainsail and, consequently, there was no lookout posted.

On September 29, 1886, a week after the tragedy, a local poet composed several lines on the tragedy, the first five stanzas are on page 100.

Notes

1. One of the earliest sea tragedies of Twillingate is associated with W. (William) Waterman and Sons. Waterman eventually had branch businesses in Fogo, Change Islands, Nippers Harbour and set up his firm in Twillingate around 1887. In 1880, Waterman equipped forty-six schooners for the Labrador fishery, and forty-one in 1890.

By 1900, Waterman and Sons was in decline and much of its property at Fogo and Twillingate was in the hands of J.W. Hodge, who had previously been Waterman's agent at Tilting.

With such a fleet and involvement in the ship trade, there were marine catastrophes. In the fall of 1890, the fifty ton *Rise and Go*, built in Halls Bay in 1877, left Twillingate. It was bound for St.

Twillingate Men Lost on *Rise and Go* in the Fall of 1890

Thomas Warr, owner and captain
George Warr, son of Thomas
Daniel Warr, son of Thomas
Abraham Earle
Elijah Sharpe
Thomas Simms

John's with a load of fish consigned by W. Waterman and Company but was never heard from again. As a result of the loss of six men, left behind were four widows and fifteen children.

2. Remnants of this story exist today in the oral version – a testament to the storytelling tradition of Newfoundland families. In October 2007, I was asked by Robert Oliver if I knew anything of the story of how the Stockwoods, Olivers, Laymans and others of Gull Island survived a shipwreck off St. John's. Basically, the story (as related above) was the same, except it was thought the ship that rammed them was a "German" ship.

Amazing really when one realizes the loss of *Mary Ann* happened 120 years earlier.

CHAPTER 28
THE STORY OF THE *PIONEER*

SELDOM-COME-BY, CARBONEAR: When the *Pioneer* pulled out of Seldom-Come-By[1] on December 5, 1902, the crew thought the voyage would be a two-day run to home port, Carbonear. Weather was fine, winds favourable and prospects looked great – but as it turned out "fine, favourable and great" were words of the exact opposite for the conditions experienced on that memorable voyage.

Pioneer, captained by William J. Kennedy of Carbonear, had been in Roddickton, White Bay, to load lumber in late November 1902. Kennedy had with him a crew made up of hard-working seamen who were, for the most part, from Carbonear and area: Nick Tobin, Dennis Kennedy, Willis Pike, Dick Reynolds and Patrick Crawford.

In fact the tale of the schooner's last voyage is told through the words of John C. Crawford, the son of Patrick Crawford.[2] One can assume that Patrick, through the oral tradition of many Newfoundlanders, had told his son this sea story. And a good deed it was; only for this re-telling, perhaps the tale of an arduous voyage and the loss of a fine schooner might have been lost forever.

During the voyage eastward from Roddickton to Carbonear, as John Crawford recalled, the *Pioneer* had to dip down into Seldom to wait out a storm. After a couple of days, Captain Kennedy set sail in company with three other schooners (*St. Clair*, *Nokomis* and *Jessie*) for home port.

The first night out of Seldom, a terrible storm came up from the northeast and it blew away *Pioneer*'s sails. As Crawford says:

> They drifted for many days. About the fifth or sixth day out while trying to secure the lifeboat, which was later lost, Captain Kennedy slipped and the lifeboat crashed on his foot, cutting off a large portion of his heel.
>
> This rendered the captain almost helpless. For the rest of that terrible voyage he had to command his ship from his bunk. To add to the plight, the ship sprang a leak and for the remainder of the trip, the crew had to man the pumps day and night. This kept the vessel afloat for a few more hours.
>
> The crew had to work just as hard to keep Captain Kennedy in his cabin. Being a true Newfoundlander, he insisted on crawling on deck and doing his part.

By now *Pioneer*, not rigged for oceanic voyages, was out on the stormy Atlantic. The crew was probably used to sailing along Newfoundland's coast, hopping from point to point during daylight hours and stopping in a safe harbour by night.

Supplies of food and water, meant to last a week or less, now had to be stretched to do for two or three weeks or longer – the crew had no idea when and how the unplanned push out to sea would end.

With the captain laid up and unable to get on deck, *Pioneer* was now short-handed. All this time sails and rigging needed closer attention as the schooner was being buffeted and driven by contrary winds. To stop pumping meant the wallowing schooner might sink and, to make matters more unnerving, they had lost their only lifeboat. Crawford continued:

> After nearly twenty or twenty-two days out, the crew saw the first ship barely visible on the horizon. In spite of all their efforts to attract attention, the vessel passed out of sight.
>
> By this time, food for the crew was dwindling and they were rationed on two cakes of hard tack and two mugs of water per day. For the next five days, they sighted six or seven ships, but none of them were close enough to see the disabled *Pioneer*.
>
> Drinking water, by this time, was rain water caught in a piece of sail. The crew – from hard work, the loss of sleep and very little food – became almost too weak to man the pumps.
>
> To "pile on the agony" as the old Newfoundland saying goes, matters became worse: seaman Nick Tobin broke his arm. This brought the work force down to four.

Yet lookouts kept a watchful eye for passing ships, for the storm had blown them into the track of transatlantic steamers. The crew sighted two more vessels, these a little closer, yet still too far away for the *Pioneer* to be sighted.

Two days went by and the men were all ready to give up; utter despair and weariness had set in. Then around midnight, Crawford says, they sighted a ship:

> It was coming toward them. Then, too, that one passed within two or three miles. Although *Pioneer* had distress lights rigged, the other ship passed on. They gave up all hope.
>
> Finally, seaman Willis Pike and Patrick Crawford (the storyteller's father) soaked an old sweater in oil and set it alight on the top of the cabin house.
>
> The flare was seen by a woman on the promenade deck of the great ship that had just passed them. She ran to the captain and told him about the strange fire or flare on the sea. My father, Patrick Crawford, and Pike were the only ones on the deck of *Pioneer* at the time.
>
> When they saw the ship turn around and head toward them, they rushed below to the cabin to tell the captain and the rest of the crew. They refused to believe the other two men. They thought my father and Mr. Pike had lost their minds.

After awhile they persuaded the rest of the crew to go on deck and see for themselves. Sure enough, the big ship was now within one mile of *Pioneer*. It turned out to be the S.S. *Rotterdam*, bound for Holland. Believe it or not, it was the last ship to sail on that run for the winter.

After thirty or forty days adrift on the ocean, the *Pioneer*'s crew fell to their knees and thanked God for deliverance. Soon they were safe on one of the largest ships afloat at that time.

Eventually, the six returned to Newfoundland. No one told or even attempted to put into words the joy and utter astonishment loved ones back home must have felt when word came (probably from a message from the steamer to Cape Race) that six Carbonear men were, indeed, alive.[3,4]

Notes

1. In the hey-day of all-sail schooners, Seldom-Come-By (or Seldom as it is referred to today) was a stopover, a place to shelter in the long runs to points further north or south. A fishing community on the southern shore of Fogo Island, the town of Seldom-Little Seldom is made up of Seldom-Come-By and Little Seldom. To the west, Stag Harbour Run was known as an especially tricky passage, not to be attempted unless conditions were favourable. Consequently, Seldom-Come-By was much resorted to by sailing schooners as they awaited fair winds. The name of the community may refer to this practice of seldom by-passing the harbour.

2. Recently, I located a description of the loss of *Pioneer* in an old newspaper clipping. The person who supplied the details was John C. Crawford of Gearyville, Corner Brook. I called the only John Crawford in the Corner Brook telephone listings and it turned out to be the son of John Crawford (and the grandson of *Pioneer*'s seaman, Patrick Crawford.) Yes, his name was John Patrick Crawford, named after his father and grandfather.

The third generation Crawford had not known his father had sent a description of the loss of *Pioneer* to the *Daily News*; indeed he had not heard the story of his grandfather Patrick's misadventures at sea in 1902-1903. He gave me permission to use his father's and grandfather's tale of the wreck; in turn, I sent him the newspaper clipping.

3. The story of the eventual fate of the other two schooners, the *Jessie* and the *St. Clair*, is found in Chapter 9.

4. Captain William S. Kennedy spent two months in hospital with his broken foot. He had, in 1898, obtained his first mate's certificate for foreign-going ships. In 1926 he went to the USA, put in two years at New York with the McAllister Navigation Company. Upon his return to Newfoundland, he lived on Field Street in St. John's and was a certified Coastal Pilot, taking large and foreign ships into any local port. As an example of the large ships he piloted, in December 1932 he stood by the Holland salvage insurance tug *Rhode Zee* to serve as its pilot if required. In September 1935, he was piloting the Portugese ship *Fayal* when the ship's captain grabbed the wheel from him, putting *Fayal* on the rocks in Western Tickle, Fogo.

CHAPTER 29
TELLING *MINTO'S* STORY BACK HOME

CARBONEAR AND GRAND BANK: By the 1900s, a marvel of technology, the telegraph, lessened the agony for Newfoundland and Labrador families waiting for news of seamen involved in marine disasters. Ever since the mid 1860s the Anglo-American Telegraph Company (AAT) had exclusive rights to the line in Newfoundland and had concentrated its business with transmitting the news from Cape Race to the rest of North America. By 1899, the Newfoundland government began to acquire telegraphic service of its own and, in a few years, had extended service to the major communities. In 1902 the government installed new cable on the pole line between Whitbourne and Port aux Basques and, after AAT's monopoly expired, extended it from Whitbourne to St. John's.

On June 30, 1905, a telegraph message came to St. John's from New Brunswick, advising shipping authorities that Captain Edgar Burke, his wife, their young son and all crew were safe and on dry land. There was considerable relief and joy over this especially in the town of Carbonear, as nothing had been heard of Burke's ship *Minto* for several weeks.

Details were scanty, but the message of safe delivery from the sea was welcomed news. Burke and his group were on the way home and then the full story would be told of what had happened.

Minto, with 180 ton of cargo aboard consisting of coal and iron goods, left England on May 13, 1905. The Burkes and the five crew had great weather. So many sunny days and fair winds had them believing in a speedy safe passage. Nine days later that all changed as head winds from the south southwest, shifting to the north west with heavy seas became the order of the day.

At 11:30 on May 31, another storm, more intense than the first one they had just sailed through, hit *Minto*, carrying away the bowsprit with bollards (posts for securing ropes) and nearly everything else forward. The bulwarks, stanchions, and skylight were damaged or torn off. Worse, the stem was split and the schooner began to leak.

The name of a great seafaring family name is rare in Carbonear today and only exists in Grand Bank in the name of a street and a school.

Burke ordered *Minto* to be put before the wind and the main boom, mainsail and all available gear was cut loose to lighten the schooner aft. The crew pumped constantly. As soon as the sea moderated somewhat, they removed the hatches and all the cargo they could get at was thrown over the side.

Meanwhile, Burke posted a lookout for passing ships and on June 1, the lookout called out, "Steamer ahead! About five miles to the windward." But despite all the signals the crew could muster, the ship passed over the horizon without noticing the water logged schooner, now lying very low in the troughs of the sea.

The next two days were dark and dreary. Hopelessness began to pervade the minds of all and Captain Burke began to have doubts of the wisdom of bringing his wife and small child on a perilous journey across the broad Atlantic. But the fading of hope did not mean the crew did nothing. Using tackles, they secured canvas outside the stem, figuring that would lessen the inflow of water.

On June 4, the lookout spied a barque in the distance and, after a short time, it became evident it had seen the distress signals flying on *Minto*. The barque came down and maneuvered to the weather side of the wallowing Newfoundland schooner. *Minto*'s weary crew prepared a lifeboat. At 5:00 p.m. Captain Burke, his wife and child and the crew, taking whatever clothes they could safely carry, rowed over to the waiting ship.

Before he left, Captain Burke set his ship afire so the water logged hulk would not drift about the ocean and become a menace to other ships. The ninety-nine-ton *Minto*, owned and insured by Munn and Company, went to the bottom near longitude 43 North and latitude 49 West.

The barque, commanded by Captain Olsen, was the *Telefon* and it was en route from Liverpool to Miramichi, New Brunswick. On Thursday, June 30, 1905, when *Telefon* reached Chatham, New Brunswick, *Minto*'s complement disembarked and immediately sent a telegram to St. John's informing shipping authorities and relatives of a safe rescue.

They took the train from New Brunswick to Sydney, Nova Scotia, crossed the Gulf of St. Lawrence on the S.S. *Bruce* and came by Reid's Newfoundland Railway Company train from Port aux Basques to St. John's. On Saturday, July 8, they arrived in the city.

Nearly two months had elapsed since they left Europe for home; it was quite a draining and traumatic experience for Mrs. Burke and the child. When asked what had happened for a staunch ship to not weather a typical Atlantic storm, Edgar Burke could only surmise that his good ship went the same way as did another previous schooner, the *Harold*, which he had lost in mid-ocean some years previously. The bowsprit was carried away by heavy seas and that, in effect, split the stem open, causing uncontrollable leaking.

The Burke family of mariners had a long and honourable association with Conception Bay and the sea. Author Frank Saunders has done very creditable work documenting Carbonear's marine history in his excellent book *Sailing Vessels and Crews of Carbonear* (1981) and recounts some history of the Burke seamen.

They were all born, Saunders says, in Burke's Lane, Carbonear. There were captains Mark, Samuel, James, Edward Horwood and John Edgar (of the *Minto*) Burke. Thomas Burke, of the same family, was father of Doctor John Burke, who was a physician in Grand Bank for forty-one years. In 1961, the Grand Bank high school was named "John Burke High" in his honour. The Burke name of Carbonear and Burke's Lane is all but extinct there today.

Delawana II (above). At the time of its loss, this coaster was owned by Captain Guy Earle of the Earle Freighting Service, Carbonear. Captain Saul White of Twillingate was skipper of *Delawanna II* for several years and at one point had a young Phil Earle as mate. One spring, between 1959-1961, the schooner was en route to Newfoundland from Halifax with a load of fertilizer. It began to leak during some heavy weather off the southeast coast of Cape Breton. A plank worked loose in the storm. Water could not be held in check and the crew beached the vessel, running into in Gabarus, Cape Breton. When wrecked, the crew was Captain White, mate Frank Poole, Belleoram; cook Tom Reid, Carbonear; and engineer Ron Snow, Bell Island.

CARBONEAR: The flag signal **NC** (- _   - _ - _), an international code which stood for "In distress; want immediate assistance," was flying from some ship in the distance. Captain Busch of the S.S. *Belvernon*, while steaming along 210 miles south southwest of Cape Race, first sighted the ship on the morning of February 3, 1923.

Although the weather was very stormy, *Belvernon*'s captain and officers thought nothing of seeing a ship in the distance at first. As it moved closer the lookout spied the distress signal aflutter in the topmast of a two-masted schooner. Busch immediately steamed down to the vessel and, being informed it was sinking, he signaled that the distressed crew should leave in their own boat.

From a distance, those on *Belvernon* watched as the boat was unshipped and put over the side. Heavy seas smashed the boat to pieces before anyone could get into it. Volunteers from *Belvernon*'s crew – mate Llewellyn Lush, seamen H. Curran, Seward, and P. Crotty – rowed their large lifeboat to the rescue.

As they neared the foundering vessel, which by this time they had learned it was the Newfoundland schooner *James O'Neill*, the lifeboat nearly swamped. Again, on a second attempt, *Belvernon*'s lifeboat came within inches of completely filling with water. Finally on the third attempt and only then after a long and hard pull on the oars, five Newfoundland sailors were safe on the deck of *Belvernon*.

James O'Neill left Oporto on January 15 bound to Harbour Grace with crew: Captain Joseph Davis, bosun John Moores, cook Herbert Legge, seamen Robert Forward and Harry Ash, all from Carbonear.

The *James O'Neill* sailing behind the *Olwen*.

Photo courtesy Maritime History Archives, MUN Accession # PF-008.083

Fine weather was the order of the day for the first half of the journey, then it was one spate of storms after another. When the schooner reached the waters of the Grand Banks, it encountered ice and attempted to circumnavigate the field. Unfortunately *James O'Neill* was caught in a grip of Arctic ice that had pushed its way around Newfoundland to extend south of St. Pierre.

Weather was still stormy and ice ground against the sides of the small ship. In a storm on Friday, March 2, the transom stern was carried away. There was no way the crew could handle this disaster, but there was more to come: the port bow was stove in by rafting pans of ice. They knew *James O'Neill* was doomed as it reached and lurched under reefed storm sail and double reefed foresail. Captain Davis ordered the men to the pumps and they were hard at it, when the *Belvernon* came in sight.

Before leaving the wreck, mate Lush set fire to the hulk. In addition the rescue gang removed the hatch covers. Before *Belvernon* left the scene, the vessel foundered; first listing down to the port, then back to starboard, finally sinking head foremost.

James O'Neill had been purchased by William Munn's business of Harbour Grace in 1922. By then the 118-ton schooner was already seventeen years old. It was built in Connah's Quay, North Wales of the finest English oak. It was ninety-one feet long and twenty-two feet wide.

Belvernon first landed in Halifax, then proceeded on to St. John's, landing the wrecked crew on March 5. Captain Davis and crew took the train for Carbonear, but not before the captain had this letter published in the local paper: [1]

Capt. Davis Thanks Captain Busch
Appreciation from Mariner to Mariner

I wish, through the columns of the *Evening Telegram*, to express my deepest thanks to Capt. Busch and crew of the S.S. *Belvernon* who rescued my crew from the schooner *James O'Neill* crushed in ice off St. Pierre...They treated my crew to the best they had on board, and we cannot be too thankful to them.

Joseph Davis,
Master Schr. James O'Neill
St. John's, March 5, 1923 [2]

Notes

1. Many years before, it was the turn of a Harbour Grace ship to receive accolades for rescue. On October 17, 1881, during a mid-Atlantic storm, the schooner *Kestrel*, belonging to John Munn and Company of Harbour Grace came across a sinking brigantine, the *Busy Bee* of Nova Scotia. Captain Joyce swung his vessel around to help. The ten aboard *Busy Bee*, nine men and a woman, were frantic as the vessel would go down any hour and there was no lifeboat.

Three of Obadiah Gilbert Joyce's crew – second mate Joseph Brazil, seamen Thomas Bemister and John Butt – put the dory over the side. There was a very high sea on at the time, and the boarding of the wreck was extremely difficult, the three gallant seamen took off four people.

Night closed in and Brazil, Bemister and Butt decided it was best to wait until daylight to finish the work. *Kestrel* stood by the wallowing Nova Scotian all night. At daylight the same men went out again to finish their good work. It was still as rough and dangerous as the night before.

Complete success was the end result, for they plucked off *Busy Bee*'s remaining five men and one woman. In September 1882, the Government of Canada presented a silver watch to each of the four men involved in the rescue.

2. It is interesting to note that a brief record of this award given to *Kestrel*'s crew is mentioned in a unique Newfoundland book, James Murphy's *Newfoundland Heroes of the Sea*, published in 1923. Information on the *James O'Neill* came from the newspaper *The Evening Telegram* of March 5 and 6, 1923.

HARBOUR GRACE: In late summer, hurricanes originating near the Tropic of Cancer lash their way northward devastating parts of the southern United States. Hurricanes Rita and Katrina in recent years are vivid reminders of nature's power.

By the time these violent winds reached the Maritimes, much of their fury was spent, but the final flick of the hurricane's tail across the fishing grounds and into exposed harbours came suddenly and with deadly results for schooners. In Newfoundland, the weather phenomenon became known as the "August (or September) Gales."

Such was the case Sunday, September 13, 1891, when a tremendous storm swept across the whole of Newfoundland and the seas off Labrador. By early October, as fishing ships reported from the offshore or Labrador banks, reports of destruction came in.

On its return from the northern run, the government steamer *Volunteer* brought news that several schooners had been wrecked on the Labrador, as illustrated in the chart below.

No lives were lost; thus the owners and crew were considered lucky. The news from Notre Dame Bay was more tragic. In that mid-September gale of 1891 the schooner *Percie*, Captain John Cull Kane, was lost with crew. The crew of six or seven, nearly all related, belonged to Pound Cove, Trinity Bay, about nine miles from Greenspond.

Ships Lost on the Labrador in mid-September 1891

Vessel	Tonnage	Owner	Place
Sir John Glover	89 tons	Thomas Stone	Catalina
Bella B	40 tons	James Bryden	St. John's
Emily Jane	42 ton	Joseph Hopkins	Heart's Content
Swallow	73 tons	John Lowe	Nova Scotia
Ida	50 tons	John Rorke?	Carbonear
Ocean Brides	39 tons	P & L Tessier	St. John's
Nymph	19 tons	Thomas Hodge	Twillingate
Advocate	44 tons	?	?
Jos.	40 tons	?	?
Alice H.	51 tons	?	?

In the same storm the schooner *Amazon*, Captain James Noble, out of Fair Island, Bonavista Bay, was lost with three crew at Lumsden – Captain Noble and two men, Cutler and Wicks.

The *Blossom*, under the command of Joseph Marsh with his six crew, was lost about midnight of Tuesday, September 15, 1891. The six, all including Marsh belonged to Purcell's Harbour, Twillingate Island, were James Witt, George Gidge, Joseph Ings, Obadiah Vining, Arthur Langdown and a girl, Priscilla Langdown (often spelled Langdon). When the vessel struck rocks at Gull Island Cove in the Bay of Exploits, only one person survived – Joseph Ings.[1]

Up to the 1940s, long range forecasting and the tracking of hurricanes from the tropics to its northern ranges were non-existant. Skippers and crew were caught out in the gales often at a great distance from land and a sheltered harbour.

By early October 1891, loved ones and shipowners were gravely concerned about two banking schooners, unreported since the great storm. The battered *Florence Silver*, owned by John Roberts of Brigus, limped into port on October 10. In the storm Captain Lacey lost two dories, four sets of trawls, about thirty fathoms of cable and one anchor. Lacey was thankful no lives were lost.

The *Sherbrooke*, after landing six hundred quintals of fish at Harbour Grace, collected a supply of bait at Carbonear and left for the offshore banks on September 12 – a day before the gale pounced without warning.

This schooner had been built in Nova Scotia in 1866 and measured seventy-one feet long and twenty-one feet wide. Its net weight was sixty-six tons. It was registered to Thomas H. Ridley of Harbour Grace and carried a crew of sixteen under the command of Captain Kearney.[2]

The next day, September 13, a violent storm swept the deck of the schooner, carrying away the fore and main masts, i.e. they were broken off just above the deck. This happened 150 miles off Cape Spear, so a quick dash into port to escape the onslaught was not possible.

Crew of Sherbrooke, September 1891, of Harbour Grace and Vicinity

William Brennan
George Leahy
Bernard Clarke
Charles McCarthy
George Clarke
Archibald Mercer
Matthew Coombs
Samuel Parrott
Richard George
John Sparkes
Captain Patrick Kearney
Thomas Williams
Anthony Leahy
John Wiseman

With his vessel almost a helpless wreck, the captain figured his best bet was to find a relatively shallower place on the banks and drop both anchors. He rigged up a jury (or temporary) mast, managed to sail eastward for some distance and found a position to anchor in eighty fathoms.

The wind veered to the northwest, blowing at hurricane force. *Sherbrooke* began to leak at an alarming rate. Kearney ordered his men to the pumps which they manned around the clock, but the water flowed in faster than it could be pumped out.

In the mad seas foaming across the deck, all dories, except one, were smashed. The captain and crew realized their position was very risky: should seawater reach the salt, it would be impossible to save the ship as the pumps would clog with brine. Sixteen men in one dory would be madness. Surely no dory would live in the seas and gale; just to get it over the side without it smashing on the side of the schooner would be almost impossible.

Knowing they were in the track of liners and transatlantic ships, the crew ran distress flags up to the top rigging. Just when *Sherbrooke* was its greatest crisis, the lookout on the S.S. *Nova Scotian* saw the signal. The steamer, under the command of Captain Hughes, was en route from Halifax to England. Hughes ordered the course changed and the steamer bore down to the assistance of the wallowing schooner.

Captain Kearney was reluctant to leave his schooner while there was some chance of saving it, but Hughes, seeing the hopeless condition of the vessel, advised all to abandon ship. After a time, Kearney agreed and at 11:00 a.m. on September 17 and about ninety miles from St. John's, all were taken from *Sherbrooke*.

Kearney said after, "We received the kindest attention aboard the *Nova Scotian* and were also treated very well at the Liverpool (England) Seamen's Home. When the *Nova Scotian* left for Newfoundland a few days later, we took a passage on the steamer."

As a footnote to demonstrate the humanity of others toward destitute sailors – and the Harbour Grace seamen were just that, for they had saved nothing from the sinking *Sherbrooke* – other Newfoundlanders aboard organized a shipboard concert. This was conducted by W. J. Clapp and organized by James H. Stewart of the St. John's business J. & W. Stewart. *Sherbrooke*'s shipwrecked crew were presented with $14 each.

Captain Kearney returned thanks for the donation. He then offered up a prayer to divine providence that no one aboard *Sherbrooke* had lost a life in the clash with the September Gale of 1891.

Notes

1. A long tale of the loss of *Blossom* and the description of the storm and wreck can be found in the book *Raging Winds...Roaring Seas*, Creative Publishers, 2000.

2. Thomas Harrison Ridley was born in Harbour Grace. He entered the family business as a young man and in 1849 he took over most of the firm's day-to-day operations. Under his direction, the firm of Ridley and Sons expanded from Harbour Grace to Catalina and Rose Blanche, and into the Labrador fishery. In 1866 he was the first outport merchant to use a steam vessel in the seal fishery. The following year, he had two such vessels, the *Retriever* and the *Mastiff*.

CHAPTER 32
DELLECNAC, A LITANY OF BLUNDERS AND NEGLECT

HARBOUR GRACE: In 1917, the Newfoundland Shipbuilding Company began constructing ships at Harbour Grace. Beginning with the 379-ton *Armoreal*, launched in 1917, this firm built six terns, or three masted schooners. In 1919, the yard burned. Few schooners over 600 tons were built in Newfoundland, but in its two years of existence the Newfoundland Shipbuilding Company produced one of them – the 613-ton *Dellecnac*. This ship, however, had less than an auspicious maiden voyage and a controversial demise.

Dellecnac was equipped with engines as well as sails, making it, in effect, an auxiliary vessel capable of steaming under engine power or canvas when the wind was fair. It slid down the Harbour Grace ways in May 1919 and was registered on the 30th of the month; three months later off Bay Bulls, it slipped to the bottom. Its first voyage began unceremoniously on June 18, as it was bound for a port in Norway.

Its crew on that maiden voyage consisted of twelve men; the names of a few are recorded: Captain Hannevig, first mate J.W. Grey, chief engineer Arthur Wells, second engineer Pynn and third engineer Noseworthy. Captain Hannevig and his brother had shares in the Newfoundland Shipbuilding Company (which also had a branch at Norris Arm.)[1]

Dellecnac had travelled but a short distance on its initial voyage when it was discovered the wrong kind of oil had been supplied for the engines, and the ship was forced to return to Harbour Grace for a new supply. This problem was corrected and the crew changed somewhat.

It left port again on Wednesday, July 16, and was put on an east by south course. Two days later, the starboard engine became disabled, the ship was discovered to be leaking badly, plus the deck beams on the starboard and port sides of the engine rooms had been scorched, probably from the engines.

The crew charted a course to St. John's, slowing the speed down to between two and four knots. The engine was not running properly, the ship was leaking, but the pumps worked fine. *Dellecnac* reached St. John's at 9:00 a.m., Tuesday, July 22. On the 26th, the ship went on dry dock where it was discovered the pintles (bolts) on the rudder were broken, the sea cocks were damaged as was the pipe leading to the circulating pumps.

When this litany of problems, breakdowns and general disrepair was corrected, a new master and partially new crew departed St. John's at 10 a.m. on August 25, 1919, to try to steam to Norway. By noon, Cape Spear bore west five miles distant and, five hours later, the port engine stopped and the ship began to leak.

From that Monday until Sunday, *Dellecnac* drifted as the crew tried to repair the engine and to slow the inflow of water. On Sunday, when *Dellecnac* was

Final Logbook Entries for *Dellecnac*

4 a.m., engineers and engine room staff gave up the engines. Engine room flooded and five feet of water in hold.

8 a.m. similar conditions.

10:30 a.m. sighted a schooner and signaled her. She bore down on us and all came aft and refused to remain longer on the ship as she is totally unmanageable and making a large quantity of water and drifting helplessly.

12:30 launched boat and dory alongside, took off four men and remainder in lifeboat and boarded the fishing schooner "Carrie Hirtle" of Lunenburg in approximately latitude 47.54 and longitude 50.40 West. The schooner was bound for St. John's or Cape Broyle.

Set "Dellecnac" on fire before leaving her.

eighty-five miles off Newfoundland, the schooner *Carrie Hirtle* picked up the crew. The log of *Dellecnac* for August 31, 1919, records the following account of how and when the crew finally abandoned the ship (see chart above).

The Marine Court of Inquiry looked into the loss of the ship on April 17 and 19, 1920. The court found that, although *Dellecnac* was in a seaworthy condition and passed as fit by the Lloyds of London agent when it left the drydock at St. John's on August 24, the real cause of the leak was not determined.

As well, the new captain and first mate hired on at that date were not certified. The first mate was totally unfit for his position, and the engineering staff was not competent. The chief engineer had considerable experience on stationary shore engines, but had little experience on a ship. At the inquiry, it was also determined there were defects in the engine.

Although there was no evidence of misconduct or neglect on the part of the master, mate or crew, the master was severely criticized for not having kept a proper log. It was not written up until days had elapsed and, even then, it was incomplete and inaccurate.

The chair of the Inquiry, Judge Francis J. Morris and Cyril D. Fenn, Lieutenant Commander, R.N., both quoted the "Merchant Shipping Act of 1894," saying that no ship registered in Newfoundland over 100 tons shall go to sea out of Newfoundland unless the master and first mate possess certificates of competency or service.

Thus, the master, mate and owners of *Dellecnac* were liable on conviction to be fined $200 each.

Finally, the Register of Shipping submitted a report for lost ships out of Newfoundland for the past two years. In 1919 alone, 124 vessels were lost. As well, from January to April 1920, another fourteen ships sank or were wrecked, for a total of 138 vessels in fifteen months. Out of this total, only two ships were lost that had been commanded by a certified Master. Yet, certification and testing for local skippers was still three decades away, and tales of that vague news item surfaced in the 1950s.[2]

Notes

1. On February 9, 1918, the Harbour Grace Shipbuilding Company laid the keel of their first vessel. It was a large one at 600 tons displacement. The company planned to lay the keels of four others of about 450 tons each during the winter of 1918. An article in the *Twillingate Sun* for October 20, 1917, commented on the misfortunes and mishaps the Hannevig brothers had in Newfoundland:

> A Norwegian steamer went ashore near St. Shotts a few days ago, and became a total wreck. The S.S. *Norge I* was bound from New York to Harbour Grace and struck the land in a dense fog. She was owned by the Norwegian millionaire Mr. (Christopher) Hannevig, owner of the shipbuilding plant at Harbour Grace, and was a new ship. The crew was saved.

Aboard the *Norge I* was a cargo of rails, cordage and other material for the shipbuilding plant at Harbour Grace. The ship and the cargo were now on the bottom at Western Head, St. Shotts. The vessel had been carried in by the strong currents off the coast. Captain L.J. McKinnon and his crew of nine took to the lifeboats as *Norge I* began to break up. The crew had a trying time in the lifeboat, but after four hours, with the assistance of the people of St. Shotts who came out to sea to meet them, they reached land.

They were all housed for the night by the people of St. Shotts. On October 7, they traveled on to St. John's, where they were housed in the Seamen's Institute.

Yet another setback for the Harbour Grace Shipbuilding Company was the .disappearance of the steamer *Flush*, registered to the company. It was lost with all crew off Sweden in November 1919, while bound for that country with a load of lumber.

The 1474-ton *Flush*, built in Louisiana in 1917, had only one other Newfoundland connection: its captain was Marcus Simonsen, who was well-known in his day in St. John's. He was Drum Major in the CLB and was in charge of the whaler *Hawk* at the time when it did outstanding work at the scene of the wrecked *Florizel* in February 1918.

2. After Confederation with Canada in 1949, Newfoundland schooner skippers and masters had to be certified masters, as was in place in other Canadian provinces. Newfoundland skippers were examined and required to take a "harbour test" or run, i.e. sail or motor in some bay or harbour. They were also forced to write and pass an examination. Some were unable to read or write thus, experienced and knowledgeable captains were required to study material that seemed totally unnecessary for the work they did.

If they failed, their operation of a schooner was limited to within Newfoundland's three-mile headland boundary. Voyages to the Labrador or from outports to St. John's were no longer possible. As well, schooners were inspected to determine whether they were seaworthy and the government agents inquired about rotten timbers, age, tattered sails, worn running gear, faulty motors and so on. Many a schooner was "turned down," as the old sea salts termed it.

CHAPTER 33
THE TALE OF DAWE'S SCHOONERS

BAY ROBERTS AND CANN ISLAND: In the days of sail, there were (and still are) hundreds of rocks, shoals and ledges around Newfoundland that stood out as particularly dangerous to shipping. Prior to the 1940s, GPS instrumentation and radar were not yet invented, and there was no availability of accurate maps as we have today through satellite imagery. Our forefathers knew many crags, islets, and reefs either by sight and location, learned through sailing lore passed on by mariners, or as indicated on rough maps. One name associated or attached to navigational hazards was "the Brandies" and that name occurs in at least three areas off Newfoundland.

One mass of sunken ledges, the Brandies, is located about three quarters of a mile off Cape Ray. Many a ship plying the waters of the south coast and near Port aux Basques piled up there. Another dangerous location of "Brandies" lie about a mile offshore from Cape St. Francis. Ships going to and from St. John's from northern ports took great care to avoid that area.

A third treacherous shoal of rocks called "the Brandies" lie eastward of Cann Island, near Seldom-Come-By on Fogo Island. Seldom was a much-frequented port for sailing vessels making the four or five day voyage to and from the French Shore or Labrador fishing grounds to the various bays and harbours of eastern Newfoundland. To list or summarize all the ships and dates of shipwrecks that happened on all or either of the Brandies might fill a book.

Recently, a particularly tragic story came to light of a ship that ran afoul of the Brandies near Cann Island. In October 1881, two schooners owned by the Dawes of Bay Roberts[1] left Labrador for home port in company with each other. Edmund Squires commanded the *Ellen*, while his brother, Benjamin Squires, commanded the other, appropriately named *Brothers*.

On the morning of October 26, both vessels had completed a leg or section of a two or three day voyage and prepared to sail past Cat Harbour – today's Lumsden. *Ellen,* built in Bay Roberts in 1875, was fifty-four feet long and netted thirty tons. On its last voyage, *Ellen* had eight people aboard and was sailing ahead of *Brothers*.

Edmund was the last person to see the ship and his brother. He explained what he thought must have happened:

> My brother, Benjamin, was bound from the French Shore to St. John's, in company with me, when the disaster occurred. We left the same harbour together on the morning of October 24 and got along well enough until eleven o'clock that night.
>
> We were then about three miles from Cat Harbour. Here the sea became very rough and the wind increased to a gale. Indeed, so unfavourable did the weather appear that we decided to take sanctuary in

a nearby harbour, and accordingly bore away and reached the Wadham Light at half-past twelve.

It then gathered in thick and we ran for Seldom Come By. But having travelled too far Southward of the latter harbour, we were obliged to turn around and head out to sea again. I could see the *Ellen*'s light all the time. We had to crowd on as much canvas as possible to keep off the lee shore. About twenty minutes to four, when nearly clear of the leeward point, the light shown by my brother suddenly disappeared, and I fancied I saw the mainmast of his craft go overboard.

Yesterday, I received a letter from a person living near the scene of the wreck. From what he says, I am led to believe that, when almost clear of the Eastern Point of Cann Island and just at the time I lost sight of the light, a sudden squall carried away the schooner's mainmast and, drifting in on the Brandies, she went to pieces.

On Sunday last, three bodies were recovered – a young woman aged nineteen, a boy of fifteen, and one of the crew – and sent to their sorrowing friends, who received them last evening. My brother had his daughter, sister, and sister's son with him at the time. No one escaped to tell the terrible tale.

The Loss of the *Lady Jane*

Eight people perished on *Helen*. Three years later, almost to the day, in approximately the same area, the Dawe's lost another Labrador schooner. A thirty-eight ton vessel, *Lady Jane* was built in Bay Roberts in 1880 and was fifty-seven feet long, sixteen feet wide and eight feet deep.

In those days, there were no restrictions or limitations put on the numbers of passengers the Labrador fleet could carry. Quite often, schooners were overcrowded, with no extra lifeboats, no safety equipment or provisions made for passengers. Often a fishermen and his family, or two or three families, would book a passage on the closest or most convenient schooner sailing to Conception Bay. There was no room in the forecastle or cabins for such a crowd; thus, most made their accommodations on top of the salt cod in the holds.

On its voyage home, *Lady Jane* had fifty-one living people – crew, fishermen, women and children – aboard. It is said 'living' because, in addition, the schooner had two dead bodies aboard, stored in salt, awaiting burial, when the vessel arrived home.

On Wednesday morning of October 29, 1884, *Lady Jane* was sailing down the Straight Shore, heading home with a load of fish and oil. It passed North Penguin Island, but hit the shoals between South Penguin Island and Deadman's Point.

The crew readied a lifeboat to get some of the people ashore, but it immediately swamped. All night and up to 8:00 in the morning, *Lady Jane* drifted about, filling with water and rapidly settling down and sinking.

During all this time, those on board were in a panic, especially the women and children, as they expected any minute the vessel would roll over or make its final fatal plunge to the bottom. At daylight, the schooner was three quarters full of water when out of the morning mist came a rescue schooner – the *Flamingo*, Captain James Sceviour of Exploits.

Immediately, Sceviour "hove to" and began to get the people off the sinking *Lady Jane*. After the crew and passengers were aboard, some of Dawe's salt fish was taken off. Then came the transfer of the two bodies.

One of them was that of a man named William Edens, who died in Labrador in September. He was an Englishman by birth, but left a wife and child in Heart's Content, where he had been living some years. The other was that of a little child, two years old, who passed away in Labrador in July. The child's body was taken to Spaniard's Bay for burial.

Flamingo continued on to Twillingate and landed its unexpected cargo. Eventually, the steamer *Lady Glover* brought all to Conception Bay.

During the first week of November 1884, another schooner laden with fish and "freighters," as the migratory Newfoundland-Labrador fisher families were termed, went down. The schooner *Spray* of Harbour Grace, with Captain Drover in charge, struck a rock in Long Island Tickle, becoming a total wreck.

It was returning from Labrador, and intended calling at Hall's Bay for lumber, when the accident occurred. On board were a number of four crews of freighters – men, women and children. Fortunately, there was not a very heavy sea at the time, otherwise the results might have been more serious. The shipwrecked people were brought into Dark Tickle on Twillingate Island in Owen Burge's schooner. The schooner crew and freighter waited until the coastal steamer *Hercules* arrived to take them to their homes in Harbour Grace.

Notes

1. Captain Charles Dawe, born in Port de Grave in 1845, commanded several ships including the *Huntsman* and *Rolling Wave*, both of which were sailing ships, and the steamships *Greenland*, *Aurora*, *Iceland*, *Thetis*, *Bear*, *Vanguard* and *Terra Nova*. Along with his brother Azariah, Charles became involved with the catching, curing and exporting of salt fish. He moved to Bay Roberts and established the large supplying outlet C. and A. Dawe.

CHAPTER 34
THE *SWALLOW* IS OVERDUE

BAY ROBERT'S, COLEY'S POINT, BARENEED, CLARKE'S BEACH: The *Swallow* left Domino on the Labrador coast late in October and should have arrived in Bay Roberts in about two weeks. After a month, that town and others in the area where the crew and "freighters" belonged were mourning for loved ones lost at sea. They believed the vessel had gone down with all hands.

In preparation for bad news, people who had family aboard the missing ship wore black and had the window shades pulled down. Yet they lived and prayed in hope that *Swallow* would show up or those aboard would return.

The sixty-five-ton, two-masted schooner, owned by A. Fradsham and Company left Bay Roberts in June 1915 with around sixty people aboard. In the fall, the Labrador seasonal fishery was finished and six crew and eleven passengers, or freighters, sailed for home. Some of those aboard were teenage girls.

Those Aboard *Swallow* and Believed Lost at Sea, October-November 1915

Crew
Capt. John Bowering, Coley's Point
Samuel Kinsella (of Kingsley), Coley's Point
William Russell (of Richard), Coley's Point
William. Russell (of Stephen), Coley's Point
Arthur Greenland, Coley's Point
female cook, Clara King of Country Road

Passengers
Beatrice Batten, Bareneed
Henry Batten, Bareneed
Charles Batten, Bareneed
Abram Smith, Bishop's Cove
Rebecca Menchions, Bishop's Cove
John Jones, Upper Island Cove
William Dawe, Clarke's Beach
Gertrude Frost, Clarke's Beach
Fred Anthony, Clarke's Beach
Harold Moores, Clarke's Beach
(name unknown) Snow, Clarke's Beach

Swallow, with a full load of salt fish in the holds, was commanded by Captain John Bowering of Coley's Point. Luckily for posterity, Bowering wrote a long description of the troubles and ill-fortune the *Swallow* ran into. He notes his ship had reached Seldom-Come-By and left there November 15. About seven miles northeast of Cabot Island, the wind freshened from the southerly.

Then a series of wind shifts put pressure on the rigging, causing the leach rope on the foresail to break. When the crew tried to tack, high winds shredded the jib and jumbo. "For the safety of the vessel,"

Captain Bowering said, "we decided to run out to the open ocean and before the seas, which at that time were very heavy."

About twelve o'clock on the night of November 16, a great wave lifted *Swallow* and the foresail came over with such force that it carried away the starboard rigging. Ropes twisted around the halyards and the crew could not get the foresail down, which ripped apart and blew away.

By now, *Swallow* was at the mercy of the seas and one huge wave breached the deck, smashing a small boat on the deck and carrying a puncheon of molasses over the rail. Worse, one of the four casks of cod oil lashed on the quarter deck broke loose. One rolled aft and struck the steering wheel out of its place. To add to their woes, the "step" of the foremast began to move and the weary lot feared the mast would break off or dislodge the planking on deck.

To veteran seamen and the wily captain, this state of affairs made them "quite gloomy," as Captain Bowering said. However, to the young passengers, especially the women, it must have been frightening.

Work on deck now consisted not of sailing and shaping a course for Bay Roberts, but pumping out water for dear life somewhere on the high seas off eastern Avalon. Bowering says:

> We were doing everything possible to keep the vessel afloat as we thought it was almost impossible with the mast disabled to reach land in her. We kept a good lookout for some vessel passing by. We made up our mind to keep her afloat as long as we had strength to do so.
>
> On the 18th we threw away about 300 quintals (about 33,000 pounds) of fish and the next day we saw a steamer's light. No time was lost running a flare-up or signal fire to the mainmast top. Unfortunately, the steamer did not see it and passed on.

No doubt for most passengers aboard, young women, boys and men, the ordeal must have been terrifying. Any past sea journeys had travelled along the coastline from Conception Bay to Domino in the spring and back along the land in the fall. Now, they were faced with the wild November Atlantic, with mountainous seas threatening at any moment to engulf their frail ship. Not knowing which breath would be their last, it was an experience they would never forget.

Then the fate of the seventeen aboard *Swallow* seemed to change. Back home, loved ones, although frantic with worry, held fast to their faith and prayers for divine intervention continued. Out on the vast ocean, the storm had abated somewhat, but a good lookout continued to scan the horizon for passing ships.

About 10:00 p.m. on the night of the 20th, crewman Arthur Greenland shouted, "There's a light!" Another flare-up was hoisted, plus some of the crew fired off their guns at one minute intervals. Captain Bowering recalled:

> A little fog obscured the light; then it cleared and we saw the light again. We discerned the ship was coming toward us, for we could see both

its starboard and port light, as well as the masthead light. The steamer came down alongside and the captain asked if we wanted assistance.

We shouted, "Yes. We want to be taken off this wreck."

"All right. We will take you off."

He steamed off to the windward, lowered the lifeboat and the first and third mate and three Chinese sailors came to our rescue. We started to pack our clothes chests, but it was impossible to take all belongings. However, we took some clothes.

Then we got the four girls aboard and then each man got aboard. The wind was moderate. We got on board the steamer, which we found out was *Hercules* from Norway, bound to Christiania, Norway, via Kirkwall, Scotland.

I would say that about noon on November 21st, the *Swallow* was on the bottom.

On November 28th, while off Kirkwall, the British cruiser *Patria* stopped the *Hercules*. Since, in 1915, Britain was still in the throes of war and battling the attempted enemy sub blockade of the northern seas, an officer and four sailors from *Patria* came aboard to escort *Hercules* into Kirkwall. The Norwegian vessel was suspected of smuggling copper for Germany.

At Kirkwall, the Customs' Officer communicated with the Board of Trade at Liverpool and they made arrangements for *Swallow*'s crew and passengers to get to either Canada or Newfoundland. Then, it was a series of hops and jumps to various ports and passages. According to Bowering:

> We were in Stornoway (Outer Hebrides) about two days when we left in a small steamboat for Kyle. We landed in Kyle on December 3rd, boarded the train for Inverness, then changed for Perth, then changed for Wigham. At Wigham, we changed for Liverpool, reaching there at 6:00 a.m. on the morning of the 4th.

> We were directed to the Board of Trade office. They told us a steamer would be leaving for St. John, New Brunswick, on the 10th. Eleven of us stayed at the Sailor's Home; two of the men and the four girls were sent to a hotel close by.

> On the evening of the 10th, we left by the Allan Line steamer *Pretorian* for Saint John. We arrived there on December 21st, where the shipping master gave us a railway pass to Bay Roberts via North Sydney and Port aux Basques.

It was Christmas Day when all arrived at Bay Roberts. They had left Domino, Labrador, October 25th, two months previously. In late November, word had come from Inverness to St. John's, then to various Conception Bay towns that the *Swallow*'s crew had been rescued.

But that didn't dampen Christmas celebrations in Bay Roberts, Bareneed, Bishop's Cove, Upper Island Cove, Coley's Point and Clarke's Beach. Those missing loved ones for whom they had hoped, wished and prayed were home.

Captain Bowering concluded, "[I have] all sympathy for the girls in passing through such an ordeal! I praise the brave fellows who stood by me and worked so faithfully in the face of such dangers..."

CHAPTER 35
WHAT A WAY TO SPEND NEW YEAR'S DAY

BRIGUS: Captain John Clarke went up to Boston in December of 1903 to bring down a schooner for the Hiscock business enterprise of Brigus. The schooner *Winona*, described as a "fine vessel," cost $2400 and wisely, as it turned out, the owner insured it for $1800. Ship's clearance articles list all crew from Brigus: James Rose, John Flaherty, Patrick Dunn and Richard Walker.

To make the voyage down to Newfoundland more profitable, Captain Clarke had orders to fill *Winona* with coal. From Boston to the southern tip of Nova Scotia, weather was relatively fine. In the Bay of Fundy, winds increased and the well-laden ship struggled.

At 9:00 p.m. on January 1, 1904, off the south shore of Nova Scotia, the storm intensified into a blinding snowstorm, with gale force winds and temperatures dropping to well below zero. High seas pounded the vessel and it began to leak alarmingly. Captain Clarke and *Winona*'s crew fought the storm until they were off Cape Canso.

Feeling the vessel might "go to pieces," Clarke gave orders to abandon ship. In the heavy seas and intense frost, it was difficult to get the lifeboat over the side. Despite the great odds against them – high seas, cold, a foundering schooner in a pitch black night – somehow they managed to get the boat out. In the rolling seas, it struck the side of the schooner, causing the small boat to leak. The captain saved only his ship's Log[1] and sextant; all his, and the crew's extra clothes, had to be left behind in order to give the boat a little more freeboard in the wind and sea.

Bailing constantly, they pulled away, leaving their newly-acquired *Winona* behind; presumably, it sank sometime after. The nearest harbour was Port Hawksbury. Winds were offshore and it took them two hours to reach the town. Even then, it was not a matter of simply pulling up to a convenient wharf or premises and walking ashore. Clarke and his crew beached the craft on a rugged shore – a ledge or rough beach.

In the attempt to land, the boat upset. Captain Clarke and Richard Walker spent two hours in the water. Somehow they survived, only to face an equally tough and surprising turn of events.

On the morning of Saturday, January 2, five Newfoundland sailors stumbled into Port Hawksbury. Each was exhausted from their fight for survival and was drenched to the skin, with their clothing frozen stiff in the biting wind. They had no food, no cash or extra clothes; in fact, each was glad they had escaped with their lives.

In Port Hawksbury, they walked up to the first house they saw and knocked on the door, only to receive a rejection – there was no help there. A second home proved the same result, as they were turned away. At subsequent homes they explained their plight more vigorously and clearly, but were not taken in and helped.

Tern schooner *Freedom* on the stocks at Liverpool, Nova Scotia, in 1908. *Freedom* sailed from Brigus on October 17, 1924, bound for Sydney for coal. A series of violent Atlantic storms pushed the battered schooner out into the Atlantic. The *Freedom*, leaky and wallowing, had to be abandoned 600 miles east northeast of Barbados. The crew rowed into Barbados on December 1st.

The tern netted 197 tons and measured 112 feet long. A.S. Rendell, a business based in St. John's, managed the vessel and at the time of its loss was crewed by Captain Sam Noseworthy, mate Thomas Power, cook Fred Rossiter, bosun Thomas Fillier, and seamen Andrew Short, John Hearn, and Richard Kenny.

Photo courtesy of Bruce Neal

According to a report filed later:

> They called at several residences telling of their pitiful plight and begging shelter and sustenance, but, when they communicated their names and nationality, they received insolent answers. None would harbour them.
>
> They were compelled to gather what wood they could find and camp all night on the beach in the terrible weather prevailing and with nothing to protect them but their broken boat. They made the best they could of their position and huddled about a fire which they had built.
>
> ...That any person could be refused shelter on a stormy and cold night is difficult to imagine, but that such treatment could be meted out to shipwrecked mariners – wet, hungry and chilled from exposure – it is too terrible to think of.

In time and without help from the local people, they found transportation to Halifax. Yet, despite the ordeal, their general good health and physical toughness pulled them through, four caught a bad cold. Walker alone, as he had spent two hours in cold water, fell ill with a chill and inflamed limbs.

Captain Clarke remained behind at Halifax for a few days: the other four; Rose, Flaherty, Dunn and Walker, came to St. John's on the S.S. *Silvia*, arriving January 6, 1904.

Patrick Dunn seemed to live "a charmed life," as the old saying went. He had been shipwrecked time and time again and had many narrow escapes. In December 1902, just a year prior to his escape on *Winona*, he signed on the Brigus schooner *Treasure*. At the last moment, he decided he wouldn't sail on the vessel and was replaced. *Treasure* left Brigus and was never heard from again.[2]

Notes

1. Often in the stories contained in this volume and in other recorded sea tales, the captain is noted as having saved the ship's Log, perhaps saving it when there is little else that can be taken from a sinking or wrecked ship.

In essence, the ship's Log is a legal document with the legal presumption that it is an accurate reflection of what happened during a voyage. Captains were obliged to keep a Log and record all events: weather, sailing orders, course, intended port, and any work the crew was ordered to carry out, i.e. changes in the sails. It was a faithful document of a ship's voyage, momentous and trivial.

2. *Treasure* left Brigus during Christmas week, 1902, on its way to load coal at Sydney. Captain James Gushue and his five Brigus seamen were never heard from again.

There were several tales of the strange and unearthly told around Brigus home fires of the *Treasure*. One comes from *The Log of Bob Bartlett* (G. P. Putnam, 1926). It is said that three days after *Treasure* sailed, one of the crew walked in on his wife, threw his sea bag on the floor and sat down in his favourite armchair, with water dripping from his face. The poor woman tried to throw her arms around him, but grasped only thin air. The next minute, the apparition turned and walked out.

CHAPTER 36
DEATH ON THE CONCEPTION BAY ICE

NORTHERN BAY, CAPE ST. FRANCIS: In March and April, when the Arctic ice fields drifted close to Newfoundland's northern and northeastern coasts, a young man's fancy turned to "swiling." Landsmen went out hunting seals. The meat – flippers – supplemented a lean spring diet and the pelts could bring in an extra dollar or two. Sometimes hunters walked on bay ice; often, they rowed in a small open boat, generally a punt, to the edge of the ice pack.

Such were the circumstances in late March 1880, when reports came to towns along the north shore of Conception Bay that seals had migrated to the outer reaches of the bay and were nearer shore than usual.

On Friday, March 26, five young men – three Hogans, William March and a Fahey lad, the latter was a nephew to one of the Hogans – left Northern Bay[1] with the idea of getting a few seals. The wind was favourable at the onset and soon they reached the seals. This meant pulling the punt up on the ice, leaving it to walk to the seals and the sealers hunting what they needed.

By now, though, the wind had veered around and came from the northwest. It pushed the ice away from the shore and pushed the boat out toward the middle of Conception Bay. Winds were too strong for them to make shore; by late evening, they were too exhausted to row any further and made up their minds to rest until the next morning. By then, it would be known in Northern Bay they were missing and other boats, they assumed, would be out to look for them.

In order to make the best possible shelter for the night, a cold and dreary one, they took the seals out of the punt, turned it on its side to the leeward of the wind and prepared to spend a long, cold night. The exhausted men were worried.

At daylight, anxiety turned to frustration. No one had come to get them – perhaps it was not known they were missing; perhaps the search scoured the wrong area.

For the five castaways, Cape St. Francis was now the nearest point of land and they started for there on foot, walking over the rough ice. After an hour, one of the two Hogan brothers became exhausted and lay down on the ice. He could not be encouraged or convinced to get up and continue.

March had one biscuit left, which he divided into five parts and gave to his comrades. With that meager fare, most were ready to beat their way over the Arctic drift ice; except one of the Hogan men.

"Go on," Hogan said. "You can't wait for me. It is getting late in the day. The four of you have to go on to try to get to safety. Perhaps I will be found and rescued."

Now the four continued on a little farther. After a few miles, the second Hogan hunter fell down and would not get up. Three, those who had a little extra strength of body and spirit, walked on for an hour.

Fahey became ice blind and said, "Uncle, I cannot see your tracks. I must lie down."

Cape St. Francis seemed tantalizing near. So two – a Hogan and March – kept walking toward the land and the livyers who had homes in that vicinity. On the way, Hogan killed two seals and cut out two hearts. He offered one to March.

"I cannot eat it. You go on," he said.

The raw food, however, strengthened Hogan, and he was able to help lift, push and convince his companion to drag himself a little farther. Finally, about an hour before the sun went down, they reached Cripple Cove, near the tip of Cape St. Francis. Hogan was walking slowly; March stumbled along, supported by Hogan.

But, at that time of the year, no one lived in the shacks in Cripple Cove. It was merely a fishing station or place the fishermen from the western side of Conception Bay used during the summer.[2]

Hogan and March managed to get into an unoccupied house, or fishing hut, and tried to make a fire. This failed, as their matches were damp and wouldn't light.

March said, "I can't go any farther. I'm weak and perhaps I will last for awhile in this hut. You go on to the Cape St. Francis Light. It's less than a mile distance across this little cove. The lightkeeper will come and get me."

Yet Hogan again convinced his friend to go with him for that last three quarters of a mile across the cove on the ice. When both reached land again, March stayed there, convincing Hogan to go on. "Well," said Hogan, "keep moving about, for if you stop moving, you'll freeze."

On reaching the lighthouse, Hogan told the keeper he left a dying man on the ice near Cripple Cove. A boat and crew were sent out and, after searching about for some time, returned without March.

"What? You didn't stay until you found him. Go again. I'm too exhausted to help look." At this point, the survivor grew agitated with the lightkeeper, threatening to inform the authorities.

On Saturday morning, the lightkeeper telegraphed for the St. John's harbour tug *Hercules* to come to Cape St. Francis. It was Sunday before it arrived. Hogan went on board and showed them the general area where he left March. His lifeless body was soon located on the ice near the rocks.

While the body was being carried to Northern Bay, *Hercules*' crew searched the ice for the other three men. Having searched all day Sunday, the tug returned to St. John's in the evening.

Of the five who set out that March 26th morning, one survivor returned to Northern Bay; March's body was interred in his home town. He was the son of Simeon March and had attended St. Bonaventure's College in St. John's.

Then, on April 2, the magistrate at Carbonear, Israel Langworth McNeil, received a telegram from authorities in St. John's that a body had been found on the ice about four miles off the St. John's Narrows. The remains were identified as that of Martin Hogan.

Then, a week later, a man named Michael Power was out on the ice off Tor's Cove and, seeing a dark object on the ice, discovered the body of Patrick Hogan of Northern Bay. Father Driscoll requested the young man's body be brought to shore.

It was put in a coffin and covered with snow in the cemetery until Hogan's people were notified. He would eventually be interred in Northern Bay. Fahey's body was never found.[3]

Notes

1. Northern Bay, located on the North Shore of Conception Bay – the western side of the Bay between Salmon Cove and Bay de Verde – is situated chiefly along a series of low cliffs on the north side of a broad, open cove. At the head of Northern Bay is a wide sandy beach which, since the early 1970s, is the site of Northern Bay Sands Provincial Park and a popular swimming area.

2. Ironically, Cripple Cove was used by fishermen from Conception Bay towns near Northern Bay – Salmon Cove, Broad Cove. It was a rough and rocky landscape, even in summer. When the wind came westerly, the fishermen had to abandon the shacks. In recent years it is an area frequented by duck hunters.

3. There is another strange story of the ice-covered sea coming from Fogo Island. On Saturday, April 7, 1917, seven young hunters, who had walked out on the ice to hunt seals, failed to return home. Six were from Joe Batt's Arm: three brothers named Jacobs, their adopted brother Pomeroy and two others named Freake. One man, a Newman, hailed from Barr'd Island.

Searchers found Newman a week later, alive on Chaulk's Island. The two Freake sealers were possibly found alive as well, for the final word on the tragedy mentions only the Jacobs and the Pomeroy.

That week, timely and thorough searches by landsmen were slow and disorganized. By Saturday, April 14, urgent messages to St. John's requested steamers to come and scour the ice floes off Fogo Island. Authorities contacted two sealing steamers, *Bloodhound* and *Diana*, the latter being fifteen miles off the Wadham Islands, to search. Both steamed in the general vicinity, but saw nothing.

Eventually, the young men were given up as lost at sea and no trace was ever found – except for one unusual sign. On August 4, nearly four months after the sealers disappeared, word came that a fisherman, James Adey, had found a sealer's gaff floating in the sea off Western Head, a headland at the northwestern extremity of New World Island, Notre Dame Bay.

Cut into the wood, onto which the hook was attached, were the words, "Lay down to perish, April 11. J.J."

People of Joe Batt's Arm were sure the initials stood for Joseph Jacobs, the eldest of the missing sealers. The date proved that he, and perhaps others of his group, stayed alive on the ice from Saturday, April 7 to Wednesday, April 11.

Mr. Adey, not knowing the story or the significance of the gaff, put the gaff in his shed until the fishing season started. He then took the device aboard his schooner when he left for the fishing grounds.

Two things struck the people of Joe Batt's Arm as odd. If a search had been quickly and properly conducted, all may have been found in time, as they had evidently lived (as indicated by the inscription on the gaff) four days on the ice. Secondly, they said, "It also seems strange that the persons who found a gaff with writing on it made no outcry or mention of it for a long time. They should have reported it to authorities or to the nearest newspaper." The gaff, they said, should be returned to the relatives of the unfortunate men.

The finding of this object seemed to add a strange twist to a sea mystery. Then, in a peculiar ending to a tale of death on the ice, a letter dated August 25, 1917, appeared in the newspaper *Twillingate Sun*. It stated:

> Dear Mr. Editor:
>
> I am the man who picked up the gaff this spring on June 11th, off Western Head. This gaff was floating in the water with about six inches of the staff sticking out of the water and I saw it while passing in my motorboat and took it into the boat. The gaff was covered with small weeds, so I noticed nothing on it at the time. I brought it home and put it in my stage.
>
> On July 27th, I was going away to the fishery, and put the gaff on board my schooner. That evening Saturday, someone aboard noticed the words on the gaff, but there was no time to do anything, and this explains why the matter was not reported by me.
>
> The gaff was not used by me while on the French Shore and was carefully looked after.
>
> (Signed) James Adey

The gaff was sent to the newspaper and those in the office who later examined it, agreed that the initials "J.J." were clearly cut. This was evidently done by the unfortunate man, perhaps during some winter evening when he made the gaff. At the lower end of the handle, as though done by someone with little strength left, were the words: "Lay Down to Perish, April 11."

CHAPTER 37
WHATEVER HAPPENED TO THE *NEREUS*?

TORBAY POINT, QUIDI VIDI, ST. JOHN'S: Two men with heads bowed and speaking to each other in low, muted conversation walked quickly through the village of Quidi Vidi. It was 6:30 p.m. on October 19, 1909. It was getting dark and there was no time to waste if someone had to be notified to begin a sea search.

In the morning of that day, two young fishermen, Messrs. Pike and Pynn, had left with Captain William Frampton of Signal Hill Road and engineer Alexander Forward of King's Road to fish off Torbay in the steam launch *Nereus*. Now, only the two fishermen remained and they knew the *Nereus* was in trouble. They had to report to owner John William Clouston[1] as soon as possible.

Frampton had worked in Clouston's fish factory during the summer of 1909 but, in early October, had taken the *Nereus* to trawl for fish for Clouston's plant. Clouston provided his crew with the steamer, the bultows, the bait, coal for the small steam engine, food and agreed to pay $1.00 per hundred weight of fresh fish.

Not a large boat, the forty-two foot long *Nereus* was built by the Reid Newfoundland Company with a sixteen horsepower steam engine. The fishing launch had an oak frame planked in pitch pine. The little vessel and its sixteen horsepower steam engine was in excellent running condition. Yet, the steamer, according to Clouston, had one flaw – it had no canvas aboard for the single mast.

At one point, *Nereus* carried passengers, as a news item in *The Daily News* (September 14, 1907) describes, "*Nereus* is now in first class condition, and is making good trips between Bell Island and the Cove. Yesterday, she brought over a large number of passengers, and made the run in less than forty minutes."

Some time previously, Clouston had suggested to Skipper Frampton that they should get some canvas for the single mast, in case the engine gave out anytime at sea. Then, a sail would provide a means to reach shore. Now, according to Pynn and Pike, such an incident had happened.

There was plenty of fish on October 19. By 4:00 p.m., while off Small Point, *Nereus* had about 1000 pounds of fish aboard when a rope from a small boat being towed behind became entangled in the propeller. The launch was unable to steam. At first, the fishermen Pynn and Pike got in the boat and towed the *Nereus* for half an hour.

Then, Frampton asked Pynn and Pike to row ashore to get help and to contact owner Clouston. *Nereus*, without power, drifted away in the encroaching evening. The two fishermen reached shore and hurried to Clouston's premises.

When they found Clouston, he engaged Mr. Chaulker's motorboat. Pynn, Pike, Matt Byrne and William Moore went out at 7:30 in the evening to search, returning at 10:00 without having seen any trace of the boat or missing men.

Of course, they reasoned it was possible Frampton may have attempted to moor and wait for help. Aboard was a chain of forty-five fathoms (270 feet) with an anchor,

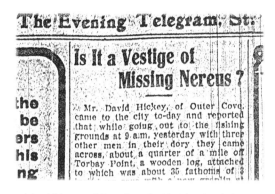

A local fisherman of Outer Cove, David Hickey, found what may have been debris or equipment from a missing ship (*The Evening Telegram* November 5, 1909).

The image shows a newspaper clipping reading:

The Evening Telegram, St.

Is It a Vestige of Missing Nereus ?

Mr. David Hickey, of Outer Cove, came to the city to-day and reported that while going out to the fishing grounds at 9 a.m. yesterday with three other men in their dory they came across, about a quarter of a mile off Torbay Point, a wooden log, attached to which was about 35 fathoms of

as well as sixty fathoms of three inch bass rope.

In the search, which extended from Torbay's Southern Point to an area off Signal Hill, the two fishermen could not understand why a light or lantern from *Nereus* was not seen. This, along with the fact the sea was too rough for the motor boat to stay out, was an ominous sign. Could the launch have swamped? Could it have drifted past Cape Spear and into the open ocean beyond?

On the morning of October 20, the harbour tug *D.P. Ingraham* went out to search. It went south and east from Cape Spear to Bay Bulls, with the crew scrutinizing the coves and creeks without seeing anything. By now, thoughts, as yet unspeakable, were that *Nereus* had filled with water in the north northeast winds of Tuesday night.

One ray of light remained: the schooners coming to St. John's from the outlying bays – Conception, Placentia, St. Mary's, Trepassey, Fortune – may have

The harbour tug *D. P. Ingraham* which in October 1909 went in search of the missing *Nereus*. In this photo it assists the sealing steamer *Vanguard* which has a number of sealers gathered at the bow.

Photo courtesy Maritime History Archive, MUN Accession # PF-316.014

seen *Nereus*. Although it was improbable, perhaps, maybe... the launch had drifted out past the northern and eastern Avalon and was still afloat somewhere.

Meanwhile, two families were grief stricken over the strange event and the lack of any news. William Frampton had a wife and three children. Alexander Forward, a son of John Forward, had a brother George in St. John's and another, Harry, in New York. Kate, his sister, lived in Boston.

In time, the search tapered down and ended. Then, on November 5, one piece of mute evidence of a disaster appeared. David Hickey of Outer Cove fished a quarter of a mile off Torbay Point and had pulled up a wooden log with about 35 fathoms of three inch bass rope attached. John Clouston believed it was from the missing *Nereus*.

From that evidence it could only be concluded *Nereus* made it into comparatively shallow water when the men aboard dropped anchor. In the heavy seas which came up later, the rope must have broken. *Nereus* either struck the rocks and swamped or filled with water offshore. At any rate, the mystery of the missing *Nereus* still lies locked in the seas off Torbay.[2]

Notes

1. Clouston's Experimental Fish Plant – John Clouston, who lived in St. John's, had patented a design which became a model for his two subsequent experimental fish processing plants; one on a small scale at St. John's in 1907, and later a full-sized facility operated at Bay Bulls. Clouston was a pioneer with work in boneless processing, shredding, and packaging codfish. To supply fresh fish, he had small fishing crafts operating off St. John's.

2. In the late evening and night of October 19-20, when *Nereus* went missing, there was quite a wind storm off the Avalon, which is shown through this clipping (*The Evening Telegram* October 20, 1909). The schooner *Candace*, with Captain Eli John King, left St. John's on Tuesday evening for Trinity. While attempting to cross Conception Bay, *Candace* was blown 250 miles off the coast. Its mainsail was torn to shreds and the jib ripped. By Friday, October 22, it turned around and headed home, arriving in Trinity Saturday evening.

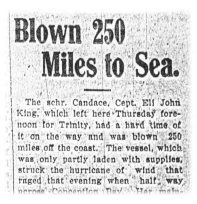

Blown 250 Miles to Sea.

The schr. Candace, Cept. Eli John King, which left here Thursday forenoon for Trinity, had a hard time of it on the way and was blown 250 miles off the coast. The vessel, which was only partly laden with supplies, struck the hurricane of wind that raged that evening when half way across Conception Bay. Her main-

ST. JOHN'S AND SABLE ISLAND: Edwin Duder Jr. took over his father's shipping business in 1881. In the 1880-90s the firm, based mainly in St. John's, owned a large number of ships and was believed to have the largest fleet of any company in the world. Duder eventually expanded to Twillingate, Fogo, Herring Neck and Change Islands.

But any business or person who goes "down to the sea to do business in the great waters" with a fleet of ships, must experience tragedy and ship losses. That is the way of the sea; the price to be paid to the treacherous ocean.

Captain Kendrick sailed from Pernambuco, Brazil, for Sydney on August 21, 1886. There, he would load coal for Newfoundland. He was in charge of one of Duder's vast fleet: the 251 ton *Olinda*, a bark built in Greenock, Scotland, in 1859. Kendrick had a crew of ten.

At noon Saturday, September 18, the ship's position was 43.35 North, 60.55 West. According to the course proposed by the captain, *Olinda* should have cleared Sable Island by twenty-eight miles to the westward. Not taking any chances, Kendrick hove to and sounded the bottom with the lead weight – fifty-two fathoms. The ship was well off any land.

Olinda kept on its northeasterly course. Winds were fresh from the southwest. All sails were set and *Olinda* was making about four and a half knots an hour. At 2:00 a.m., the mate took charge of the ship; Kendrick went below for some rest, as he expected to be up all the next night. At 3:00 a.m., he asked the cook, who had

The bark *Olinda*, above. As a bark (or barque) it has three or more masts: fore and aft rigged on aftermast, square rigged on all others.

Photo courtesy Maritime History Archives, MUN Accession # PF-008.082

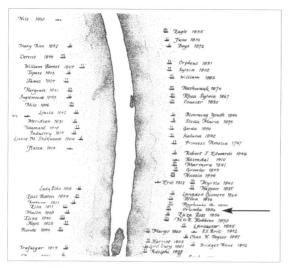

Map of Sable Island showing the Location of *Olinda*'s wreck, right, and the "Salt Lake" bottom center.

come to his cabin, if it was clear on deck and he replied that it was. Then disaster – as Kendrick recalled:

About twenty minutes later, I heard a cry from the deck, "Breakers ahead!" I immediately rushed to the deck and called all hands to bring the ship about, but she refused to stay. I then let go both anchors and took off sail.

Shortly after, a heavy sea struck her on the bow, and the starboard chain carried away the outwater. *Olinda* struck aft and the breakers hove her in broadside. The starboard anchor was then slipped and the port chain put. As she was being fast buried in wet sand, I ordered out the boats.

The ship, as she lay, formed a breakwater, which enabled us all to land in safety. The fog was so thick at this time that we could not see the outline of the island and did not know on landing where we were.

At 5:00 p.m., the fog lifted and we found we were on the south side of Sable Island, about a mile and a half from the main lifeguard station. The superintendent of the island (Robert J. Boutillier, who was superintendent of the island's lifesaving station from 1885 to 1912) came down to the wreck and advised us to leave the ship. The wind was then blowing strong on shore and a heavy sea running. Nothing could be done, he said.

Captain Kendrick knew it was impossible to refloat *Olinda* so he and his crew stripped the derelict of all gear. When the hulk was pared and lightened, Boutillier and his staff had, at great risk to their safety, tried in every way to refloat it. It was not to be; the bones of *Olinda* remained in the sand.

The Nova Scotian steamer *Newfield* made its regular run to Sable Island and the Newfoundland crew were taken on board and carried to Halifax, landing there September 27, nine days after *Olinda* became a wreck on Sable Island.

A Mysterious Disappearance

There appears yet another strange footnote to the tale of *Olinda*'s wreck. On September 24, 1886, less than a week after the bark grounded, Superintendent Boutillier sent William Guinane, one of his employees, to the wreck site. Guinane, with a cart pulled by a team of oxen, was to haul one of the lifeboats belonging to

Olinda in St. John's harbour, circa early 1880s.

the wreck to the other side of the island. From there, the lifeboat would be put aboard the S. S. *Newfield*.

Guinane finished attaching the lifeboat and began his return to the station. On the road, he had to cross a salty bog-like lake, situated in the center of Sable Island. Though one end of the lake was fordable, that is a team of oxen could travel over it, the oxen returned to the station without its driver.

No trace of Guinane could be found. The cart trail could be seen where it entered the lake, which was at the deepest part. He had vanished. Those on the island performed a long and intense search, but neither the man nor his body had been found up to the time the *Newfield* left. Guinane, about fifty and married, lived in Halifax.

ST. JOHN'S: The word panic is defined as, 'overpowering fright, leading to hasty measures.' Captain Rogers and his crew saw panic in the actions and heard it in the shouts of seamen on another ship. Rogers' vessel, the banking schooner *Charlie F. Mayo*, anchored down on the banks in latitude 46.38, longitude 49.30, on a stormy Saturday night, September 19, 1896.

It was a wild night as the storm increased to a howling fury, but nothing that his schooner couldn't manage. Rogers had taken all precautions and anchored with nearly all cable out – 250 fathoms. The more cable out, the less strain on it and on the ship and the greater chance of staying in one spot. To go uncontrollably adrift in high winds was tantamount to disaster.

About 9:00 p.m. the French brigantine *G.C. 12* board bore down toward them. To say its crew was alarmed would be putting it mildly; their shouts and motions confirmed that to Captain Rogers. At the time, it was very dark and a heavy sea was running, i.e. white-capped waves broke in cross currents with the sea in a turmoil. Rogers could only hope the brigantine, which appeared loaded with cargo, as it was well down in the water, would not run too close to *Charlie F. Mayo* at this time.

Charlie F. Mayo, at seventy-four net tons and seventy-eight feet long, was built in 1868. It was one of an extensive fleet of banking schooners registered to Kenneth Prowse, a partner in the fishing business of Robert Prowse and Sons of St. John's. If the French vessel struck or collided with Rogers' schooner, there was a possibility both vessels could go down. Soon, Captain Rogers saw – and heard – the problem.

"Take us off! We are sinking!" Those aboard *G.C. 12* lined the rails, shouting in French, English and a combination of both languages. It was obvious the vessel, weather beaten and with decks awash in an Atlantic storm, was about to go to Davy Jones' Locker.

Rogers called to them, "Stay close. Hang around until daylight and we'll take you off your ship." He knew a daylight rescue would be easier and safer for the panic-stricken Frenchmen and for his own crew. Perhaps, too, by morning seas might have abated.

But near midnight, the screams and actions aboard *G.C. 12* intensified. According to Rogers, "The crew of the sinking vessel seemed to lose their presence of mind." Some fell on their knees in prayer, others rushed around, cried and shouted continually.

"Heave up the cable!" Rogers told his crew, as he knew he would work up to the windward side of the brigantine. About ten to twelve fathoms was up when the cable burst and the remainder, including the anchor, was lost. But now *Charlie F. Mayo* was maneuverable and the crew worked it down alongside the troubled ship.

Rogers sent a dory over, intending to bring the crew over to his schooner, one dory load at a time. But he saw that, in their anxiety, all those aboard the sinking French vessel would have piled into the dory, overloading it.

Rogers sent over three dories and the whole group, rescuers and rescued, transferred to the *Charlie F. Mayo* without mishap. Rogers decided to remain as close to *G.C. 12* as he could. Perhaps a salvage attempt was possible. Weather, thick fog and high winds became mitigating factors. He stayed until 10:00 a.m. Sunday morning, when the foundering French brigantine was lost from sight. No one was sure if and when it sank.

On the voyage back to St. John's, all hands had to be put on a food and water allowance. Provisions meant for *Mayo*'s crew had to serve nearly three times that number. As it was, Rogers and crew had lost their cable, anchor and some fishing gear. With only 250 quintals in the holds, their fishing voyage had been cut short as well.

On the way into port, the French explained that *G.C. 12*, about 140 tons, had left St. Pierre in mid-September with a cargo of 190,000 pounds of green codfish aboard. Some of those aboard were boys, 'graviers', who worked ashore, and some were the fishing crew.

The dead weight of green fish and the rough weather caused *G.C. 12* to split completely apart in the stern. No amount of pumping or temporary repair could save it. Had it not been for the fortunate sighting of the Newfoundland schooner, the ship and crew would have been gobbled up by the raging Atlantic. It is likely no one would have ever known what had happened.

On September 22, *Charlie F. Mayo* sailed into St. John's with no drinking water and little food left, but it did carry many grateful French fishermen, who were subsequently looked after by the French Consul in Newfoundland.

CHAPTER 40
CAPTAIN HOEBURG

ST. JOHN'S: He was well-known. A fine gentleman, admired by seamen along the St. John's waterfront, Captain Rudolph Hoeburg came to Newfoundland at age twenty-one from Viborg, Denmark. As a teenager, he had joined the Danish navy and, when his naval ship stopped at St. John's, Hoeburg decided to stay there.

In Newfoundland, he rose in the ranks from sailor, mate, to captain and then acquired and earned the title, 'Master Mariner.' Yet in the end, his death at sea was surrounded with questions and mystery.

His final voyage began late in the year 1920 on the tern schooner *Ludwig*. A.S. Rendell and Company of St. John's had recently purchased this fish carrier from a Danish company and Hoeburg may have had a share as part-owner in the ship. Built in 1918 in Denmark, *Ludwig* was 118 net tons and ninety-one feet long.

The captain had actually retired from a seafaring life, but the shareholders had difficultly finding a qualified captain to take the boat to Europe. Hoeburg chose to make one final voyage. With the exception of seaman Nilsen, the other crew were Newfoundlanders: mate William Johnson, bosun Jonathan Gustafsson, cook Arthur Watton and seaman Edward Boone.

Ludwig loaded codfish at St. Anthony and left November 1, 1920, for a port in the Mediterranean. As was the custom, it first had to stop at the British protectorate, Gibraltar, for further orders and to get some necessary repairs and gear. The ship experienced very rough weather all though the passage and, as a result, the foresail and jumbo were blown away and the bulwarks badly smashed.

Owing to adverse winds and strong tides, Captain Hoeburg was unable to bring his ship into dockside at Gibraltar and was pushed on up through the Strait of Gibraltar. At 7:00 p.m. on December 12, Hoeburg and his crew managed to get the damaged tern outside Malaga in southern Spain. It anchored on the eastern side of the eastern breakwater.

However, during the night, the wind came up from the southeast and at 1:00 a.m. it was blowing a gale. Seas broke over *Ludwig*, causing it to drag anchors and drift toward shore, a few yards distant. Seeing the dangerous position of the vessel, Captain Hoeburg called the crew together on deck and directed mate Johnson to get the lifeboat ready.

Shortly afterwards, he ordered them to leave the vessel, but – and this is the strange part of the tale – he absolutely refused to get into the lifeboat himself. The mate and the rest of the crew, after much work and difficulty, got the boat over the side and tied to the drifting *Ludwig*.

Despite the entreaties of the crew, calling him to get aboard and telling him that it was unwise to remain on the craft, Hoeburg stayed put. He slipped the lines of the boat, again refusing to join his crew. As the lifeboat pulled away from the drifting schooner, the last the crew saw of him, Hoeburg was standing on deck, peering into

B. Thomson's Optical Parlor, 336
Duckworth Street and being properly
fitted with glasses. Day and evening
attendance.

Old Captain's Sacrifice

(London Times)

A moving story of the devotion of a
captain to his ship was told on Tuesday by the crew of the three-masted
schooner Ludvig, of Newfoundland,
who are at present under the care of
the Sailors' Home, Well Street and

✪ ✪ ✪ ✪ ✪ ✪ ✪ ✪ ✪ ✪ ✪ ✪ ✪ ✪

The Clyde left Merasheen at 7.45
p.m. yesterday.

The Glencoe left Burgeo at 5 a.m.
yesterday, going up the coast.

Teas served Afternoon and
Evening at the Green Lantern.

The incoming express is not due
until 3.30 to-morrow morning.

For all ignition and lighting purposes use Reliable Dry Batteries and

Clip from *London Times* via *Daily News* features the "Old Captain's Sacrifice."

the darkness. He seemed quite unconcerned or unaware of his dangerous situation.

The crew barely escaped with their lives. The seas were crashing over the breakwater with great force and they had a hard fight to reach the land. Eventually, mate Johnson and the others landed safely in Malaga.

The next morning, they went to the scene of the trouble, only to find *Ludwig* had sunk. Only the ship's topmasts were above water. The crew immediately made arrangements for a search to try and locate the captain or his body. They found a diver who was willing to go down to the ship. But Captain Hoeburg's body was never recovered.

There was nothing else the surviving crew could do. They were looked after by the British Consul in that part of Spain and were sent to Gibraltar and, thence, to London. They joined the ocean liner *Saxonia* from London to Halifax, Nova Scotia. Within a few days, they joined the steamer *Digby*, bound for St. John's.

While in London, they had a wait to join the ocean liner. The venerable newspaper *London Times* heard about the news of the death of the old captain. It sent a reporter to see the crew, who were then staying at the Sailor's Home on Well Street in London.

The *Times* called the tale of the wreck and the loss of life, "A moving story of the devotion of a captain to his ship...who, in spite of the crew's entreaties, absolutely refused to leave the ship. A few minutes afterwards, *Ludwig* struck and went down suddenly, carrying her captain with her."

The crew arrived in St. John's on January 21, 1921. Then, with a heavy heart, they had to tell the tale of the wreck of *Ludwig* and the unusual manner of the captain's death.

According to *The Daily News* (January 22, 1921), "Captain Hoeburg left home at an early age and took up the seafaring life." He married Miss Mary Ann Fitzgerald of St. John's and had three children: Michael who, in 1921, was in charge of a submarine school in Newport News, Virginia. Nora was a nurse in a Boston hospital. Mrs. Alma (Hoeburg) Holland lived in St. John's.

After the death of Captain Hoeburg's first wife, he had visited or was managing vessels in Burin. There, he met and married a Miss Elizabeth Morris. At that time, Miss Morris, the daughter of Sir Edward Patrick Morris, Newfoundland's twelfth prime minister, was managing a hotel in that Burin Peninsula town.[1]

Notes

1. I first became aware of this personal tragedy of a sea captain through a conversation with Al Holland, St. John's, a descendant of Captain Hoeburg. In time, the captain's story was verified by *The Daily News* January 22, 1921, and *London Times* via *The Daily News* January 31, 1921.

CHAPTER 41
THIRTEEN DAYS AND NIGHTS

PETTY HARBOUR-MADDOX COVE, TORBAY: Frost! Snow! Wind! One of the coldest springs ever, as remembered by the older people of the southern shore, was March and April of 1857. The worst of winter weather meant extra burdens for the early pioneers of Newfoundland. Winter supplies had to last a little longer, spring planting came later and the "long and hungry month of March" – as our forefathers were wont to say – seemed to never end. For fishermen and sailors ploughing the sea, they had to endure extra hardship from bitter winter winds.

In early April 1857, there occurred a unique disaster in which three men lost their lives, attributed, in part, to the long and unusually cold conditions. That spring, the brigantine *Norman*, under Captain Lynch and with fifty men, was returning from the seal hunt.

About nine miles off Bay Bulls, the ship became stuck in ice. Thirteen of the crew, more anxious to get home than the others, thought of an idea which they put into execution. They would walk across the ice to land and then walk to St. John's. This information reached the ears of Captain Lynch. He called this crew altogether in the after part of the ship, pointing out the danger to them.

He said, "If you are comfortable here, have patience. The ice will soon shift and the vessel will free. I ask of you, nay, beg and plead for you to stay. 'Tis a foolhardy plan. Don't take such a risk."

It was all to no purpose. There was one ringleader, a man named Griffin, who was at one time a master of a vessel himself. He possessed an oily tongue and a considerable power of persuasion. Some said he had kissed the Blarney Stone, for he was a regular sea lawyer.

"You are cowards," Griffin said. "I'm not afraid to go, if two or three others will join me."

The mention of the word "coward" was enough to stir proud spirits and, about midnight, the thirteen left the ship upon their hazardous undertaking. When they arrived near the land between Bay Bulls and Petty Harbour, they found that the ice was about half a mile from the shore and open water greeting them.

Griffin said they would walk to Cape Spear. At that point, there was more open water which was in fact a gap, a barrier preventing them from reaching safety. The group had plenty of food, at least for a limited time; however, they did not count on such difficulties and hardships as they now had to face. For thirteen days and thirteen nights, they were on the ice, a good distance from land, exposed to all the cold, wind and storm that "spring of frosty weather" had to offer.

When some days out from the *Norman* – now miles away and out of sight – one of Griffin's group, a man named Healy of Maddox Cove, Petty Harbour, succumbed to the cold and died. He was reputed to be the strongest man among the crew, a man over six feet tall and of powerful physique. Not long after, two others gave up and perished.

The remaining ten men did everything possible to keep themselves alive and when all hopes were abandoned, a vessel from Conception Bay bound to St. John's to land its seals hove in sight. The castaways made signals and Captain Bussey bore down and rescued them.

All arrived in St. John's, but some were terribly frostbitten – especially a man named McAuliffe who lived on the South Side near Job's Bridge. However, not all were so afflicted. One survivor, Phil Grace of Torbay, stepped ashore from the ship as lively as the day he went on board the *Norman*. He proceeded to walk to his home, a distance of nine or ten miles.

During those thirteen days, Captain Lynch was in great anxiety over his men. He was and still felt responsible for them until they signed the ship's articles that the voyage was over. His mate or second hand, Captain French, and the master watches tried to console him with their belief that they had landed all right. At last Lynch thought so himself.

As *Norman* neared St. John's, sailing slowly through the breaking ice, another vessel bound for Conception Bay sailed quite near them.

Captain Lynch hailed them, asking the captain of the vessel, "What news in St. John's of the men who walked over the ice?

"Bad news," replied the captain. "Three of Captain Lynch's crew were brought in dead and others more or less frostbitten."

Captain Lynch took this news hard, described by relatives as in "an awful shock and he became prostrated with grief." Of course, the master of the other vessel, being a stranger, did not know he was speaking to Lynch or he would have couched his reply more carefully.

Everything possible was done for the survivors, and although some were crippled for life, others recovered quickly, showing no effects of the thirteen days and nights on open ice in temperatures well below zero. Some prosecuted the seal fishery for many years afterwards.[1]

Notes

1. One man who did think Griffin's plan was a foolish one and chose to stay with Captain Lynch on *Norman* was a Mr. Hagerty of St. John's. For many years after the disaster to his shipmates, he piloted ships and rose in rank to pilot His (or Her) Majesty's Ships, which he brought in and out of nearly every bay in Newfoundland. His services were so appreciated that the British Admiralty presented him with a silver cup for assisting British warships.

PETTY HARBOUR, SHOAL BAY, GOULDS: In January 1915, five vessels waited outside St. John's trying to get into port. They were foreign-going fish carriers, bound from Brazil. On January 25, there had been a terrific snowstorm and all five, *Earlshall*, *Clutha*, *Atilla*, *Waterwitch*, and an unnamed three-masted schooner from the southwest coast, were forced to anchor between Cape Spear and Petty Harbour. One of the five didn't make it to port, leaving its iron bones in Shoal Bay.[1]

The iron bark *Earlshall*, one of a number of relatively large vessels that was brought into the Newfoundland overseas fish trade after the turn of the century, was bought here by Job Brothers just before the start of World War I. Its career on this side of the Atlantic was a short one.

All five ships had come from ports like Bahia and Recife (known also as Pernambuco). All had made excellent time between South America and their landfall at Cape Race. The Cape had been passed on January 23; the sighting of each was recorded and reported to St. John's by the Cape Race lighthouse keeper.

Although they encountered a great deal of ice, they managed to keep well to the south of it, skirting the floes, so that by Saturday evening, January 23, after passing Ferryland Head, all five were sailing together.

Crew of *Earlshall* January 1915

Captain Samuel Coward
mate P. Odderson
bosun M. Burke
cook M. Cahill
engineer Bristow
seaman Crowe
seaman J. Hawco
seaman P. Stack
seaman J. Squires
seaman R. Thompson
seaman Winhein

Earlshall, under the command of Captain Samuel Coward, was the largest of the Newfoundland sailing fleet at that time. Coward carried a crew of twelve to sail the ship.

Earlshall was 422 tons and had been built in 1876 at Dundee, Scotland. Jobs had fitted the bark with a 150 horsepower Bolinder motor engine; thus, with both kinds of power, it was an "auxiliary" vessel.

The small flotilla managed to get quite close to the Narrows by Saturday night. Conditions didn't look good for entering – wind, ice, current were against them. So, the captains "wore ship" for the night in hope that wind and ice conditions would improve.

At this time, all five ships were quite close to each other. *Attila*, being closest to the iron bark, passed information to Captain Coward and crew. As the night passed, conditions, rather than improve, grew worse. Wind increased and it began

The *Earlshall* before engines were installed.

Photo courtesy Maritime History Archives, MUN Accession # PF-315.406

to snow. This developed into a blizzard, so much so that even Cape Spear was blotted out.

Earlshall moved away from *Attila* and drifted back; the latter and the other vessels headed for the Narrows. It was Sunday, but that didn't stop the captains from expressing their views vehemently. They were more than indignant over the fact that there was no harbour tug or tow boat out to meet them. Marine authorities knew the ships were outside St. John's in a blizzard; in fact, they knew the previous day they had passed Cape Race.

All that hindsight didn't help *Earlshall* much. About 4:00 a.m. Monday, cook Cahill came on deck, bringing the labouring crew hot coffee. Captain Coward had just "turned in" for some sleep and mate Odderson (probably a Norwegian) was on watch. By then, the bark had drifted back to a point between Cape Spear and Petty Harbour.

Suddenly there was a crash. *Earlshall* struck reefs and ledges off Petty Harbour Motion, about practically the same place the S. S. *Regulus* met its fate five years previously.[2] There was a tremendous sea running and the vessel began to pound heavily against the rocks and to leak badly. Soon, the seawater had reached up to the galley. Captain Coward was soon up on deck, directing his crew and ensuring their safety.

In no time, they had the boats over the side. During the launching, one of the lifeboats was damaged and nearly sank. When the leak was fixed, it had to be bailed continuously. After rowing eight miles, the crew reached land near Shoal Bay. They were exhausted, but yet had to face the elements in an overland trek.

From Shoal Bay, they had to walk overland to the Goulds, climbing icy hills, struggling through snow covered trees and brush. During the long and difficult walk, mate Odderson and engineer Bristow collapsed and had to be carried by the rest of the crew.

The first occupied home they came to was that of Mrs. Mills in the Goulds. There, they were given shelter, food and dry clothing. They had escaped the wreck of *Earlshall*, but had lost all belongings. The only thing saved, besides the clothes the crew stood in, was Captain Sam Coward's master's certificate.

Notes

1. Shoal Bay is located south of St. John's, on the exposed coast between Petty Harbour and Bay Bulls. The name is a misnomer, as there is no bay and little shelter for vessels. As early as 1776, Shoal Bay was the site of a copper mine.

By the 1860s, families from the Goulds and Petty Harbour were fishing at Shoal Bay in the summers. It was a poor landing place and catches had to be hoisted by cables to stages and flakes built atop the steep cliffs.

Shoal Bay appeared in the *Census* for the only time in 1869, when there were 103 people fishing for cod and salmon and raising swine and goats. Although it is not likely Shoal Bay was ever occupied year round, the common names listed were Clark, Fizel (Frizzell), Heffernan and Raymond.

According to the *Newfoundland Encyclopedia*, Shoal Bay is the setting for numerous ghost stories and pirate legends. The most often-told tale concerns a pirate ship which is said to have run aground in the mid-1700s. Most of the crew, according to the story, were lost with the ship but the captain, mate and four others made it to shore where they buried a large treasure. The four crew members were murdered on the spot, the mate was lost at sea and only the captain survived. He is supposed to have traveled to Holyrood, where, on his deathbed, he revealed the secret of the treasure. By some accounts, the Shoal Bay copper mine was merely a "blind" for efforts to find the pirate treasure. Numerous people attempted to find the treasure in later years, but all were said to have been frightened off by ghostly apparitions.

2. On October 23, 1910, the coal carrying *Regulus* went down at Petty Harbour Motion with a loss of nineteen men. Ironically at the time of its loss, two tug boats had been sent to assist the steamer. Captain Roberts of the tug *John Green* attached a brand new eight-inch hawser, but in the wind and with the heavy weight of *Regulus*, it snapped. In the darkness and storm, the steamer struck the ledges and went down, carrying all crew with it.

A wreck of more modern times at Shoal Bay, near Bay Bulls. On November 17, 1950, the Halifax-based National Seafoods steam trawler *Flatholm* grounded and wrecked. Captain R. A. Winn and his nineteen crew rowed in safely to Bay Bulls. *Flatholm* was never refloated.

Photo courtesy Leonard Howlett, Goulds

CHAPTER 43
THE MYSTERY OF THE S.S. *FALCON*

FERRYLAND: In the morning of May 7, 1851, the Royal Mail steamer *Falcon*,[1] which had a regular run between Newfoundland and Nova Scotia, steamed out of St. John's for Halifax.

Captain George Corbin, a Nova Scotian who was one of the most experienced commanders in his trade, had his family traveling with him. It would be a routine voyage. *Falcon* was deemed seaworthy in all aspects, the captain competent and experienced, and the weather civil for the month of October.

Then, much to the surprise and consternation of the general public, on the evening after *Falcon* left, this letter appeared in the St. John's newspaper *Times*.

Ferryland, 8th May, 1851
Messers. Baine, Johnson & Co.

Gentlemen:

It is with deep regret I have to advise you of the loss of the steamer *Falcon* on the north side of Ferryland narrows. She struck at about 2:00 this morning, being very foggy from the time we left St. John's.

I cannot account for the accident, as I had been steering S.S. W. two hours, S. W. by S. one hour, and S. W. ½ S. until she struck. It is the opinion of all persons here (Ferryland) that the compasses must be greatly out. The vessel is sunk in thirty feet of water, the weather rail under the surface; – she sank so rapidly that very little has been saved. I have saved the mails and will forward them as soon as weather permits. No lives lost. Mr. James Carter is rendering me every assistance.

I am, Gentlemen, your obedient servant,
George A. Corbin
Isle de Bois (Ferryland)

On May 13, Captain Corbin and his family arrived back in St. John's on a boat from Ferryland. There was still "much interest and enquiry amongst the public, but we (at the newspaper *Times*) are not in a position to say more than that." Although talk and gossip swirled around the arrival of Corbin, most people said they were grateful the mails aboard *Falcon* were saved. Shipping authorities were sure "the mystery will be unraveled."

No investigation or charges ever faced the captain. According to public statements, Corbin, "whose competency as a seaman and whose unvarying attention to life and property have ever been admitted," need not fear a rigid investigation. There was no marine inquiry, nor was it ever officially reported what caused the wreck of *Falcon*.

Captain Corbin and his family returned to Nova Scotia. The mail, saved from the wreck, was shipped aboard the chartered schooner *Lara* and dispatched to Halifax. By the end of May, the S.S. *St. George* replaced *Falcon*.

Gossip along the waterfront claimed *Falcon* was scuttled by someone without the captain's knowledge, but why? Other unanswered questions arose, adding another twist to this strange tale of the sea. Rumors, not substantiated by the local print, said that *Falcon* carried more than the customary mails, passengers' trunks, and ordinary freight.

On May 14, the following advertisement appeared in all St. John's papers. Who bought the wreck, and if attempts were made to refloat it, is not clear.

Advertising the sale of the wreck of *Falcon*.

Sophisticated underwater technology to search wrecks and to raise cargo was limited in Newfoundland in the mid-1800s. Thus, in time the mystery surrounding *Falcon* diminished and the wreck remained basically undisturbed for many years.

One other intriguing aspect of the wreck of *Falcon* remains. Early in the year 1851, the Newfoundland government, then an independent state, began recalling all foreign coins and tokens circulating around the island. This would protect the nation's economy and would increase the value of its own currency. Legislature passed an act to allow this law to take effect.[2]

As a result currency from South America, the United States, Canada, France – some of which were gold and silver coins – were collected by banks in exchange for colonial and British paper money. Much was gathered in the early months of 1851 and the first batch to be sent out was put aboard the S.S. *Falcon*. Coins, destined for Halifax to be melted down and recycled into gold or silver bullion, were now on the bottom of the ocean off Ferryland.[3]

Notes

1. There have been several "Falcons" associated with Newfoundland. Elsewhere in this volume (Chapter 17), there's a reference to another S.S. *Falcon*. This 458-ton steamer, built in 1872, disappeared in the Atlantic in 1894 with a loss of sixteen crew. The Cabot Steam Whaling Company of St. John's owned a large whaler of the same name. Several schooners were named *Falcon*, including one owned by Lake and Lake of Fortune. It was wrecked at St. Pierre on December 11, 1919.

2. In this era, tokens were outlawed but they continued to circulate for many years. Job Brothers & Company Ltd. did not stop using them in Labrador until 1927.

3. The wreck of *Falcon* was worked by Marcel Robillard in the early 1970s. In his book, *A Hundred years of Remorse*, published in 2002, he tells of his search and the removal of coins from the wreck (as well as from many other Newfoundland shipwrecks). One of the recovered coins, a 1751 George II Silver Crown is pictured here.

CAPE BROYLE, WITLESS BAY, BRIGUS SOUTH: March and April of 1857 was so cold that it was later referred to as the year of the frosty spring (as described in Chapter 41). Yet a cold spring brought the ice floes further south and this meant extra income for many Newfoundland families in those times. The seals and seal pups on the ice were a resource. A few extra supplies and a little cash could be made by harvesting seal pelts. The extra work and income helped to get families through a long winter, if the young men wanted that kind of arduous work.

Captain Thomas Carew of Shores Cove, Cape Broyle, saw the earning potential of the seal fishery and, in late February 1857, prepared the schooner *John and Maria* for the ice. On Monday, March 2, he and his crew of twenty-one sailed from St. John's for Cape Broyle.

According to local stories, Carew was going to "clear" from Cape Broyle, then head north for the ice fields and the seals. To clear meant to sign the ship's papers and to begin the record of the sealing voyage. Perhaps, too, he wished to clear from Cape Broyle, as he may have needed to pick up some extra crew.

Local knowledge says the ship was known as *John & Marie*; yet its registry says the official name was *John and Maria*. By 1855, when Carew bought it, the sixty-four-foot long *John and Maria* was already an old vessel. It had been built on Cape Breton Island in 1827.[1]

In the run down the southern shore, *John and Maria* ran into a typical winter storm – easterly wind, then a few flurries, increasing by late evening to a full fledged blizzard. Temperatures were well below freezing.

Although the captain and many crew knew the sea and the area, visibility was reduced to zero. *John and Maria* struck a rock at Herring Cove Point on the western side of Brigus harbour (today named Brigus South to avoid confusion with Brigus in Conception Bay).

When it struck the rock, the storm was at its height with blinding snow. The crew managed to get the boats out, while Captain Carew and a young fellow, James Greene, went up to the top rigging, perhaps to try to determine what land they had struck.

In the attempt to get the boats out in the paralyzing cold and with the freezing spray coating the men time and time again every minute, many men succumbed to the elements. After an hour or so, the ship filled with water and sank; any seamen still alive on deck quickly drowned or perished.

In the morning, when the snow storm cleared away, people of Brigus South breathed a sigh of relief and hoped that it was the last blizzard for the winter. Mr. Thomas Battcock looked out of his window and saw something unusual to the seaward. It was a ship with the top masts showing above water. There were two still figures on the top of the foremast. Battcock quickly raised the alarm and soon all the able-bodied people of Brigus South went out to rescue the men from the wreck.

That was a task in itself; seas were still mad and Brigus gut or channel was covered with slob ice. It was hard work, trying to row open boats out to the wreck, but they reached seventeen-year-old James Greene and Captain Thomas Carew who were still alive.

As soon as they were able, both survivors said that *John and Maria*'s full crew had been twenty-four and that only they had survived. All nineteen bodies were recovered near the entrance to Brigus harbour. All were made ready for burial in Brigus. However, as most belonged to Witless Bay, a town twenty kilometers to the north, and the people from that community came with horse and cart to bring their men home for burial.

On March 6, Coroner John Stephenson, together with a Coroner's Jury, examined several bodies from the *John and Maria*. The jury found, as expected, that James Reed, Andrew Armstrong, William Nichols, Nicholas Gahvan, a Mulloy man and six other men whose names were unknown, had drowned in the wreck.

Despite his terrible experience as a young man on his first trip, James Greene went back to the sea and spent many springs at the seal fishery. He became a "Master Watchman" and served under Captain Arthur Jackman of Renews. Greene also fished in the rugged offshore Grand Bank fishery. When he died in the early 1930s, he was over ninety years old. His many descendants say he loved telling of his adventures and misadventures at sea.

But for Captain Thomas Carew, who was fifty years old at the time, that was the end of his venture into sealing. If the voyage had been successful, *John and Maria* would have been the first vessel to prosecute the seal fishery from Cape Broyle. Carew lived for many years after his ordeal of spending many hours in a snow storm on the mast of his vessel. He became the Justice of the Peace for Cape Broyle and was a Special Constable for many years. He died in 1883, at age seventy-six.[2]

But what a trauma and a heart-wrenching ordeal for the captain. He saw nineteen men perish, many of whom he knew well. In the anguish of his letter to the paper *Newfoundland Ledger,* he briefly attempts to tell what happened:

Cape Broyle
March 3, 1857

　　It is my painful duty to relate the loss of John and Maria *between the hours of 11:00-12:00 on Monday. We made Brigus Head. It was very thick and heavy with snow and sea, and in wearing the ship around, they unhooked the throat halyards of the mainsail.*

　　I let go both anchors but before they grounded, she struck on a sunken rock and after a few minutes she filled with water and went down and melancholy to relate, the crew was all lost but one boy and myself.

Signed
T. Carew, Master [3]

For hundreds of years the ships of Southern Shore were sailing brigs, schooners and sealing vessels. Around the 1980s, the type and style changed dramatically as the great oil rigs appeared on the coast, as evidenced by the *Glamor Grand Banks* moored in Bay Bulls, June 2003.

Notes

1. Actually *John and Maria*, according to the ships' registry, was a brigantine. Sailors of the area called the vessel a "Beaver Hat"; named for the configuration of the two yards on the foremast, which looked like a hat from the distance.

The vessel had another name. Stories passed down from James Greene recall him saying, "I once spent eighteen hours on the mast of the Hammer."

2. In the year 1875, there is a record of a sea tragedy from Cape Broyle. Three people lost their lives on June 6. They were John Aylward, the son of Patrick Aylward, Joseph Grant, a descendant of the first Grants to settle in Cape Broyle. The third victim was a boy of only fifteen from St. John's, who had come to the town to earn a few dollars in the summer fishery.

The boat or "jack", as it was termed, sailed out of the Cape Broyle narrows for the first time. Boat and crew never returned. It was a new vessel, built during the previous winter.

That June day was a poor one for handline fishing. The sky was covered with heavy clouds, the morning was windy and the water was cold, like ice.

It was late in the day when John Aylward and his two crew arrived on the fishing grounds. Most other boats were preparing to return to Brigus. Aylward spoke to two boat crew who were fishing on the inside fishing ground. They said fishing was poor, as the water was too cold and there were no fish. John Aylward said he would go to the Bantam fishing ground, about one and quarter miles east by south from Cape Broyle Head.

Soon after, the wind increased from the west and gusted up to about forty miles per hour. All other boats reached port safely. As the day advanced, there was no sign of John Aylward and his two crew. Local fishermen thought they must have anchored behind Brigus Head or in some cove, but they never returned.

Lost were the three men and a new boat on its first day out fishing. Of the latter, Brigus fishermen said the boat was never tried for wind. It must have upset in a squall of wind.

3. It is believed this story of *John and Maria* was passed down by Jim Joe O'Brien. It was verified by sealing statistics in the papers of the day and by Carew's letter in the *Newfoundland Ledger*.

CHAPTER 45
HOT SOUP FOR THE WRECKERS

CHANCE COVE, CAPE RACE: Chance Cove, some four miles northeast of Cape Race, is a small open bight on an exposed stretch of coastline marked by headlands and cliffs which are the highest (152 m or 500 ft) in the vicinity of Cape Race. The area is subject to strong winds, rain and fog. Chance Cove, and the adjacent coves of Clam Cove and Frenchman's Cove, have been the sites of many spectacular wrecks.[1]

The *City of Philadelphia* was one of the first wrecks in that area of which someone wrote a detailed description of a forced landing on a foreign and desolate shore. On August 29, 1854, the new Inman ocean liner left Liverpool on its first, or maiden, voyage across the Atlantic. It carried sixty crew and 540 passengers bound for Philadelphia.

One of the passengers was J.W. Gadsby who wrote of his experience in a narrative called, **"Wreck of the Steamer City of Philadelphia."**

On the 24th of September, Gadsby says a heavy rain began to fall and the atmosphere became so densely clouded that no observation of position could be taken that day. About 11:30 p.m., when nearly all passengers were in their berths and the ship was travelling at over ten knots per hour, it hit a sunken rock.

Instantly the ship was alive; from every hatchway, the passengers – men, women, children – poured over the deck in the wildest confusion and distress, many in a near primitive state of nudity, rending the air with shrieks and manifesting every symptom of mortal terror.

Then the seamanship of the captain and crew came into focus as they tried to free the *City of Philadelphia* from the rocks. When the water depth was sounded, it was found that there was deep water on both sides of the ship. It had struck a rock on the port side, near the bow.

While one crewman checked to see how fast the water was rising, the ship's carpenter and his crew, with oakum and blankets, attempted to plug the hole. This was deemed impossible, as the hole was some six feet long and four feet wide through which water poured like a river.

Captain Leitch determined the ship had struck off Cape Race. When the crew had the steamer backed off its perch, the captain announced he would head for Chance Cove, some seven miles northward. No sooner had the ship reached the cove, when the second compartment flooded and the fires for the steam were put out. Gadsby reports how the great ship was beached:

> During all this time, the sea was calm as a mirror, but the fog was so dense that objects could not be distinguished a ship's length distant. After the boats were launched and a ship's party reached shore, they surveyed the beach, saying it had a fine sandy bottom.

City of Philadelphia grounded about three quarters of a mile from shore and the anchors were let down. The lifeboats were hoisted out and the passengers, who by this time mostly had come to their senses, were carried ashore.

The 2100-ton ship *City of Philadelphia* was new and had several innovative features: it was an iron ship and had screw propellers, whereas many transatlantic ships of this era were wooden paddle steamers. The ship had built-in compartments, so that if one section flooded, others would not; thus, the ship would stay afloat longer in case it was damaged or holed. But the concussion when the great steamer struck was so violent that the bulkheads were started and rendered useless. Gadsby described how over five hundred passengers reached the beach at Chance Cove:

> The women and children were carried in first and, after them, the male passengers. The loading of the boats was done with utmost care to prevent any accident and this kept in check the excited crowd. They would have otherwise rushed into the boats and swamped them. The whole of the passengers reached shore at 4:30 a.m.
>
> The shelter and provision for so large a number of people thus thrown upon a desolate shore, some sixty miles from the nearest village or town (Renews) was the next consideration. Sails, spars, provisions and fuel were sent ashore, tents rigged, fires lit, food cooked and everything possible was done for the comfort of the castaways.
>
> By night, mattresses and bedding enough for the women reached the shore; for the men, large fires and close quarters had to suffice.

A desolate shore – at that time there were no permanent livyers in Chance Cove (the first permanent settlers came in the 1870s). Those English passengers who had never set foot in Newfoundland before had a look around. The small cove, small dent in a rugged coast and exposed to all wind and sea, has a shore line nearly void of vegetation except for bog and small coniferous trees stretching for miles. There is no record of whether or not the visitors climbed the high hills to view the surroundings.

Yet the news of a wrecked ship has a way of getting to towns and villages along the coast. Soon the crew and passengers would meet the people from towns to the north and south.

First though, Gadsby said, some crew, who were given responsibility of getting passengers' trunks and luggage ashore, were arrested. They had ferreted away some valuables, but they were caught and put in irons. Then, on September 25, as Gadsby noted, wreckers, or "wrackers" as they were termed locally, appeared:[2]

> On the following day, the *City of Philadelphia* was surrounded by a fleet of fishing smacks, the crews of every one watched every opportunity to steal property. I am informed that they did carry off considerable.
>
> Some of the more audacious wreckers got broken heads and a treat to some scalding soup thrown over them from the cook and his crew.

After the effects of the passengers had been gotten safely ashore, the work of breaking out the cargo commenced, but this was slow work, as most of it was submerged in water. On Saturday a small mail steamer, the *Victoria*, which carried provisions between the different posts of the Telegraph Company, came in sight. Being signaled by Captain Leitch, hove to and when it was boarded, a deal was made. Passengers would be carried to St. John's at $5 a head.

That night, 250 passengers embarked on it and the remainder the day following. The luggage was sent after them to the same place, St. John's.

At St. John's, Gadsby and all other passengers were given the best accommodation the city had. Gadsby said that "The townspeople demanded double price for every necessary accommodation. Eventually all reached Halifax and then their intended destination, Philadelphia. As for the *City of Philadelphia*, its bones remained in Chance Cove.

Notes
1. Chance Cove, today an abandoned community, is not to be confused with Chance Cove, Trinity Bay.

Chance Cove near Cape Race has been the scene of several dramatic shipwrecks. In 1863, the *Anglo-Saxon* ran aground in breakers near the cove and 238 of 444 passengers and crew were drowned when the ship broke up on the rocks. More than 100 bodies were reported to have been buried on the bank of Clam Cove Brook near Chance Cove. Fourteen years later, the French brig *Alice Marie* wrecked near Chance Cove with a loss of eight lives. Other wrecks include the *Askill*, the *Royal*, and the schooners *Manutter* (1872), *Laura* (1894) and *Iolanthe* (1895) and, in the 1920s, the Bonavista Bay schooner *Joseph*.

Between 1884 and 1891, the settlement was abandoned. According to *The Newfoundland Encyclopedia*, "The abandonment of the settlement was a dramatic one. Following a series of disastrous years in the fishery, practically the entire community in great disgust moved away to Maynard, Massachusetts, leaving their houses, furniture, bridges, stages, boats and gear behind them, just as they were."

John W. White reported visiting the abandoned settlement in 1897. He found "On the beach, north, south, east and west of the cove...portions of wrecked steamers. The houses, at least most of them, are in splendid condition, and it can't be poverty that drove them away."

White speculated that the settlement was haunted by the ghosts of the many people who had lost their lives on the shores of Chance Cove and Clam Cove. Two years later, he revisited the settlement and found that "a large number of northern fishermen...had gone ashore at this place and, having used the houses all the season, set fire to them in the fall previous to their leaving for home, and razed nearly every one of them to the ground."

In the early 1970s, Chance Cove was created a Provincial Park.

2. Although the word 'wracker' does not appear in *The Dictionary of Newfoundland English* as a legitimate word, there is ample evidence of the use of

the word wrack and shipwracking. Judge Prowse, who made a career of apprehending and bringing wrackers to justice, noted:

Seafaring people looked upon wrecks as their lawful prizes, gifts sent to them direct by Providence, and their views about these fatalities were characteristic. Mostly the vessels contained valuable cargoes, but occasionally it was otherwise. I heard an old Irish-Newfoundland woman declare about one 'wrack', "I don't know what God almighty is thinking about, sending us a terrible bad fishery, and then an old Norwegian brig full of nothing but rocks!"

Chapter forty-eight has more to say about wrackers and Judge Prowse.

TREPASSEY, ST. MARY'S: Hoax – the Oxford Dictionary describes it as 'a deception by way of a joke; a mischievous falsehood.' The words joke and mischief may be too mild to describe what happened in Trepassey many years ago. The effect the lies and tricks had was demonstrated in headlines in a Newfoundland paper (*Colonist* of mid-October,1891). It read:

City of Rome Story: James Brennan, the Survivor, Startles Two Continents. Is the story true?

The story described the effect the news of a substantial wreck had on news reporters: "Yesterday we were startled by the report received to the effect that a large steamer named the *City of Rome* had been lost on Monday night at a place called Marine's Cove, St. Mary's Bay.[1]

"The news comes from Trepassey, fifteen miles from the scene of the wreck and the story of the disaster come from the lips of the only survivor, a man named James Brennan, who said that forty-two people had gone down with the ship..."

Brennan also said he belonged to Sligo, Ireland, and claimed the ship left Montreal on October 7, bound for Dundee, Scotland, with a cargo of flour, corn and 575 head of cattle. Brennan said there was fog at the time of the accident, and declared that the captain, officers, and engineers were all drunk.

As if to substantiate the tale of a great calamity, *The Evening Telegram*, left, carried further descriptions of death and disaster under its headlines on October 14. Brennan said that the sight of cattle and men struggling in the water and crying for help would terrify you. No help, however, could be rendered, as no person but Brennan himself was an eye witness to the event.

Furthermore, several men and boats from Trepassey left the town to get to the scene of the wreck.

Latest by Telegraph.

TERRIBLE TRAGEDY

At Marine's Cove.

THE "CITY OF ROME"

Lost With All Her Crew,

EXCEPT ONE MAN.

An Awful Sight.

(Special to the "Evening Telegram.")
& A Heart-Rending Tale;
Trepassey, This Afternoon.

Evening Telegram in its October 14, 1891, issue headlines the loss of the *City of Rome*. It turned out to be a horrid hoax perpetrated by one man, himself a survivor of another shipwreck.

The story of the wreck S.S. *City of Rome* (above) turned out to be a sick joke played out near Trepassey and Marine's Cove.
Photo courtesy Capt. Hubert Hall, Shipsearch MARINE

Could the story be true? Immediately Bowring Brothers, agents for Lloyd's Insurance, sent a telegram to Montreal to ascertain if the *City of Rome* had cleared from that port on October 7. In time, they received an answer saying that no such vessel had left port on that date.

Furthermore, Montreal said that there was only one ship named *City of Rome*. It was owned by Anchor Line, was plying between the ports of Liverpool and New York and had never carried cattle.

With this information, Bowring representatives contacted Trepassey or Cape Race to enquire if the information was authentic or not. Soon a message from Trepassey – yes, the story was true if Brennan could be believed. However, now Brennan claimed he was so frightened and upset by the sight of wreck and death that the recollection was confused. Thus, he may have made a mistake on the name of the vessel. (Remember that Brennan said he had sailed on this vessel from October 7 to Monday, October 12, when it was supposedly lost near St. Shotts).

Other messages came from Trepassey; one from the commissioner of wrecks, A. Simms, who said he was sick and could not get to the supposed scene of the wreck. Five wires in a row came from Trepassey from Magistrate Carey, saying that he was investigating Brennan's tale. When Brennan was asked about the location of the wreck, he replied that it was not visible, although the weather was clear at the time of the disaster.

Within forty-eight hours after telling his story, Brennan left Trepassey after dark, heading for St. John's via Renews. At this point, he should have been taken into custody for his own safety's sake. He had already admitted he was confused, in a pathetic state of mind, and crying continuously.

Furthermore, the men of Trepassey had returned home after searching for the wreck of *City of Rome*. They found nothing and had nothing to show or tell despite a round trip of approximately forty kilometers. Soon news shifted to their frame of mind with the details under the heading **Trepassey Men Indignant**:

> The boats and men that left here yesterday, overland, for Marine's Cove returned this morning, no wreck or vestige of wreck being visible. Brennan was going about here, but could not find the Commissioner to get lodgings, so he started overland to St. John's.
>
> He is about five feet eight inches high and rather stout. He has dark hair and wears a dark felt hat and a pilot-cloth reefer jacket. Well for him he is not here today, or he would fare badly.

The story told by James Brennan was finally labeled as a fraud by a message written by Magistrate Carey on October 15, 1891, addressed to Honorable (later Sir) Robert Bond, the Colonial Secretary. It stated clearly: "No truth whatever in report of steamer *City of Rome*; hoax perpetrated by half-witted cowboy of the wrecked steamer *Mondego*."[2]

Notes

1. Marine (or Marine's) Cove, on the eastern side of the town of St. Shotts, is an unoccupied inlet surrounded by high cliffs. Mainly, it is noted for the scores and scores of wrecks that happened there in the era of sailing ship and steamers. One of the most tragic was the British ship *Harpooner* on which 206 people perished on November 10, 1816.

2. Yes, there really had been a wreck of a steamer in that area – the steamer *Mondego* on September 16, 1891. Captain J. Rowell said his steamer left Montreal on September 10 with a little over 82,000 bushels of rye and 554 cattle aboard destined for Dundee.

The first report of wreck came from Joseph Hyland, a foreman on board, who telegraphed John Crowe, the owner of the cattle, that ten cattlemen and a crew of thirty had landed at St. Mary's. *Mondego*, valued at $150,000 and owned in Glasgow, Scotland, struck the rocks

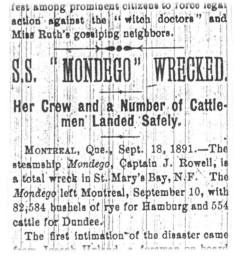

fest among prominent citizens to force legal action against the "witch doctors" and Miss Ruth's gossiping neighbors.

S.S. "MONDEGO" WRECKED.

Her Crew and a Number of Cattle-men Landed Safely.

MONTREAL, Que., Sept. 18, 1891.—The steamship *Mondego*, Captain J. Rowell, is a total wreck in St. Mary's Bay, N.F. The *Mondego* left Montreal, September 10, with 82,584 bushels of rye for Hamburg and 554 cattle for Dundee.

The first intimation of the disaster came

Headlines of the loss of S.S. *Mondego* from a local paper of October 5, 1891.

and had gone to pieces in a storm. In fact, *Mondego* had been the third Canadian grain/cattle ship that had gone to the bottom in 1891 with very heavy loses on livestock. Insurance rates had gone up accordingly.

With the *Mondego*, a magistrate was sent to St. Mary's from St. John's to prevent pillage, but that was a seven day journey away. Assistance and accommodations had been made for the cattlemen and crew, some of whom were destitute. Most had been transported to St. John's, except for James Brennan. He had decided to remain in Trepassey and to create a little excitement there. However, the men of Trepassey had other ideas about his future.

CHAPTER 47
ROBERT LOWE: TWENTY-TWO
SURVIVED, EIGHTEEN LOST

LA MANCHE, ST. MARY'S, ST. VINCENT'S: In 1866, the Anglo-American Telegraph Company (AAT) laid the first successful trans-Atlantic telegraph cable between Ireland and North America at the landfall of Heart's Content. In 1873, the Company installed a land line from Heart's Content to Placentia Bay, which connected via a new submarine cable with St. Pierre and Nova Scotia where, in turn, it connected with the Western Union system in the USA.

Actually, the overland portion from Heart's Content emerged near La Manche, Placentia Bay. The cable ship commissioned to extend the underwater telegraph cable from Island Cove, near La Manche, to Placentia was the AAT cable steamship *Robert Lowe*.[1]

Robert Lowe finished this work on November 18, 1873. On the 19th, it left Placentia for St. John's, where it would tie up for the winter. Captain James Tidmarsh had, with his crew of thirty, one passenger aboard, as well as a technical person. G. E. Wickenden, a young man, brilliant, skilled, and highly esteemed by all who knew him, supervised the joining of the cable and other intricate operations.

It was the winter season and weather conditions along the rugged seacoast of Newfoundland could turn about face within hours. Upon leaving Placentia, *Robert Lowe* ran into what was described as "...thick and boisterous weather, a heavy southwest gale, bringing with it high seas, dense fog and a stronger easterly set of the tide." It was a combination of circumstances – weather and tide – which was greater than the determination of the ship's officers and stronger than the constitution of the ship itself.

Captain Tidmarsh gave the steamer a considerable course to the south and then eastward and put on all steam. Ordinarily, it would have gotten *Robert Lowe* well out to sea. Yet the steamer struck at full speed on a place called Sculpin Cove Point, near St. Mary's.

It was quarter past four on the morning of November 20, twelve hours after leaving Placentia. Seas were high when the vessel hit a ledge and, immediately, the after part of the ship was submerged in the towering whitecaps breaking near shore.

At once, the crew attempted to get out the lifeboats, together with the ship's boats. It seemed impossible to get the lifeboats into the water, due to their weight and being cumbersome, plus they were almost under water in the location near the stern.

The crew quickly launched a smaller boat and a pinnace. Some of the crew, officers along with passenger W. Miller eventually reached shore in these. Others, not wanting to face the mad seas and figuring it was safer aboard the half submerged wreck, stayed aboard *Robert Lowe*. They hoped someone, some livyer, some people of the area, would see them. Taking to sea in a small boat seemed a sure way to die.

The first indication of the marine calamity reached Holyrood (today St. Vincent's), when the smaller boat made land there. Some time elapsed before the St. Vincent's people reached the scene of the disaster, but when they did arrive, it was too late to do anything for those aboard the *Robert Lowe*. Even if they been hours sooner, it was doubtful if any line or boat from shore could reach the stranded steamer. There was no one left alive on or near the stranded steamer.

The ship's pinnace was at sea and those on shore signaled to the safest spot for landing. This was on a shingle, a cobblestone beach, at the base of a cliff. Those survivors in the pinnace had to climb hand over hand up a rope that had been thrown down from the top – a climb of three to four hundred feet.

Several of *Robert Lowe*'s survivors were too exhausted to accomplish this feat and had to be hoisted up by ropes tied around their waist.

As all this transpired, sections of the S.S. *Robert Lowe*, its captain, several crew and the telegraph technician, were swept away by a remorseless and cruel sea.

Twenty-two survivors were taken to St. Mary's on Sunday, November 25, 1873. As soon as Alexander McLellan McKay, the Anglo-American Telegraph Company's General Superintendent, heard the news, he sent the St. John's harbour steam tug *Cabot* to St. Mary's to bring them to St. John's. Many survivors reached shore nearly naked, but the people of the St. Mary's-St. Vincent's area had given them every kind of attention and generosity, including clothes and food.[2]

On December 4, seven bodies had been recovered and brought to St. John's – one of whom was Captain Tidmarsh. These had washed ashore at Sculpin Point, St. Mary's. Like the other bodies, Tidmarsh's remains were broken, bruised and stripped of most clothes. The captain could only be identified by a tattoo of an anchor on the arm and a ring on the right little finger. Dr. Renouf, Her Majesty's Coroner in St. John's, proclaimed the person had drowned.

Thus was communication, commonplace today and taken for granted, established between the old and new world, landing at great cost in lives and a ship on the rugged coast of Newfoundland.

Notes

1. The population of La Manche – approximately four kilometers south of North Harbour, Placentia Bay – rose dramatically about the time of the laying of the trans-Atlantic cable. The town made its first appearance in the *Census*, with Little Harbour (East) in 1836, at which time, there were twenty inhabitants in the two communities.

La Manche became the site of a galena or lead, mine around 1857. The ore vein was presumably being discovered by men searching for an appropriate location to land the cable in Placentia Bay.

The mining property, initially owned by the Ripley Company, with which Cyrus W. Field (a financier of a cable company) was associated, was transferred to the Placentia Bay Lead Co., and then to the La Manche Mining Co. in 1863. By 1874 the community had 142 people, all of them dependent on the mine. The mine closed shortly after.

In 1900 and in the late 1940s, the mine re-opened for brief periods. Mining, like the sea, is a dangerous occupation; on May 10, 1947, Patrick Whiffen was killed at the site.

In the 1950s, the mine closed permanently and the population of La Manche dropped to twenty-five. Today, it is an abandoned community.

2. However, there is a strange story to be told about the wreck itself. At low tide, much of abandoned ship was exposed and, after assisting the survivors, crowds of fishermen boarded *Robert Lowe*. One of the wrackers found his way into the electrician's room (electrician Wickenden perished in the wreck). The wracker was surprised at the array of unfamiliar wires, tubes and batteries. Out of curiosity he began handling equipment and objects and touched a powerfully charged battery. The shock left him writhing on the floor.

A companion, not knowing what had happened but realizing his friend had been hurt by a strange object, commenced to batter everything in sight with his axe. Unwittingly, he destroyed thousands of dollars worth of valuable and innovative electrical equipment. (Adapted from *The Southern Gazette* July 30, 1991)

CHAPTER 48
WRACKERS

ST. MARY'S BAY: According to mariners of the day, St. Mary's Bay was one of the most dangerous spots on the eastern seaboard, that is up to about the 1930s. Canadian and American shipping authorities claim more ships piled ashore there than on any other part of the south coast. It is at a southeast point of Newfoundland, just between Cape St. Mary and Cape Race. Unwitting seamen, thinking they were rounding Cape Race and steering northerly, found themselves ashore in St. Mary's Bay.

Two other factors made the coast a fearsome one for foreign mariners. In the late 1800s, the signal station there gave out a weak signal and communication was difficult; secondly, the area was known to be inhabited by fishermen who, when a vessel went ashore, became wreckers, or as pronounced locally, wrackers.

Although thirty years apart, two tales of the sea help verify this.

In 1869, politician and lawyer Daniel W. Prowse was appointed as judge and magistrate. In his judicial functions, he went into uncommonly wide-flung communities, in diverse capacities, throughout Newfoundland. He took an interest in protected wildlife and curbing the illegal activities of ship wreckers. He became a expert of the ways of "wrackers" of abandoned vessels and their cargoes on the long stretches of the island's rocky coast.

S.S. *Micmac* before falling prey to the wrackers of St. Mary's Bay.

Courtesy Capt. Hubert Hall, Shipsearch MARINE

During Prowse's term as judge, magistrate, constable, all rolled in one, St. Mary's Bay became seriously involved with the law for the crime of "wracking." It was not the first time. On May 1, 1873, Judge Prowse was ordered to proceed to St. Mary's with such policemen as he should deem necessary, to investigate a complaint of "wrecking a vessel called the *Florence*."

The *Florence* was a brigantine from Charlottetown, Prince Edward Island, on a voyage from Boston to St. John's with a load of general cargo. On February 8, 1873, a sudden storm forced the captain to run for St. Mary's Harbour. The wind being southeast, he was unable to beat in the harbour, so he beat up for Mall Bay and came to anchor in seven fathoms of water.

On the 9th of February, the storm continued and the vessel dragged its anchors. Being unable to bring the ship around, the captain put out a kedge (a small anchor) and hove it taut. The tide was falling, however, and the vessel began to touch bottom, not yet enough to endanger it.

At noon on the ninth, three boats came out from the shore with a large number of men but, until dark, were prevented from boarding the vessel. After dark, the men forced their way aboard, cut the line to the kedge anchor and carried it away. Then they broke into a storeroom and took a mainsail, while others went aloft and loosened the top-gallant sails on the ship.

Frustration turned to anger. The captain did everything in his power to make the band of desperadoes desist. Soon the whole group, armed with sticks and hatchets, took complete possession of the vessel, forced open the hatches and unloaded most of the cargo of flour, Indian meal, pork, and furniture, none of which was damaged in the slightest way. They took 369 barrels of flour, ninety-two barrels of meal, thirty-four barrels of pork and one barrel of kerosene.

In the meantime, the captain sent one of his boats for the local magistrate at St. Mary's; however, by the time that gentleman arrived, the boat was stripped and the plunderers all fled.

When the tide rose, the Captain succeeded in getting his ship afloat and moved it to the mouth of the river at Riverhead, near St. Mary's, where he completed sufficient repairs to get to St. John's. Police were sent to arrest the marauders, but they had taken refuge in the woods and the police were unable to flush them out, or find out where they were hiding.

By the time Judge Prowse arrived, there was nothing to investigate and no one to try for wracking.

Thus ended the wreck of the Prince Edward Island ship *Florence*. In the governor's letter to the Colonial officer, he said that it appears the practice of wrecking ships in Newfoundland, in order to obtain their cargo, was very common.

In the third week of August 1907, a rumour spread around the southern Avalon Peninsula that a steamer had gone ashore at Broad Cove in St. Mary's Bay and it was being looted. This report, at first, was said to be greatly exaggerated. Yes, the S.S. *Micmac* was ashore in that place; however, the articles removed from the wreck were taken when there was no one aboard. As with all abandoned ships, the people of the area had salvage rights; beside that, they said, the looting began with the crew.

S.S. *Micmac*, a steel, screw-driver vessel of 2,500 gross ton, had a cargo of deals (blocks of squared timber) aboard and carried only two passengers – two women. It had been built in Glasgow in 1893 for the Micmac Steamship Company of Scotland. *Micmac* had indeed become a total wreck at Broad Cove on August 15.[1]

The government tug *D.P. Ingraham*, intent on taking off cargo, reached the scene on August 18. When the *Ingraham* arrived back in St. John's, it had some of the wrecked steamer's gear which had been salvaged by men hired by the MHA for Ferryland and area, Michael Patrick Cashin. *Micmac* had not yet gone to pieces. Reports were local fishermen had taken food, gear and other items from *Micmac*.

By August 24 and 26, 1907, the newspaper *Daily News* stated:

> It is likely some arrests will be made today, in consequence of alleged stealing at the wrecked steamer *Micmac*. It is said that considerable amounts of the ship's gear, her furnishing and stores were stolen before the police arrived at the scene.
>
> The names of the eight suspected persons have been secured by the Underwriters' Agent and the matter will be placed in the hands of the proper authorities this morning. Sergeant Peet and Constable Lawlor left St. John's to find and detain the looters.

On August 28, Judge James Gerve Conroy left St. John's for Placentia. From there he travelled by the government steamer *Fiona* to St. Mary's Bay where he held a full investigation into the wreck and the alleged looting.

Within a week, the eight brought before the judge were released for the lack of evidence. The clash with the law was enough for the St. Mary's Bay men and there was no more trouble with looting or wracking the *Micmac* after that.

The final word on *Micmac* came on October 23.

> The men working at the wrecked steamer *Micmac*, were very successful last week and, to date, have salved over three quarters of a million feet of timber, which has been landed at St. Mary's. The wreck was still in the same position Monday, but the storm is supposed to have done some damage.
>
> The wrecking steamer *Amphitrite*, Capt. Larder, is at St. Mary's and, when the weather moderates, an attempt will be made to refloat her. The *Amphitrite* has some powerful pumps on board and if the steamer has not been injured by the storm, it is expected that it will be possible to lift her off the rocks.

Notes

1. There is an odd story of *Micmac*'s name. At the luncheon given in Glasgow on the occasion of the steamer's launching, Mr. Dunsmuir, the builder, rose to speak. He remarked that its name was a double compliment to the two great Celtic races: "Mic" for the Irish, and "Mac" for the Scotch. Perhaps Dunsmuir was making his own joke.

Captain Richard Meikle explained that "Micmac" was the name of a well-known band of native North Americans living in Nova Scotia. However, newspapers and reporters tend to get information garbled, saying that the ship *Micmac* was called after a mixed tribe of Indians in Nova Scotia who were half Irish and half

In the summer of 1935, residents of certain Placentia Bay towns saw a unique sight – a four-master and one of the largest schooners ever owned in Newfoundland. At 832 net ton and 187 foot long, *R.R. Govin*, (above at St. George, New Brunswick) was purchased and brought down from New York state by W. W. Wareham of Placentia Bay. Shortly after, Wareham sold it to the Monroe Export Company of St. John's where the vessel began its foreign-going career.

R.R. Govin made newspaper headlines in Scotland in April 1938 when the vessel was storm-driven into Loch-in-Dale. Its crew at that time: Captain Harry Thomasen, Grand Bank; Philip Stone, Fortune Bay; Frank Witherall, Fortune; Tom Coffin, St. John's; Rae Hadley, Cole Harbour, Nova Scotia; bosun Harold Samson, Grand Bank; cook Norman Chaytor, St. John's and mate John Ralph, Grand Bank. Navigator Henry Burke belonged to Lunenburg.

In the fall of 1939, *R.R. Govin* went to Labrador, buying salt fish and supplying fishermen. On October 26 it struck a reef off Snug Harbour while leaving port and sank, eventually going to pieces.

Photo courtesy Shipsearch MARINE, Yarmouth, NS

Scotch!

BURIN, EPWORTH, MORTIER, MARYSTOWN, GARNISH, STONE'S COVE:
By the 1940s, many South Coast fishermen worked on schooners out of Lunenburg,
Nova Scotia. Wages on the "Lunenburgers" were higher and the crew was paid in
cash; whereas, in many outports in Newfoundland, fishermen were required to "take
up" or accept credit from the merchant. Often, they saw no cash or dollars, only
food and supplies from the merchant's, store exchanged for work.

Then, too, food on the Lunenburgers was of a higher quality and more of it.
Working conditions were better. One improvement certainly made a labour
intensive job a little lighter. Most Nova Scotian fishing vessels employed a
"dressing crew," that is two to four men whose only work was to dress – gut, clean
and salt – the cod when it came from the dories. Thus, the dory fishermen did not
have the extra work and long hours of dressing or salting fish after it came aboard.

However, danger from the sea was still a common denominator with all vessels
and the Lunenburg fleet was no exception. This became all too evident when the
distressing news of the fate of *John H. McKay* first appeared in the St. John's
newspaper *The Evening Telegram* on July 21, 1941.

Wreckage Sighted Off Cape St. Mary's

The banking vessel *Freda M*, Captain George Follett, a day from the
banks, arrived in port yesterday and reports that at 7:00 p.m. on Saturday
(July 19) when about 93 miles south of Ferryland Head, he passed the
wreckage of the Lunenburg banker *John H. McKay*.

Wreckage May be Lost Equipment Of Fishing Vessel

LUNENBURG, July 23—Wreckage of the Lunenburg schooner John H. McKay, reported lost by members of the Newfoundland fishing schooner Freeda last Saturday may have been deck equipment washed overboard from the McKay on her recent Spring trip to the banks, it was learned today.

While coming from a Newfoundland port with last baiting for the Spring trip, loose deck equipment was washed overboard by a heavy sea. Captain Crouse made efforts

The vessel sprang a leak during a storm and had to be abandoned. There was no sign of the crew, the Captain reports, but it is believed that they took to their dories and have been picked up by some other vessel.

"There was no sign of the crew" – distressful words indeed. And there was no word of twenty-one men for nearly a month. They had been picked up, but where were they and who was aboard?

Captain Moyle Crouse of Lunenburg had Newfoundland fishermen with him, several from the south coast. Captain Follett

John H. McKay, leaving a Nova Scotian fishing port and most of the fishermen are standing on the forward section of the vessel. Five dories are nested of the port side (and five starboard) and much of the gear, trawl tubs, for the dories is stacked on top of the cabin (under the main boom). In this era, circa 1930s, there was no wheelhouse aft over the steering wheel.
Photo courtesy Capt. Hubert Hall, Shipsearch MARINE, Yarmouth.

of Grand Bank, who had sighted the wreckage, may have known one man aboard *John H. McKay,* who was from his home port – George Herridge.

Hardy and experienced south coast fishermen manned the vessel. Wilson Evans was an experienced and well-liked cook aboard. Lunenburg vessels employed dressers; that is, two or three men who split and cleaned the fish so the dorymen would not have to do that extra work when the dories offloaded the catch. Richard Long was one of the best and fastest splitters. The complete crew is given in the chart below.

John H. McKay fished off Cape Race; Captain Crouse and his crew were doing well – seas were relatively calm, fish was plentiful, as he had 1700 quintals already salted down. However, an ever present antagonist hung around — thick fog. By the summer of 1941, the war at sea was in full swing. More North American ships than usual crossed the Grand Banks, carrying supplies to Europe.

On the morning of July 19, the Dutch steamer *Kentor*, while at position latitude 45.30 North, longitude 51.45 West, rammed the Nova Scotian fishing vessel. Captain Crouse said later:

> There was thick fog when the vessel hit us about one hundred miles off Newfoundland. We were en route to the Banks from Newfoundland and we had a harrowing escape.
>
> It was all over in a matter of six or seven minutes. *John H. McKay* went down like a rock. We just had time to jump into the dories and get out of the way. After bobbing around for an hour, the ship that hit us came back and picked us up.

The 100-ton *McKay*, a nineteen-year-old schooner owned by Lunenburg's Zwicker and Company, was on the bottom; the crew was en route somewhere toward Europe. Word came back to concerned shipowners that the crew was safe, with no injuries; however, due to wartime restrictions, it was difficult to communicate with the captain or crew.

The questions were, to what country or port had the *McKay*'s crew been carried? When and how will they get back to Nova Scotia and Newfoundland? Within a few days, all that shipping authorities in Nova Scotia could gather was the crew, all accounted for and safe and sound, was in Iceland.

It was equally hard to squeeze information from shipping authorities in Halifax or St. John's. Wives, families and loved ones in Newfoundland had no news.

James Mallay's wife thought he had surely perished at sea, he had been

Crew of *John H. McKay*, Cut Down July 19, 1941

Captain Moyle Crouse, Lunenburg
engineer Paul Crouse, Middle LaHave
Richard Kavanagh, Pleasantville, NS
Dawson Corkum, Lunenburg
cook Wilson Evans, Belleoram
mate John Flaherty, NL
Leo Kilfoy, Marystown
Maurice Power, Marystown
John Walsh, Marystown
E? Walsh, Marystown
James Mallay, Marystown
T. Hilliard, Marystown
George Duffney, Burin
Richard Long, Burin
Thomas Nicholas Lundrigan, Burin
Raymond Mayo, Burin
Nicholas Power, Mortier
Samuel Hiscock, Epworth
George Herridge, Grand Bank
Ambrose Synard, Parker's Cove
Anson? Banfield, Garnish
George Pope, Stone's Cove
N. Williams
G. Hogan[1]

gone so long. They were expecting a call any day about his death. One evening Mrs. Mallay was at the home of Mrs. Maurice Power. Maurice was also on *John H. McKay* and both women with their children met and perhaps discussed the loss of the ship and crew. Then, one evening Maurice walked in. Mrs. Mallay asked, "Where's Jim?" Jim had gone to his own home.

Many prayers of deliverance had been answered: the missing men were safe. Although there was little or no compensation for the accident and the crew returned home without pay, James Mallay had pleasant memories of the experience. There was a dentist on the ship that rammed the schooner and he removed several of Mallay's troublesome teeth.

Other crew recalled that live cattle and hens were kept aboard the *Kentor* to be killed for fresh food when needed. Another family which recalled anxious times

LUNENBURG, N. S., WEDNESDAY, AUGUST 13th, 1941

CAPT. MOYLE CROUSE AND CREW RETURN

Schooner John H. MaKay Hit Broadside By Freighter

Awarded Grade XII Certificate

Mrs. Olivette Zinck, teacher at Second Peninsula, is receiving the congratulations of her many friends

After a harrowing experience, when their vessel was

A Lunenburg newspaper tells only the ship facts; the human element of missing crew and the trauma inflicted on families is not presented.

was that of George Duffney, Burin. According to George's son, the family knew the schooner had been sunk by a freighter and the crew had been carried to Iceland. George Duffney, like the others, was gone quite awhile. He, like all *John H. McKay*'s fishermen, lost all extra clothes except for what he stood in.

In addition, they "lost their voyage"; in other words, the catch of 1700 quintals went down with the ship. Since the fish represented wages, there was no money or payment from the owners to the shipwrecked fishermen.

The first newspaper report that all the crew had arrived back in Nova Scotia came on August 11 in bold headlines – **John McKay Lost in Crash on Foggy Sea**. According to one source, the south coast fishermen reached home months later and they had been landed in Argentia.[2]

Notes

1. There was some confusion over exactly who the twenty Newfoundland fishermen were and there were two or three conflicting lists given out by Nova Scotian sources. Thus, some question marks still remain on several first names or place of residence. For example, papers listed Anson Banfield, Garnish, but no one seems to know who this is; another source gave his name as L. Banfield.

Help in researching the Newfoundland crew of this harrowing tale of the sea were Howard Mallay and family, Marystown; Bill Duffney, Burin; and, Randell Pope, Grand Bank. Newspaper accounts were in *The Evening Telegram* July 21, 1941, and *The Halifax Herald* July 23 (which had an incomplete crew list) and August 11, 1941. Curator Ralph Getson of Lunenburg's Museum of the Atlantic sent several important newspaper articles of the event.

2. As strange and coincidental as it may sound, the crew of another fishing vessel had a similar experience around the same time. The banker *Andavaka* foundered on the Grand Banks on July 9, 1941, during a storm. The eighteen crew were picked up by various vessels and taken to Iceland. Three were south coast

men: Arch Keeping of Belleoram; Celestine Dominaux, Bay du Nord; and, Stanley Drake, Lally Cove.

Unlike *John H. McKay*'s crowd, they returned to Newfoundland much earlier, arriving in St. John's on July 31. There, H.B. Clyde Lake arranged to look after them until they returned to their homes in Fortune Bay. The fifty-seven-ton, seventy-foot- long *Andavaka*, owned at that time by Joseph R. Burdock of Belleoram, was built in Garnish in 1935 and first registered to James Anstey of Garnish.

GRAND BANK: There is an old saying, "Any town that sends a fleet of ships down to the sea, pays a price in lost ships." In its long association with the sea, Grand Bank had an extensive fleet going down to the sea and grieved through many marine disasters. In a space of one hundred years, twenty-eight ships were lost with crew – with several, some questionable debris had been found, but no sign of bodies or positive identification of the ship. Others disappeared without a trace.

One vessel, which unfortunately fits the latter category, is the *John McRea*. It set sail on a voyage from St. John's to Grand Bank in mid-December 1917 and was never heard from again. There was little evidence to say exactly what happened. Seemingly, the sea had swallowed another victim and its entire crew.

In 1905, the seventy-nine net ton *John McRea* was built in Mahone Bay, Nova Scotia. The sailing vessel was nine feet in depth, twenty-four feet long, with an overall length of eighty-six feet. In 1907, it had come under the registry of George A. Buffett of Grand Bank. The same registry shows its "Reason for Closure," or what eventually happened to the vessel, as **Missing/Not Heard of Again/Disappeared**.

Strangely, its Newfoundland registry shows the name as "J. McRea" and the one or two times the little schooner is mentioned in newspapers, it is as *J. McRea*, although town and family history always refer to the vessel as *John McRea*.[1]

It was a banking schooner, probably carrying six or eight dories. The fishery report for 1911 lists *John McRea* as bringing in 1300 quintals under the command of Grand Bank's James Forsey. Like most schooners of its era, in the fall it delivered the salt fish to larger centers and brought provisions, food and supplies from St. John's to outports like Grand Bank. Coasting, or bringing supplies, was precisely *John McRea*'s work in December 1917.

Four seamen took the schooner to St. John's: Captain Josiah "Joe" Hiscock;[2] mate Charles Hickman; George Butler; all of Grand Bank, and, Edward "Ned" Follett of Grand Beach – a town twelve miles east of Grand Bank. On the return voyage, *John McRea* had a passenger and his story is a lamentable vignette of the tale.

George Hiscock, the son of the captain, had been in training in St. John's in order to become a Salvation Army officer. The cadet could have taken the coastal boat, leaving St. John's for points west along the south coast. With its community stops and delays, the trip home on the steamer would have meant days lost during the upcoming Christmas season. Cadet George Hiscock decided to wait and to return home with his father on the *John McRea*.

John McRea sailed from St. John's laden with winter supplies, but never arrived in any port. Days lengthened into weeks. It became way overdue. The Christmas

Schooner *John McRea* (taken in 1911) with a cutwater stem. Three crew are out on the long bowsprit stowing away the jib. There seems to be four dories nested on the starboard side, indicating (with four on the port side) it may be an eight-dory banker. In those years, there would not have been a wheelhouse at the stern over the steering wheel. There seems to be a lookout barrel on the mainmast.

Photo courtesy PANL

season came and went. There was no word from the schooner; no message from any of the five people aboard. It had not been seen by any other vessel. There was talk that unidentified pieces of a schooner drifted into Placentia Bay in January 1918, but no one knew for sure.

Mate Charles Hickman probably wouldn't have gone on the winter voyage, however the shipowner promised him a chance to skipper a banking schooner in the spring of 1918. Would he sail as mate on *John McRea* on its last coasting trip for the season and then go captain of a banker next spring? Yes, he told the owner.

Charles was married to Mary "Minnie" Millington and had five children: Alice, age thirteen; twins Bella and Clarence, ten; Edith, seven; and, Lucy was a new-born, just eight months old. Lucy (Hickman) Woodland, today living in St. John's, recalled the family stories of the loss of *John McRea* and the difficult times her mother had making ends meet and surviving in the 1920s' and '30s:

> My mother knew the schooner was missing. Then there was a word, a message saying, *John McRea* left St. John's, but had returned there some days later. Mother knew this couldn't be true, as Charles would have wired if there had been a delay or a return to port.
>
> There might be some hope the schooner had been intercepted by a German submarine or warship. The crew may be captured, but that was unlikely. When the war was over and all prisoners of war were released, all hope of any return of the crew was given up.

True, during the war at sea in World War I, some larger Newfoundland schooners delivering salt fish to Europe or salt to North America had been attacked by the Germans. Some crews had been imprisoned in Europe. Never had there been a report of smaller schooners hugging the coast lines of Newfoundland being sunk by the enemy, much less the crew being captured.

1918 Shipping Losses.

Forty-three sailing vessels and steamers, all locally owned, and engaged in the foreign trade, have been lost or sunk by submarines during the past year. The insurance companies have had to pay out several millions of dollars. The names of the vessels are: S.S. Florizel, S.S. Kite, S.S. Beverley, S.S. Erik, S.S. Gordon C. (burned at sea); sailing vessels, Forbin, Seth Jr., Maid of Harlech, Marion Silver, Albert A. Young, Lottie A. Silver, Maggie Sullivan, Emily Anderson, Lucania, Minnie, Bessie R., Tatler, Dunure, Jorgina, Archie Crowell, Moran, Watauga, W. C. McKay, Assurance, Latooka, Ruth Hickman, Sidney Smith, Attila, Waterwitch, John E., Ada D. Bishop, Cecil L. Shave, Oregon, Fisherman, Jessie Ashley, J. McRae, W. S. Wynot, Lila B. Hurtle, Jose, Hawanee, Adriatic, Elsie Burdett, Lizzie M. Stanley.

Evening Telegram lists the 43 Newfoundland shipping losses for 1918. *J. McRea* was probably lost in Dec 1917, but officially declared "Missing" in February 1918.

"By February of 1918, the vessel had officially been listed as lost with crew and mother received a small allowance from the government's Marine Disaster Fund, or the Widows' Allowance, of seven dollars every three months. Ship and crew insurance and personal insurance were unheard of. When brother Clarence, who was ten when the *John McRea* was lost, reached eighteen, he was considered the breadwinner and even that pitiful small allowance – the Widow's Order – was cut off. But with Clarence working, he always sent money, usually to buy coal."

Mrs. Charles Hickman was a victim of a sea disaster. As a symbol of her grief, she always wore dark clothes, black or navy blue. She wore a black bonnet when working on the beaches curing fish. If there was one thing she wanted to avoid, it was handouts, welfare, or social assistance. Indeed, most families of this era tried to avoid formal government assistance and proudly made a living by sheer industriousness in a variety of types of work.

Mother had to go out to work. Alice and Bella looked after the younger children. Mother could do much work at home (located on Citadel Road). We kept three or four sheep and she sheared them, washed the wool, carded, spun and then knit socks, mitts, sweaters, caps, whatever from the wool. Double knit mitts, with a finger and thumb, sold for fifty cents. She would hem pants for twenty-five cents.

All the girls learned to knit at an early age. I did at age twelve and sold my first pair socks for fifty cents, giving me a little money for Christmas.

We had three gardens: one behind our house; another near Cemetery Road, and when the Commission government cleared and distributed farming land, we cleared another garden near Farmer's Hill. From the gardens, we had plenty potato, carrot, turnip and cabbage. We always kept hens for food and eggs. The sheep gave us mutton. In later years, we kept a cow as well.

My mother had to work on the fish beaches, making fish, laying it out in the sun, turning it, piling it in great pooks in the evening. This work often began in March, when the bankers first went out, and lasted sometimes until October. A day's labour began in the morning and often went until dark, depending on the amount of fish to be cured.

Mrs. Lucy (Hickman) Woodland holds the model of the schooner *John McRea* after the dedication of the Mariners' Memorial statue and gardens in Grand Bank on August 8, 2007.

Photo courtesy of Lucy and Rhodie Woodland

In the spring, mother would always "set out" other people's gardens – plant their potato; set carrot, cabbage seeds and so on. For this work, she was often paid in kind, or goods, such as carrot and cabbage seed, in lieu of money. Not wanting to lose her place on the beach when she set out gardens, I would have to work on the beach in her place. My two older sisters were already working on the fish drying beaches. I would have to miss a day or two of school.

We had very little, but our family was never hungry. Mother always put the best side out, wanted no pity and avoided handouts. If Uncle Harry (Hickman) came to visit, she always placed the butter dish on the table with butter in it to show him we had butter. When he wasn't there, it was put away.

Then, in the 1930s, conditions became worse for all Newfoundland families. With the advent of world depression, "The Dirty Thirties" became a time to go reluctantly on relief or on the dole. There were few paying jobs and very little hard cash.

One feature of the 1930s, often remembered by those who lived through it, was the "relief" flour – a brown flour, enriched and cheaper than white flour. It was issued in one hundred pound bags and distributed by the Newfoundland government.

Through the sheer dint of hard work and thrift, times and conditions improved. As Lucy (Hickman) Woodland recalled:

The author and Mrs. Lucy (Hickman) Woodland, September 2007. This lady, whose mother was widowed by the sea and who had several small children, grew up in the 1920s and 30s. It was an era of tough economic times and hard work.
Photo courtesy of Sadie Parsons

Mother, through her industry and independence, was able to get white flour. People would come to exchange their brown for white. Mother would mix both kinds and bake bread.

Then there was other work, like cleaning schooners in the spring. They carried coal or supplies in the fall or winter and, to get them ready for fishing, schooners would have to be scrubbed. My mother cleaned homes often in exchange for beef or other food: the homes of Dr. Allan MacDonald, who lived on Camp Street; and the home of Mrs. Addie (Captain Reuben) Thornhill.

In 1936, I left Grand Bank to go to school in St. John's as a "pupil teacher." This was a system in the Salvation Army where you completed formal schooling in St. John's and then went teaching in an outport Army school. I was posted first to Change Islands and the next year to Hickman's Harbour.[3]

Such was the aftermath of a sea disaster. The loss of *John McRea* meant hardship for a community and an epic struggle for survival for a young mother and her children. No one ever determined exactly what happened to the schooner. The best guess is that it struck St. Mary's Keys, or Lamb's Rock, or the Bull, Cow and Calf, all treacherous crags and rocks off the southern Avalon.[4]

When tern schooners like *Frank R. Forsey* (above) sailed to Portugal, waterfront artists in Oporto would quickly paint the schooner and offer the artwork at an affordable price to the Newfoundland sailors. Built in Liverpool, Nova Scotia, in 1917, this foreign-going vessel was 157 net ton with an overall length of 116 foot and was registered to Steven Will Forsey, Grand Bank.

On its return journey from Oporto in January 1923, *Frank R. Forsey* collided with the Grand Bank lighthouse during a snowstorm. Its crew at the time: Captain Charles Rose, mate John Vaters, his brother Phil Vaters, cook Tom Thorne and John James Hickman, all of Grand Bank.

Photo courtesy Don Forsey

Notes

1. The name of the ship *John McRea* sounds like the name of the writer of "In Flanders Fields" – John McCrae, a Canadian physician. The poem remains to this day one of the most memorable pieces of writing ever composed. It was written in May 1915, two years before the ship *John McRea* was lost. It is possible that over the passage of time the official and proper name of the ship, "*J. McRea*" changed in Grand Bank to "*John McRea*."

2. Captain Josiah Hiscock, originally from Winterton, was married to Phoebe (Evans) Hiscock of Grand Bank. They had another son, Harry Charles Hiscock. (born in 1897 and later married Amelia Anstey), and daughters Mary "Minnie" Hiscock (later Dodge) and Lilly Hiscock, a long-time teacher in Grand Bank.

3. I went to see Mrs. Lucy (Hickman) Woodland on September 3, 2007, in her St. John's home and I am grateful to her for the background of *John McRea*, its crew, and most especially for her memories of life after the ship was lost.

As I said to her that day, "It was a story of survival of the 1920s and 1930s when a father was lost at sea and a mother with a young family was left behind to cope. There are few instances today where one can find such a touching, yet wonderful story of life in that era." Other information came from Mildred (Dodge) Loveless, Grand Bank.

Actually, I boarded with Lucy and Gordon Woodland on Cornwall Crescent, St. John's, when I attended Teacher Training Summer School in July 1963. It is quite possible we talked back then of Grand Bank ships and men lost at sea, and I probably heard the story of *John McRea* (but didn't listen).

4. The table in Appendix C puts the loss of *John McRea* in context with other marine disasters of Grand Bank.

CHAPTER 51
A KILLER STORM

LANGUE DE CERF, ST. BERNARD'S: In Newfoundland and Labrador, many communities have been abandoned over the years and the reasons for this vary. Between 1950 and 1975, government sponsored programs, Resettlement and Centralization, convinced long-established families to leave small isolated towns and to move to larger centres. Other towns were abandoned when a resource became depleted, employment ceased, and families relocated. Since the 1950s, it is estimated that about three hundred towns have disappeared from Newfoundland and Labrador maps. However, a community in Fortune Bay, Langue de Cerf (often pronounced Long Surf or Long de Surf), can mark the beginning of its population's decline and eventual abandonment to the disappearance of a vessel. The *Newfoundland Encyclopedia* says of Langue de Cerf:

> ...the rapid decline of Langue de Cerf's population in the early twentieth century was in part consequent on the drowning of some of the community's fishermen on September 15, 1900. After the wreck of the *Maygo,* some of the widows moved back to their original communities with their children. (St. Joseph's, Placentia Bay)

The ship was *Maygo*; however church records (whose clergy sometimes corrupted or changed spelling), record the ship as *Omega*. The name itself is unique. Oral sources and descendants of the fishermen say the schooner was quite a while under construction in a place called "Collins" in Western Harbour near St. Bernard's. "She's been there so long on the stocks," the people said, "that she may go or she may not go." Thus, the banking schooner was christened *Maygo.*

Whatever the name, the schooner never returned from a September fishing voyage to the Grand Banks. A destructive gale swept over the island and the offshore banks between September 13-15 that year and all of *Maygo*'s crew perished.

The loss of several breadwinners on *Maygo* left the community devastated and nearly all the employed men, the breadwinners, were gone forever. Widows, many with young families to provide for, had little or no support. Several went back to communities where their parents lived, mainly Fox Cove, a community near Langue de Cerf, renamed in 1915 to St. Bernard's.

By 1911, more than half of the forty-four inhabitants at Langue de Cerf at the turn of the century had relocated, mainly in St. Bernard's, about three kilometres away. According to the *Census*, its population decreased further by 1935 and the community did not appear in any subsequent *Census*. It is believed that the family of Austin Whittle was the last to move out of the community to St. Bernard's in 1947.[1]

What of this storm that claimed at least one ship and caused people to abandon or move away from the town they had established and lived in for years?

Crew from Langue de Cerf Lost on *Maygo* in the September Gale, 1900

Name	Age	Place of Birth
George Power	26	Fox Cove
George (John?) Power	56	Harbour Breton
Edward Power	24	Fox Cove
William Cox	21	Fox Cove
Stephen Power	32	New Harbour
Edward Stewart	25	Langue de Cerf
Charles Whittle	19	Placentia Bay
William Whittle*	48	Placentia Bay

*Both Whittles were living in Langue de Cerf, but were born in Port Elizabeth, Placentia Bay.

In the days before the death-dealing calamity hit Newfoundland, the hurricane of September 1900 had caused much damage and hardship in the United States. It was later labelled "Isaac's Storm," named for the meteorologist Isaac Cline, who erroneously predicted the storm was of no consequence. When the 135 mile per hour winds hit Galveston Island, Texas (where Cline lived), on September 8, the storm surge and waves destroyed half – roughly 3,600 – of the homes and buildings in Galveston and killed over 8000 people. (After the flattened Galveston was re-built, a sixteen kilometre seawall was constructed to protect the low-lying city from any future surges.)

Isaac's Storm roared up through central United States, bringing hurricane force winds to Chicago and Buffalo and killing several loggers and riverboat men in the area. Winds downed so many telegraph lines, that communication throughout America's Mid-west came to a standstill.[2]

On September 12, the storm sank several ships and took many lives as it crossed Northumberland Strait, between New Brunswick and PEI, then moved stealthily, with killer intent, over Newfoundland.

It first ravaged Saint Pierre et Miquelon, the French islands near Newfoundland. On the ships sunk in Saint Pierre harbour, no lives were lost, but nine fishing schooners at the offshore banks had nowhere to seek shelter. They failed to return to port and 120 French fishermen drowned.

The tale of one of these ships is particularly gruesome. The *Ali Baba* was a Saint Pierre schooner that fished the Saint Pierre Banks on September 13. It seemed to have disappeared in the hurricane and was missing for weeks. According to John Reid in *The Galveston Hurricane in Canada* (1975):

> The fishing fleet of Saint Pierre was decimated. With the 120 men reported lost, there were fifty children left without fathers. One of the

capsized schooners, the *Ali Baba,* was towed into port at Saint Pierre, with thirteen bodies inside so bloated that only one was recognizable.

The final body count and list of missing ships in New Brunswick, Prince Edward Island and Newfoundland was staggering. *Maygo* of Langue de Cerf became one of several Newfoundland ships simply swallowed up in the storm. Like *Maygo*, they were defenceless in the onslaught.

Two factors accounted for this: firstly, in this era, there was no long-range forecasting. No one knew the hurricane was coming until it was too late. As well, scores of fishing ships were on the fishing banks, far from shelter. Others were at sea, finishing up trading voyages or travelling to home port.

Secondly, the Collins' schooner and Burton's schooner, the latter a thirty-ton vessel out of Bay de L'eau, failed to return home after the gale. The *William Burton* carried seven men. It was last seen fishing on St. Mary's Bank in company with the Marystown vessel *Alexander*, belonging to M.T. Flynn.

Capt. John Walsh, in trouble in the gale, had his *Alexander* go adrift when anchors dragged and *Alexander* lurched down near the Burton vessel. Captain Walsh, whose vessel survived the onslaught, thought the Burtons went adrift shortly after. They were never seen again.

Collins' schooner, the sixty-ton *Barbara Heck* fishing in the neighbourhood of Cape Pine, had not reported. It was last seen fifteen miles off Cape Pine and is believed to have struck Nixons Rock. A report in the October 2, 1900, edition of *The Evening Telegram* said, "It is believed to be lost with all hands."

Late reports showed the gale had widespread effects all over the island. Between Belle Isle and Englee, forty-two fishing ships were driven onto the rocks; about half were never refloated or repaired.

Newfoundland Ships Which Disappeared in the September 1900 Gale

Ship	Home Port	Number in Crew
Maygo	Langue de Cerf	Eight men
Lillydale	Catalina	Capt. William Edgecombe and nine other crew
P.K. Jacobs	St. Lawrence	Capt. Jacobs and eight others
Goodwill	Carmanville	Capt. John Carnell and four others
Lizzie	Burgeo	Capt. Vatcher and six others
Barbara Heck	Burin	Twelve men, schooner owned by Collins[3]
William Burton	Bay de L'eau	Six men

Initial reports from William Cunningham, the Justice of Peace at Tilt Cove, indicated no loss of life. By September 20, this changed when he received news that five men were lost at Pacquet, a fishing harbour located on the north shore of the Baie Verte Peninsula. The Catalina schooner *Lillydale* disappeared while fishing off the Avalon Peninsula; the *Goodwill* was driven on the rocks and all crew perished near the Straight Shore.

Then, within an hour or two, it was over. The reign of terror ended as quickly as it came. By the next day, September 14, winds moderated and crippled survivors sailed into port, many greatly damaged, others with a man or two lost. These were the lucky schooners; at least seven known or recorded schooners, including the *Maygo* of Langue de Cerf, disappeared without a trace.

One hundred years ago, a terrifying face of nature, a cold killer, slipped away from our island and headed north, arcing across the seas off Greenland and finally disappearing somewhere over the northern seas.[4]

Notes

1. Langue de Cerf, about three kilometres from St. Bernard's in the bottom of Fortune Bay, is believed to have been named for an abundance of the Langue de Cerf (or Deer's Tongue) plant in the region. Captain James Cook, who surveyed that part of Newfoundland's coast, mapped one fishing stage at Langue de Cerf in 1765. By the first official Census in 1836, there were seventeen permanent settlers in the community.

2. The effects of the storm that nearly annihilated Galveston is now the subject of Erik Larsen's book "Isaac's Storm," published in 1999.

3. Most sources say twelve crew perished on *Barbara Heck*, of which ten are identified.

4. A more complete story of *Lillydale* and *Goodwill* can be found in the book *Raging Winds...Roaring Sea* (Creative Publishers, 2000). In 2005, a TV program, *Disasters of the Twentieth Century* (produced by Man in Motion, Regina), documented the origins of the storm and its effects on Newfoundland. The author of this book was featured in the program.

Vessel	Crew Lost	Dependants
Barbara Heck	Capt. W. Kirby	wife, 12 children
	Thomas Collins	wife, 5 children
	Frank Collins	single
	J. Brett	wife, 2 children
	W. Dowell	2 children
	Isaac Kirby	single
	Howard Kirby	single
	Thomas Moulton	single
	Thomas Watts	single
	Thomas Brown	single
William Burton	Capt. Patrick Burton	Unknown
	Edward Burton, brother	
	James Gaulton, cousin of Burton	
	John Gaulton, cousin	
	William Day, Trinity Bay	
	Maurice McGrath, Little Harbour, near Oderin	
Lizzie	Capt. John Vatcher	Unknown
	Hugh Dominey	
	Charles Hann	
	Harry Parsons	
	George V. Rose	
	Henry Dicks	
	Joseph Gunnery	
	(name unknown) Simms, Hunt's Island	

CHAPTER 52
ONE NEWFOUNDLANDER
TO TELL THE TALE

BELLEORAM, CODROY, CONCEPTION BAY: On Saturday, August 8, 1908, the German Cruiser *Freya* steamed along on the edge of the LaHave fishing banks, approximately sixty miles southeast of Halifax. Drifting fog around 11:30 made the night all the more dark. Then, directly in front of them, the officers on the bridge of the cruiser could see the lights of a ship. Only seconds went by, not minutes, when the bow of the *Freya* impaled itself in a schooner amidships. Four of the schooner's crew were located in the dark waters and these were rescued, still alive. Nine could not be accounted for.

It was the Gloucester schooner *Maggie and May* and it sank immediately upon impact. *Freya*'s commander, Maas, stayed at the scene, but wired the German consul in Canada, M.C. Grant, to inform him of what had happened.

Maas said *Freya* had been sailing at seven knots through drifting fog. The steam whistle sounded at regular intervals. Then the crew heard a fog horn, seemingly coming from the port side. *Freya* was put to the starboard to avoid a ship, as of yet unseen. The last blast came, he said, two points from the port.

At that moment, a blue pilot light could be seen on the schooner directly ahead and an instant later, the cruiser, with all its five thousand ton, went crashing through the timbers of the schooner as if, said Maas, "it was deck of cards." It sank almost immediately, bow first.

Captain Erick McCathran and the whole of *Maggie and May*'s crew were all on deck, as they could clearly hear the whistle of a large ship. Like Commander Maas, his lookouts were confused by the signals which seemed to come from different points.

Upon impact, *Freya*'s engines were reversed and Maas gave orders to launch lifeboats to pick up survivors, if any. Of the thirteen aboard the schooner, nine were on the bow. Near them, the great foresail was flapping idly in the calm air.

These nine men began to get the dory out right away and might have succeeded had it not been for the foresail. *Maggie and May* went down bow first and the sail fell over on the men, covering them in such a way that they could do nothing in their last few moments of life.

The German sailors – many of whom were students, as *Freya* was a training ship (school ship) – threw ropes to the struggling fishermen. Only one that been on the schooner's bow caught a rope and he was the first to be saved.

Within two minutes, *Freya*'s lifeboats were over the side. By now, a section of *Maggie and May*'s stern showed above water. Four of the schooner's crew were standing aft on the vessel's deck. As *Maggie and May* went down, they grabbed anything they could reach to help them stay afloat. Three of these were rescued by those in the lifeboat.

NINE BRAVE MEN MEET WATERY GRAVE
SIXTY MILES OFF HALIFAX HARBOR

The Gloucester Schooner Maggie and May Cut in Two in a Fog by German Protected Cruiser
Freya and in Two Minutes She Goes to the Bottom With Nine of Her Crew of Thirteen
—There Was Confusion as to the Direction of the Sound From the Schooner's
Fog Horn, Which Seemed to be From Port, Whereas the Vessel Was Di-
rectly Ahead, and Was Cut Down Almost at Right Angles—Five of
the Victims are Yarmouth Men, One is From Lunenburg
And Two From Newfoundland.

Nine men, five of whom were Nova | that The Mail is indebted for its flapping idly in the culm air. These

Local papers headline the loss of *Maggie and May*.

Maas said afterward that he couldn't understand how this fourth man at the stern perished. There was so much wreckage, debris and pieces of wood floating about, he could have found something to hold on to. Possibly, the man was injured, either before he left the sinking schooner or he may have been struck by debris while in the water.

Freya's lifeboats stayed in the area and its searchlights scanned the water for two hours. Finally and reluctantly, Maas headed toward Halifax. He had to report to the German consul and to Canadian shipping authorities. On the way in, Maas consulted with the four survivors, one of whom was a Newfoundlander, to ascertain who was on the schooner. The nine who went down with *Maggie and May* were Captain McCathran of Gloucester, five Nova Scotian fishermen and two from Newfoundland: Patrick English, whose place of birth is given only as Conception Bay and Walter Fiander from Codroy.

Maas' story is basically presented above, but there were four survivors, one of whom was a Newfoundlander. He was not reluctant to give his version of the story.

The survivors came into Halifax on the cruiser *Freya* – Silvian White, John and William Muise of Eel Brook, Nova Scotia, and a man identified as Leo Farn of Belleoram. (This may be a misinterpretation of Yarn, as that surname is a common one on the Connaigre Peninsula. For the purposes of *Maggie and May*'s story, his name will be Leo Yarn.)[1]

Maggie and May left Gloucester on Thursday, August 6, for Arichat, Nova Scotia. There, it would pick up more crew and a supply of bait. By Friday, they ran into thick fog right up to the time of the collision. Leo Yarn and others heard a ship's whistle, but the direction of it seemed to vary. All hands were called to the deck; some kept the schooner's foghorn going, others were on lookout.

"The captain of *Maggie and May* was on deck too by this time," said Yarn. "When the huge hull came in sight, he called out an order to the helmsman to starboard the helm."

But in a minute, the stem of the school ship struck the schooner near the fore rigging, staving in the sides. Yarn said there was no time to lower a boat:

> I was alongside Captain McCathran on the deck as *Maggie and May* sank and the captain went down with his lantern in his hand.
>
> I am a good swimmer, but I was drawn down by the suction and I think I was nearly two minutes under water. I swam to the utmost of my power to get clear of the suction and finally did so.
>
> I got to the surface where I grabbed a piece of wreckage and finally reached a life line thrown by *Freya*'s crew. After our schooner sank, I saw nothing of the captain and the others of the crew, except the three rescued. I think the nine were carried down by the suction.
>
> The officers and men of the school ship searched the vicinity for two or three hours, and we helped them. There was plenty of wreckage, but no sign of other survivors. We were treated with every attention and kindness on the school ship.[2]

Notes

1. The Yarns were prominent seafaring and shipowning people in Mose Ambrose and Belleoram. Henry Yarn of Belleoram co-jointly owned the *Bessie M* in 1901; the other shares being registered to Margaret Yarn of Mose Ambrose. At Mose Ambrose, just a few miles from Belleoram, some of the more prominent seamen, captains and shipowners who lived there were James Yarn and Chesley Yarn, who both owned ships in different decades. Captain Philip Yarn of Mose Ambrose was lost on the *Mary Carmel* in 1939; Mose Ambrose's Captain William Yarn was shipwrecked on *Francis L. Spindler* in 1938.

2. Newfoundlanders had found employment on the Gloucester wooden fishing fleet from the 1880s right up the end of the dory fishery in the 1950s. Many Gloucester schooners and crews were lost at sea; scores of Newfoundland fishermen manned them.

One example of this was the sinking of the banker *Mildred W. Lee*. It sailed from Gloucester to the Grand Banks on January 30, 1895, and never returned to port. It was thought the schooner was lost in the great storm of February 3 and wreckage picked up near Sable Island about that date was identified as belonging to *Mildred W. Lee*. By April 5, 1895, it was officially declared "Lost with Crew."

Half of the sixteen crew were Newfoundland men, all of them unmarried: George Grant, Burgeo; brothers Thomas and Richard Williams, Bay Bulls; Fenwick Williams, Bay Bulls; Michael Connolly, Tor's Cove; Lawrence King, St. Mary's; John Carey, Witless Bay, and Patrick Fahey, Fermeuse. Fahey's father, mother, brother and sister lived in Blackstone, Massachusetts.

CHAPTER 53
FINAL IMAGES OF
MAUREEN & MICHAEL

CONNAIGRE PENINSULA: The fresh fishing industry, with trawlers and otter trawls, had become well-established by the 1950s. These vessels were equipped and able to fish all year round, including the rough and stormy winter months. With the loss of several offshore trawlers in February, this utterance soon became commonplace: "February is the cruelest month for the draggers." On February 23, 1967, several offshore bank fishers were battered by a violent storm. Four ships went down off Nova Scotia; one of them was *Maureen & Michael*.

It is not often one finds the tale of a shipwreck presented, for the most part, in images.[1] This is one.

The Nova Scotian fishing vessel *Maureen & Michael* (above, in the mid-1960s at Yarmouth, Nova Scotia) was crewed by Newfoundland fishermen.

Courtesy Capt. Hubert Hall, SHIPSEARCH Marine, Yarmouth, NS

Caught in the severe winter storm of February 21-23, 1967, the eighty-two-foot long *Maureen & Michael* begins taking on water on the fishing grounds. Captain Max Fiander had already put out a distress call as the vessel settles at the stern.

The U.S. Coast Guard *Castle Rock* arrives on the scene, puts out a powered life raft and takes off five of eight crew on the sinking *Maureen & Michael*. By this time, mad seas wash over the stern and the rescue vessel's raft is situated near *Maureen & Michael* midship.

Two U.S. coast guard personnel from *Castle Rock* had to put on diving wet suits and take a rubber life raft to get the last remaining crewmen of *Maureen & Michael*.

Rescuer Pettek of *Castle Rock* said afterwards, "The stern was going down as we got there. One guy jumped aboard the raft...the raft drifted away and we had to pull it back to get the other man. We were only about fifty yards away in the raft when the ship sank."

Maureen & Michael takes its final nod and sinks. Only the tip of the bow and some floating debris shows. In the same storm three fishing vessels were lost with crew: Lockeport's *Polly and Robbie*, which was steaming to help *Maureen & Michael*, disappeared with seven crew, including three Newfoundland-born men. The Nova Scotian dragger *Cape Bonnie* was driven on the Sister's Ledges and all sixteen crew were lost. *Iceland II*, out of Souris, PEI, ran aground near Fourchu, Nova Scotia. Its ten crew perished.

Castle Rock's rescue life raft is pulled alongside.

One of the rescuers or rescued reaches out to climb the safety net lowered. Personnel from *Castle Rock* stand at the side (out of camera shot) to assist the weary and hungry shipwrecked men in over the side. Most of *Maureen & Michael*'s crew saved no extra clothes or personal belongings.

From the left, Conrad Mills (with bandaged hand), William Hardiman and Isaac Bartlett relax in the rest room of *Castle Rock*. They were given clean and dry clothes – ship-issue work shirts and blue denim jeans.

The eight photos above courtesy Con and Alma Mills and the U.S. Coast Guard

Back row (l-r) William Dominiaux, Bay L'Argent; Seward Bartlett, Coomb's Cove, residing in Grand Bank; Captain Max Fiander English Harbour West and William Hardiman, Bay L'Argent; Middle row (left) John Tom Tibbo, Harbour Breton and later resided in Ecum Secum, Nova Scotia. Front row (l-r) Isaac Bartlett, Coomb's Cove; Conrad Mills, Lolly Cove, then Belleoram and later Albert Bridge, NS, and John Ben Strowbridge, Jersey Harbour, residing in Harbour Breton. Although this photo, courtesy of Mary Bartlett, was featured in another book, *Survivors and Lost Heroes*, it is shown here to present these resilient and hardy heroes of the sea.

Notes

1. This story had its beginning in the summer of 1999, when Mrs. Mary Bartlett, whose late husband Isaac was a crewmember on *Maureen & Michael*, gave me a photo of the eight shipwrecked sailors who had been rescued from *Maureen & Michael*. When I attempted to identify them, I received help from Seward Bartlett as well as Conrad and Alma Mills in Albert Bridge, Nova Scotia. Con and Alma later sent several pictures of the vessel sinking. These eight images were most likely taken by a sailor on the U.S. coast guard ship *Castle Rock*.

APPENDIX A

Ships of Newfoundland Lost in 1918, as reported by *The Evening Telegram*, January 22, 1919. Those in **BOLD** were lost with entire crew.

Ship	Fate
Ada D. Bishop	Left Twillingate January 10; missing in North Atlantic with five crew
Adriatic	Stranded near St. Lawrence, September 1918. Captain Frank Pine and crew survived.
Albert A. Young	Abandoned in mid-ocean, Captain Clarence Dodman and crew rescued February 27.
Archie Crowell	Abandoned in mid-ocean in April, Captain Sam Taylor of Carbonear and crew rescued.
Assurance	Unknown
Attia	Unknown
Bessie R.	Wrecked St. Mary's Bay, February 17. Captain Sandy Thistle and crew safe.
S. S. Beverley	Missing in mid-ocean with twenty-two crew, many from St. John's. Left Harbour Grace January 21.
Cecil L. Shave	Sunk March 1 by enemy ship; all six crew perished.
Dunure	Unknown
Elsie Birdett	Sunk by enemy sub on March 30, 1918. No survivors. Most crew were from Burgeo and area.
Emily Anderson	Abandoned in mid-ocean, Captain Leonard Miller and crew rescued February 1.
S. S. *Erik*	Sunk by enemy sub off Saint Pierre on August 25. Captain Lane and crew survived.
Fisherman	Sunk by enemy sub in July. Captain Nichol and Carbonear crew survived.
S.S. *Florizel*	Wrecked on Horn Head Rocks, Cappahayden with a loss of ninety-four people on February 26.
Forbin	Unknown
S. S. *Gordon C.*	Burned while laden with coal on September 13. Captain Perry and crew were uninjured.
Hawanee	Sunk by enemy sub on October 28. Captain King and crew imprisoned and released.
J. McRea	Missing since late December 1917 to early 1918 with four crew, 1 passenger, all of Grand Bank.
Jessie Ashley	Unknown
John E.	Unknown
Jorgina	(Or *Georgina*) Sunk by enemy sub on March 24. Captain Josephus Osmond and crew survived.
Jose	Unknown
S. S. *Kite*	Sealing steamer wrecked off Gaspe coast August 12. Captain House and crew, no loss of life.

Latooka	Unknown
Lilia B. Hirtle	Unknown
Lizzie M. Stanley	Missing since late December 1917 to early 1918 with six Burgeo seamen.
Lottie A. Silver	Abandoned in mid-ocean; Captain J. Rogers and crew rescued January 27.
Lucania	Ran aground and sank near Ferryland on February 18. Captain Norris and crew survived.
Maggie Sullivan	Unknown
Maid of Harlech	Torpedoed in Mediterranean Sea in March. Captain Moore and crew safe.
Marion Silver	Collided with *Margaret Lake*, September 24. Captain H.B. Clyde Lake and crew rescued.
Minnie	Abandoned in mid-ocean late January. Captain Yarn and crew taken to Corunna.
Moran	Abandoned in mid-ocean late January. Captain Colford and his Carbonear crew rescued.
Oregon	Abandoned at sea. Captain George Rose and crew survived.
Ruth Hickman	Torpedoed by enemy in late May. Captain Snelgrove and six crew survived.
Seth Jr.	Abandoned in mid-ocean, Captain Weston Keeping and crew rescued January 1.
Sidney Smith	Disappeared in the Atlantic, early January. Captain Taylor and crew all perished.
Tattler	Abandoned mid-ocean; Captain Burden and crew survived (probably happened in March 1917).
W.C. McKay	Sailed from Twillingate January 10; missing with seven crew, three of whom were from St. John's.
W. S. Wynot	Lost at Hermitage on February 18.
Watauga	Sunk by enemy March 27 off Lisbon; five crew perished.
Waterwitch	Unknown

In addition to those listed from media reports, several other Newfoundland ships were abandoned at sea, sunk by the enemy, or wrecked in 1918:

Blanche with Captain McLean lost near Bonne Bay on January 8; *E.S. Hocken*, Captain Courtenay, abandoned at sea on January 9; on January 26, Captain Haynes and the crew of the abandoned *Thomas A. Cromwell* were rescued; *Commander* of Great Burin wrecked at Port au Port, May 28; coastal steamer *Susu* wrecked on Pilley's Island, November 25; schooner *Mary Lloyd*, Captain Penny, burned at sea on December 7; *Success*, Captain Rafuse, lost while entering Oporto, December 9; *Paragon*, Captain Kean, abandoned at sea on December 10; *Eva C*, Captain Lodge, sailing from Cadiz to St. John's, abandoned in mid-ocean on December 11; *Winnifred* of Grand Bank wrecked on December 14, no loss of life; *Donald G. Hollett* of Burin abandoned at sea on December 17 and *Pauline Martin*, Cadiz to St. John's, abandoned at sea on December 20.

APPENDIX B
Survivors of the *Viking* Disaster of March 16, 1930

Adams, George - Brigus
Adams, Patrick - St. John's
Antle, Bennett - Brigus
Ayles, Israel - residence not given
Bartlett, William (of John) - Georgetown
Batten, Walter - Bareneed
Batten, Harold - Bareneed
Berg, Peter - Wesleyville
Best, Fred - St. John's
Bishop, Harold - Burnt Head
Boland, John - Calvert
Boone, William R. - Bareneed
Bradbury, Thomas - Torbay
Bradbury, Isaac - Brigus
Bragg, Edgar - Pouch Cove
Brown, Patrick - Colliers
Brown, Dan - Brigus
Brown, Henry - St. John's
Brown, Joe - Colliers
Burke, James - Colliers
Burke, Patrick - Colliers
Burry, Sydney - Greenspond
Bursey, Walter - Lower Island Cove
Butt, Alfred - Freshwater
Carew, Walter - Flatrock
Chaulk, David - Catalina
Coady, James - Outer Cove
Codner, Henry - Torbay
Cole, Robert - Conception Harbour
Cole, Joe - Colliers
Cole, William - Colliers
Conway, Dick - Colliers
Conway, Edward - Colliers
Dalton, Edward - Western Bay
(Patrick Oliver held this man's ticket)
Dawe, James - Burnt Head
Dawe, Frank - Bay Roberts
Day, George - Little Harbour, Placentia Bay
Doyle, Alphonso - Gull Island, C.B.
Doyle, William John - Gull Island, C.B.
Doyle, John - Gull Island, C.B.

Dyke, Abram - St. John's
Efford, George - North River
Efford, Issac - Bareneed
Fifield, Alfred - Trinity
Fleming, William - Bonavista
Fleming, Dan - Spillar's Cove
Flemming, Thomas - Bonavista
Flynn, Frank - Brigus
Fowler, Richard - Burnt Head
Fowler, William - Burnt Head
Fry, James - residence not given
Gahaney, Benjamin - Colliers
Gardner, Mike (stowaway) - St. John's
Garland, Simeon - Caplin Cove, C.B.
Garland, Eli - Caplin Cove, C.B.
Gosse, John - Torbay
Green, Louis - residence not given
Gushue, Patrick - Conception Harbour
Gushue, Ronald - Brigus
Hawco, Vincent - Torbay
Hicks, Victor - Bonavista
Johnson, William - Job's Cove
Johnson, Stanley - Job's Cove
Kean, Al. - Valleyfield
Kean, Capt. Abram, Jr. - Brookfield
Kennedy, Wilson - Western Bay
Kennedy, John - Brigus
Kennedy, Thomas - Brigus
Kennedy, William - St. John's
King, Clayton - Brigus
King, Richard - Brigus
Kinsella, Michael - Outer Cove
Lambert, James - St. John's
Lambert, John - St. John's
LeDrew, Roland - Bauline
Linthorne, Arch - Georgetown, Brigus
Linthorne, George - Georgetown
Loveys, Gordon - Western Bay
Lush, Stephen - Georgetown
Martin, Michael (of Thomas) - Torbay
Martin, Michael - Flatrock

Martin, Chesley - Bonavista

Martin, Wm (or Wilfred?) - Flatrock

Martin, Michael - Flatrock

McGrath, Charles - Colliers

Morgan, Samuel - Seal Cove

Mouland, Yetman - Bonavista

Murray, James - Pouch Cove

Newell, John - Georgetown

Newell, Jacob - Pouch Cove

Newell, Ernest - Burnt Head

Oliver, Joseph - Gull Island, C.B.

Oliver, Edward - Gull Island, C.B.

Oliver, James - Gull Island, C.B.

Payne, Fred - Brigus

Pearce, Israel - Bonavista

Pearcey, Fred - Brigus

Pearcey, Ira - Brigus

Power, Walter - Flatrock

Quinlan, Jerry - Red Head Cove

Ralph, Jacob - St. John's

Richards, Arthur - Brigus

Roberts, Jack - Brigus

Roche, Nicholas - Middle Cove

Ryan, Herbert - Port Rexton

Soper, John - Carbonear

Sparkes, Harry - Brigus

Sparkes, Albert - Sibley's Cove

Spracklin, Albert - Brigus

Spracklin, Simon - Brigus

Spracklin, Edward - Brigus

Spracklin, Edward - Brigus

Spracklin, Thomas - Brigus

Spracklin, Charles - Brigus

Spracklin, George - Brigus

Spracklin, Ernest - Brigus

Spracklin, Patrick - Brigus

Street, James - Bonavista

Tippett, Nimshi - Catalina

Walker, Richard - Brigus

Way, Noah - Bonavista

Way, Alfred - Bonavista

Whalen, Patrick - St. John's

White, James - Greenspond

Whitey, Jack - Georgetown

Youden, George - Brigus

Young, James - St. John's

APPENDIX C
Grand Bank Ships Lost with Entire Crew

Ship	Date Lost	# Aboard	Owner
Watchword	1862	4	Robert Forward
Elizabeth	March 1870	4	Benjamin Lawrence
Prince of Wales	Dec 1872	4	George and Thomas Symes
Daisy Dean	Nov 1873	5 or 6	Captain Robert Courtney
Idler	Oct 1876	5	Captain William Henry Buffett
Sarah Jane	Aug 1886	8-10	William George Evans
Ernest J.S. Simms	Dec 1887	4	Thomas A. Hickman
George Foote	Aug 1892	17	Thomas Foote/Samuel Patten
Maggie Foote	Aug 1892	5	Thomas, John and George Foote
Clarence T. Foote	Aug 1893	5	Morgan Foote
Mikado	Oct 1897	5	Captain Thomas A. Hickman
Nellie Harris	Nov 1906	6	Samuel Harris
Tubal Cain	Jan 1907	8	Simeon Noel Tibbo
Orion	Oct 1907	17	George A. Buffett
Elfreda May	Dec 1910	7	Walter Patten
Dorothy Louise	Nov-Dec 1911	5-6	George C. Harris
Arkansas	Dec 1911	5-6	George C. Harris
Jennie Duff	Jan 1917	5-6	Lionel B. Clarke
John McRea	Dec 1917	5	George A. Buffett
General Horne	Dec 1920	5-6	George C. Harris
Jean and Mary	Dec 1921	6	Aaron F. Buffett
General Plumer	March 1930	6	Sam Piercey, George C. Harris, Lionel B. Clarke
Alsatian	March 1935	25	Samuel H. Patten
General Gough	Nov/Dec 1935	6	George C. Harris
Partanna	April 1936	25	Grand Bank Fisheries Ltd.
Mabel Dorothy	Nov 1955	7	Forward and Tibbo Ltd.
Blue Wave	Feb 1959	16	Bonavista Cold Storage Ltd.
Blue Mist II	Feb 1966	13	Bonavista Cold Storage Ltd.

This list shows the known (or documented through gravestones and/or newspaper accounts) twenty-eight ships lost in a hundred years' span. Of the five earliest disappearances – *Watchword*, *Elizabeth*, *Prince of Wales*, *Daisy Dean*, *Idler* – little was recorded in local history or in the papers of the day. For example, of *Idler* family history says it was located in October 1876, drifting bottom up near Pass Island with no sign of the crew. The newspaper *Courier* barely mentions its loss in the December 9, 1876, edition with this brief comment:

"We (at the *Courier*) learn by letter from Grand Bank of the loss of the schooner *Idler*, owned by William Buffett, the master, and built at Grand Bank last winter. The owner and four hands were lost with her, leaving two widows and five orphans."

In human terms, twenty-eight missing ships translates into approximately 230 mariners lost. The question marks indicate no one is entirely sure how many were on a certain vessel. No complete list was carried in church records, shipping lists, family oral history or in newspaper accounts of the day.

In addition to these losses of full crews, the freighter *Administratrix* was cut down in 1948 and five of its seven crew perished.

INDEX OF SHIPS, TOWNS AND LANDMARKS

Princeton 66
Psyche 63
Pubnico Belle 95
Puffin Island 52
Purcell's Harbour 116
Purtian 51-53
Quidi Vidi 139
Raleigh 17
Random Island 69-70
Regulus 157
Renews 164, 168, 172
Retriever 117
Rhoda Zee 105
Richard Wainwright 4
Riverhead, St. Mary's 181
Rise and Go 101
Rita Windsor 44
River of Ponds 5
Robert Freddis 40
Robert Lowe 175-177
Roddickton 31, 103
Romeo 4
Rose Blanche 117
Rossland 20
Rotterdam 34, 104
Royal 169
Roy Algar R. 67
R.R. Govin 182
Ruth Hickman 23-25
Sable Island 144, 205
Sagona 66
Sally's Cove 13
Salmon Cove 69, 137
Salvage 59
Sam 44
Sandy Point 4
Saucy Arethusa 23
Saurel 49
Saxonia 150
Scotch Lass 59-61
Scotsman 17
Sea Bride 39
Seal Cove, Bonavista Bay 81
Seattle 86
Seldom-Come-By 27, 31, 76, 103-105,

123, 127
Sherbrooke 116
Shoal Bay 155-158
Shoe Cove, Cape Race 67
Signal Hill 140
Silver Point 3
Silvia 133
Sir John Glover 115
Sir William 65-68
Somerset 99-101
Southport (Fox Harbour) 69
South River 69
South West Arm 58
Spaniard's Bay 44, 125
Specular 35
"Splinter Fleet" 79
Spray 125
Springdale 8, 23-25
Springfield 69
Stag Harbour Run 105
St. Andrew's
  (Little River) 1
St. Anthony 75, 149
St. Bernard's 197-201
St. Brendan's 71
Star 39
St. Clair 31-34, 103
St. George 160
St. John's 20, 21, 27, 31, 42, 52, 55,
63, 79, 81, 89, 93, 97-98, 115, 119,
136, 143, 147, 149-151, 154, 169, 189,
193
St. Jone's Within 75
St. Lawrence 18, 45, 199
St. Lawrence River 1
St. Mary's 171-174, 175-177, 179-182,
205
St. Mary's Keys 193
St. Paul's 13
St. Paul Island 47-49
St. Pierre 85, 112, 148, 161, 198
St. Shotts 121, 172, 173
St. Vincent's 176
Stone's Cove 183-187
Straight Shore 27-29, 124, 200

INDEX OF NEWFOUNDLAND AND LABRADOR SURNAMES